Ramesh S. Balsekar is known and loved by seekers from around the world as an eloquent master of Advaita, or Non-duality. After retiring as president of the Bank of India, Ramesh translated many of the daily talks given in the Marathi language by his guru, Nisargadatta Maharaj. Ramesh started teaching in 1982 after Maharaj had twice directed him to talk; since then he has written over twenty books on Advaita.

Books by Ramesh S. Balsekar

Wisdom of Balsekar (2004)

Guru Pournima (2003)

Peace and Harmony in Daily Living (2003)

The Ultimate Understanding (2001)

Advaita, the Buddha and the Unbroken Whole (2000)

It So Happened That ... The Unique Teaching of Ramesh S. Balsekar (2000)

Sin and Guilt: Monstrosity of Mind (2000)

Meaningful Trivialities from the Source (2000)

The Infamous Ego (1999)

Who Cares?! (1999)

The Essence of the Bhagavad Gita (1999)

Your Head in the Tiger's Mouth (1997)

Consciousness Writes (1996)

A Net of Jewels (1996)

The Bhagavad Gita – A Selection (1995)

Like a Large Immovable Rock (1994)

Ripples (1994)

Consciousness Speaks (1992)

From Consciousness to Consciousness (1989)

The Final Truth (1989)

A Duet of One (1989)

Experiencing the Teaching (1988)

Explorations into the Eternal (1987)

Experience of Immortality (1984)

Pointers from Nisargadatta Maharaj (1982)

CONFUSION NO MORE

For the Spiritual Seeker

Ramesh S. Balsekar

WATKINS PUBLISHING

LONDON

This edition published in the UK 2007 by
Watkins Publishing, Sixth Floor, Castle House,
75–76 Wells Street, London w1t 3qh

Text Copyright © Ramesh S. Balsekar 2007

1 3 5 7 9 10 8 6 4 2

Designed and typeset by Paul Saunders

Printed and bound in Great Britain

British Library Cataloguing-in-Publication Data Available

isbn: 978-1-905857-14-2

www.watkinspublishing.com

CONTENTS

Events happen, deeds are done.
There is no individual doer of any deed.

❄

Enlightenment means the end of suffering.

❄

There is no soul.
Therefore there is no transmigration of souls.

THE BUDDHA

CHAPTER ONE

CONFUSION IN SPIRITUAL SEEKING

W HAT IS SPIRITUAL seeking all about? Who is seeking what? Obviously, the seeker, in whatever kind of seeking, must be the 'me', the ego. In spiritual seeking, what does the ego want? The obvious answer would be: freedom. The 'ego' means identification with a particular form and name as a separate entity, who considers himself in control of his own life. The freedom which the ego seeks is not, as is generally misconceived, freedom from itself. This can never happen. Even after the total understanding, (enlightenment, Self-realization or whatever) the ego has to live the rest of his life as that particular separate entity: the sage does respond to his name being called even after the fact of Self-realization.

The idea of the ego seeking freedom from itself (!) has been the cause of enormous confusion. So what is the freedom sought by the ego? It must surely mean freedom from the 'other'! And yet, freedom from the 'other' seems as confusing as freedom from itself: the relationship with the other – 'me' and the 'other' – is the very basis of life and living. The 'other' can be as close as the father or the mother, wife, or son or daughter, or as distant as a total stranger.

This is the basic conundrum – the enigma – which every seeker faces at some time or the other. And yet, this aspect of the seeking has not received the attention it deserves. What is sought is not freedom from the 'other' – as impossible as freedom from the 'me' himself – but freedom from the problems which the relationship causes in its functioning. And, one must emphasize that the problem exists even in a very close relationship, perhaps even more intensely than a relationship with a comparable stranger: the closer the relationship, the more intense the pain caused by a 'faulty' relationship.

The core of the problem in spiritual seeking thus centres around the basic cause in a faulty relationship between the 'me' and the 'other'. Is there a basic cause in almost all relationship? If you analyse the many instances of faulty relationships, you will be astonished to realize in how many cases, the cause comes down to something like:

1 Why should she have said that?

2 Why could he not have done this for me?

In other words, the basic cause of almost all faulty relationships arrives at something someone did to hurt the other or something someone did not do to help the other: *the sense of personal doer-ship*. And the relationship can work smoothly only if there is a total acceptance that, in the words of the Buddha, 'Events happen, deeds are done, but there is no individual doer of any deed.'

The fact of the matter is, that while in reality the ego does not 'exist', for all practical purposes it is the ego who is the seeker and it is the ego who needs to be convinced that his 'existence' is merely a matter of divine hypnosis, and that his notion of free will or volition is based on the programming in the body-mind organism – genes plus environmental conditioning – over which he has had no control.

It is only when the ego himself comes to the conclusion, from personal investigation into his own personal experience, that his every single action has been based on some prior happening over which he has had no control, that he is finally compelled to surrender his sense of personal doership, that no one is the doer of any action, neither himself nor the 'other', that all that happens at any moment, through any body-mind organism is brought about by the Primal Energy functioning through each body-mind-organism, according to God's will or the Cosmic Law.

It is only with this *total* acceptance of personal non-doership that the ego ceases to blame anyone for any event – neither himself nor the 'other'; and the relationship between 'him' and the 'other' can run smoothly. What causes the rupture in any relationship in day-to-day living is the heavy load almost every individual carries, of guilt and shame for his own actions and the load of hatred and malice towards the other for his actions.

There is an enormous complexity in our day-to-day living that gives rise to stress and strain almost continuously. Our present-day living has lost all its simplicity and we are bewildered by the complexity and multiplicity of choices in almost whatever we do. And yet, deep down it is everyone's experience that while we try to shape our day-to-day living, what actually happens is that events seem to happen in a unique way, which is not explained by our usual reason. And, in that odd moment, the thought occurs: why do I bother? Why don't I just float along the flow of living instead of struggling against it?

It is clearly everyone's experience that all one can do is to make a choice and, thereafter in spite of all one's efforts, what actually happens – or does not happen – has never been in one's control. Indeed, the more one thinks seriously on these lines, one cannot help coming to the conclusion that the absolute limit of one's free will is to make a decision and try one's best to transform that decision into action. Whether the efforts succeed or not has never really been in one's control. It is quite clear, therefore, that the strain and stress of life is the result of our *expectation of our efforts to succeed.* Therefore, why not, in our own interest, make our best effort and leave it at that? Expectation of results leads to frustration.

Another constant underlying feeling – a result of modern hectic living – is a feeling of uncertainty which constantly haunts anyone who is not naturally a slob: have I left something undone? It is my experience that it really helps to get into the habit of doing immediately whatever can be done at once, instead of putting it forward to another time. I remember a very dear friend of mine saying that his father was always at him, when he was young, yelling some bit of advice or the other all the time, and that he had managed to forget most of such advice which was, of course, meant to make the father's life easier. But he had never forgotten one piece of advice that he has been following scrupulously as long as he could remember: do it now!

Which of us does not remember the many times we have uttered the words of anguish: 'If only I had done it when I thought of it,' or, 'Why did I not do it earlier?' Would it not contribute a lot of peace and harmony in our daily living if such anguished expressions became an exception than a rule?

It is quite a usual experience that one makes a decision in a responsible way, but there is a lingering doubt: have I made the right decision? In such a situation, the really vital point is that there cannot ever be a 'right decision'. One's supposed 'free will' extends only towards making a decision. It is everyone's actual experience that, having made a decision and having made the necessary effort, what happens subsequently has never been in one's control, because other forces in the circumstances come into effect, over which one cannot possibly have any control. And, what is even more extraordinary, the actual results affect not only the apparent doer of the deed, but many other people who were not directly concerned. And this is the fact that produces considerable confusion and uncertainty in life, leading to a continuous sense of discomfort in daily living.

The only answer to this situation is to try and have an awareness of the present moment, a realization of the fact that one's place in the fabric of all that exists in the moment has never been in one's control. What this realization means in effect is that in the moment, every single moment, 'all living things of the Earth open their eyes wide and look Me in the eye'. It is the simple realization that whatever exists in the moment is precisely as it is supposed to be, according to the Cosmic Law that is forever beyond the conception of the human intellect.

This radically realistic and experiential approach to Reality, although more prevalent in the East – especially in India – was not unknown to the great mystics and authentic creative artists all over the world. The summit of Awareness cannot be different in the East and the West. The ninth-century Irish mystic, John Scotus Erigena, knew: 'Every visible and invisible creature is an appearance of God.' And Meister Eckhart in thirteenth-century Europe said: 'The eye with which I see God is the same eye [seeing] with which God sees me.' Eckhart's 'eye' is the very same that in the East is called the 'Buddha eye', or what the Upanishads speak of: 'Verily, oneself is the eye, the endless eye.' It is the eye not of the 'me', but of 'God born in man's soul', of the true Self. In other words, it is not the eye with which one human being sees another, not the eye that operates in a subject-object relationship in relative phenomenality.

In one of the *abhangas*, the saint Tukaram said:

> *Where God abides, let us hasten,*
> *There let us seek our restful haven,*
> *To him our weal and woe we must surrender.*

These lines, said so confidently by the saint, raise wonderful expectations in the heart and mind of the ordinary human being, living his day-to-day life that is usually full of competition and conflict. At the same time, the word 'surrender' is not an acceptable word in the background of the usual conditioning of the modern man. There is, therefore, a certain confusion in one's mind. What is man to surrender? Is he supposed to surrender the identification with the body-mind organism as a separate entity – the ego? This is unthinkable because without that identification as a separate entity even a sage would not be able to live the rest of his span of life, whatever role he is supposed to play in life. So long as one has to live in society, identification as a separate entity must necessarily be there.

Why is the identification to be surrendered? Presumably because it signifies the stifling source of separation that is the cause of the burden the human being feels in his daily living. What one has to consider carefully is where exactly the burden lies, and then it becomes clear that it does not lie in the mere identification as a separate entity, but that it actually lies in the sense of personal doership or volition that usually goes with the identification. The burden is in fact the burden of responsibility for one's individual actions.

The real question to be considered, therefore, is: to what extent does the human being really have free will or volition? Is his action really 'his' action? It is everyone's experience in life that free will actually means the free will to make a choice, a decision. How many of one's decisions have in fact been translated into actions? And among those that have become actions, how many have had the precise results expected when the decisions were made? The answers to both these questions would clearly indicate that the free will that the human being values so highly – and which is the cause of so much guilt and shame, and hatred and ill will – is in fact actually just an illusion. All it does is to create the burden that would be instantly lifted if it were possible for the ego genuinely to surrender its volition or sense of personal doership.

Such surrender means the total and absolute acceptance that it is the will of God – according to a Cosmic Law – that prevails all the time. In other words, the genuine surrender of one's free will and personal doership means, in effect, the clear acceptance of the Buddha's declaration: 'Events happen, deeds are done, but there is no individual doer of any deed.'

What the saint has suggested is that we should abandon conceptual thinking, which is the basis of all our anxiety – 'on Him we shall rest our cares and fears' – and surrender our volition to Him for the simple and obvious reason that our will, our wants, would necessarily be short-sighted. What we think we want in the immediate future may not be in our own interest in the long run. Perhaps an excellent illustration of what the saint means could be found in the fact that, at a certain level of magnification, the cells of an organism would appear to be engaged in a fierce and relentless battle for individual survival, but if the organism were to be observed as a whole through a different level of magnification – a different perspective – it would be clearly seen that what appeared to be a conflict at a lower level was indeed harmony at the level of the entire whole organism.

The sculpted figure of the Dancing Shiva – with its four arms and their gestures, so dynamic and yet so superbly balanced – very beautifully exposes the rhythm and unity of life as such. It personifies the ceaseless flow of Primal Energy passing through infinitely different patterns, merging into the totality of the phenomenal activity of the noumenal Brahman through the ceaselessly changing myriad manifestations in the phenomenal world. Even more impressive, in the same manner, is the sculpted figure Mother Kali in action – Primal Energy personified.

What the saint actually means by his words, 'On Him we shall rest our fears and cares,' is that Whatever-is at any given moment is precisely what is supposed to happen according to the Cosmic Law. Accepting this means resting our fears and cares on Him who is the ocean of bliss and cheer. We do not like the short legs of the duck but they cannot be lengthened even with considerable discomfort to the duck; the same thing applies to the long, ugly legs of the crane that we do not like. Similarly, we have to accept our own imperfections as right and proper in the larger perspective which we may not quite see as such.

The beautiful aspect of such a wider vision is that it restrains our tendency to constantly conceptualize and to compose and judge the What-is in the present moment, and thus becomes conducive to a surrender to the Totality and its natural functioning. This surrender is not the abject surrender of defeat but the elevating surrender of our volition as nothing but the stupid usurpation of the pure subjectivity of the Source. When the subject-object relationship is seen in the correct perspective, we experience the present moment in which we see ourselves as mere units through which happens the universal functioning.

Such an acceptance does not come easily because of the conditioning over thousands of years that a human being is a separate entity responsible for 'his' actions. The confusion – the real problem – for the seeker, even after accepting the fact of non-doership, is: how do I live my life in this world as a separate entity who is held responsible by society for his actions? The problem seems very real until it is realized that in the absence of conceptualizing, as a result of the understanding, all thought and all action at once assume a noumenal nature: whenever action is needed, the working mind provides the necessary thinking and action, without any interference from the thinking mind, concerned only with the results and consequences in the future. In other words, when the understanding – that in all daily subject-object relationships there is really no subject and both are objects – becomes deeply entrenched in the psyche, all actions become spontaneous and natural without the taint of the separation between 'me' and the 'other'.

As the Chinese sage, Huang Po, says: 'If you were to practise keeping your mind motionless at all times with the aim of not creating any thinking, the result would be an absence of dualism, no dependence on others and no attachment; if you would allow all matters to take their own course throughout the day as if you were too ill to bother, without the specified desire to be known or unknown to others, with your mind like a block of stone that mends no holes, then the Universal Law would deeply impregnate your understanding. And, very soon you will find yourself firmly unattached and your reactions to phenomena rapidly decreasing and your ceaseless flow of thought coming to an end.'

Thus the important fact is that the purity and naturalness of one's actions cannot but evoke a sympathetic response from the 'others' concerned even though these actions may not in fact be in their immediate interest. In short, a deep understanding, working mysteriously, miraculously, would make life unbelievably more pleasant and considerably less complicated.

To come back to the practical confusion and problem: in any given situation, what is one to do? The answer is extraordinarily simple: do whatever you think you should do, irrespective of the consequences, over which you have no control whatsoever. Whatever happens – *and the consequences* – would undoubtedly be strictly in accordance with the Cosmic Law. No confusion, no problem.

When the first principles of non-doership in the world of duality become intellectually acceptable – that all actions are happenings based on the will of God-Cosmic Law, and not the doings of any individual doer – there arises some confusion, some difficulty in day-to-day living. It is the ego, with the sense of personal doership still very much present, who has to face this confusion, this problem which seems very real indeed: I like the concept of non-doership very much because I no longer have to accept the responsibility either for the action or for the consequences; but the society in which I have to live still holds me responsible for what it considers as my action.

The answer to this confusion is astonishingly simple: let the ego, with the sense of personal doership, do whatever he thinks he should do. There is neither any confusion nor any problem when one remembers the basic fact – and everyone's personal experience – that no one has any control either over the actual happening (whatever the decision) or over the consequences. Both the actual happening and the consequences, whomever they might affect, would obviously be according to the will of God-Cosmic Law, and have to be accepted as such. Whoever is affected will be affected strictly accordingly to his own destiny, depending upon the will of God-Cosmic Law. There is truly no confusion at all. One simply has to accept the verdict of the society about the action and the consequences.

The confusion really concerns the concept of responsibility for one's action. If I still have to accept responsibility for my action to the society in which I live, where is the big deal about the acceptance of non-doership? What is the real benefit I am supposed to have by accepting totally that no one is the doer? The answer is vital: one's responsibility to the society can never be removed, but what is removed totally is the more unbearable *responsibility to oneself*. The acceptance of non-doership means I no longer have to carry the massive load of guilt and shame for my action, nor the load of hatred and malice for the actions of the 'other'.

In other words, once the ego has done a thorough and honest investigation into his own personal experience, he will have come to the unequivocal conclusion that every single action that he thought was 'his' action has turned out on investigation to be merely the consequential reaction to an earlier happening over which he had absolutely no control. Soon, the simple action of scratching his nose turns out, on investigation, to be the reaction of the brain to an itch over which he had no control. Thus the ego, who had earlier enormous anxiety that the removal of personal doership would endanger his very existence, is soon convinced that not only does his existence as a separate entity continue unhampered, but that his day-to-day living has now become enormously simpler, with the load of personal doership removed: total absence of any guilt and shame for his actions and of the hatred and malice, jealousy and envy towards any 'other'.

Even more importantly, the ego now finds that in order to be in direct harmony with the oneness of Reality, all he has to remember – and even this has become natural and spontaneous – is that there is only one Reality functioning through every single body-mind organism, while the body-mind-organism as a separate entity continues to function as an essential part of the One Whole. The provocative Persian philosopher, Omar Khayyam, has depicted the human condition this way in the *Rubaiyat*, in the following words:

> *We are no other than a moving row*
> *Of visionary Shapes that come and go*
> *Round with this Sun-illumined Lantern held*
> *In Midnight by the Master of the Show;*
>
> *Impotent pieces of the Game He plays*
> *Upon this chequer-board of Nights and Days;*
> *Hither and thither moves, and checks and slays;*
> *And one by one back in the closet lays.*

To live in this realization that all there is in phenomenality is the One Infinite Universe – all definitions and divisions, all confusions have vanished – is to live anchored in the peace and tranquillity of Self-realization.

The average person cannot help seeing in day-to-day living the fact that a few people, generally known as kind and wise people – sages – seem to live their lives enjoying the same pleasure and suffering the same pains and miseries as the ordinary person; and yet, deep down, they seem to be anchored in peace and harmony. And the ordinary person is confused as to how this could happen. He has somehow been under the impression that enlightenment would produce a big change for the person concerned; he does not know exactly in what way. The word that has confused him is 'bliss'. It is his impression that the enlightened person has no more problems in life, that God looks after him and that he is always in 'bliss'. And yet here is the sage suffering the same kind of pains in his daily living as he himself does. This he finds utterly confusing.

It is true that the sage seems generally relaxed not only in his own daily living but also remarkably comfortable in his relationships with other people, even with those who are supposed to be difficult to deal with. What is more, the very presence of the man of wisdom – not the man of learning who very often is proud and arrogant – seems to exude peace and harmony in spite of the fact that he seems to respond to outside events with an absolutely normal reaction. And yet, there is nothing extraordinary about the sage. The confusion is: what is the big deal about 'enlightenment'?

The question about the enlightened person which bothers the spiritual seeker is: how does the Ultimate Understanding translate itself into action in daily living? What makes the ordinary person feel such peace and relaxation in the sage's company? The simple answer is that the sage is constantly aware of the 'happening' of life effortlessly; and this 'being aware' keeps functioning even when thoughts, feelings, desires arise in the body-mind organism. Because they are merely witnessed as they arise and take their course, there is no involvement through an egoic reaction to the thoughts, feelings and desires: there is no sense of personal doership about any happening – neither himself nor the other, no blame to either.

The true understanding absorbs the realization that, like the clouds that wander through the sky, thoughts and feelings floating through the mind have neither any home nor any roots. Once Consciousness is understood as the substratum of everything phenomenal (including sentient beings and 'their' thoughts and actions), discriminatory judging – and blaming – ceases because no thing is seen to have any real independent existence. Then the virtues and vices are seen not as opposites as such, but as polaric counterparts that negate each other when superimposed.

All action becomes spontaneous, being the operation of virtuality as latent power that exhibits itself in the miraculous fruition of plants, the formation of eyes and ears, the circulation of blood and the reticulation of nerves. Such force or power is generated without any conscious direction – it is a natural and spontaneous working force, of which, for instance, electricity (no one knows its nature even if we know how it works!) is only one aspect.

This miraculous natural force – the basis of which is the absence of personal volition – virtuality (which has nothing to do with siddhis or spiritual powers) has been beautifully described by Lao Tzu:

> *Superior virtue is not (volitionally) virtuous, and thus is virtue.*
> *Inferior virtue does not forsake being virtuous, and thus is not*
> *   virtue.*
> *Superior virtue needs no force, but nothing remains undone,*
> *Inferior virtue uses force, but achieves nothing.*

Virtuality is steeped in ordinariness and anonymity, and it is precisely for this reason that the ordinary person is confused and puzzled when he comes across it in day-to-day living. It is this same force or power that brings out the genius in various people in various fields of life, which cannot be explained in mundane terms through the step-by-step linear method.

When action is spontaneous, without the slightest hesitation or wavering, there is no room for thinking about the future. The curious fact is that the chances of survival are best where there does not exist any undue anxiety to survive: the special force of virtuality is available to those who do not tire themselves out through anxiety. And the joke is that 'anxiety' includes the positive effort to stop the worry. It is the spurious individual ego-doer who does the worrying. True understanding accepts whatever life brings and responds to each experience without resistance or recoil. Thus, speaking of the death of his master, Lao Tzu, Chuang Tzu said: 'The Master came because it was time. He left because of the natural flow.'

In other words, the senses, feelings and thoughts must be allowed to operate in their natural flow because any attempt to control them could only result in worsening the disturbance. As Lord Krishna has said in the *Bhagavad Gita*:

> *The man who is one with the Divine and understands the Truth believes 'I can do nothing at all' because in seeing, breathing, speaking, emitting, grasping, opening and closing the eyes, he holds that it is only the senses that are concerned with their respective objects.*

It is only through true understanding – the principle of non-doership – that any change could occur in thoughts, emotions and desires; any muscular effort at controlling them would necessarily be futile because the nervous system is essentially electric circuitry and not muscle.

The deep and clear ultimate understanding – not the intellectual comprehension at the linear level – of What-is leads to true humility and the annihilation of the sense of personal doership in the ego entity. This means, in effect, natural and spontaneous action which reflects the fact that human intelligence – not the mind-intellect – is very much an inherent aspect of the whole organism of the phenomenal universe, which maintains the functional order in dynamic balance through the operation of the Consciousness that is the substratum of the entire phenomenal manifestation. This balance in the functional order of the phenomenal manifestation is maintained through the natural mechanism of polarity between apparent opposites or counterparts. Conflict based on stark, irreconcilable opposites of good and evil, subject and object, 'me' and the 'other' would, therefore, be not only superficial but basically unacceptable to the essential culture. What this really means is that this entire phenomenal show of the universe – the *lila* – cannot have any real purpose and it is futile to seek a goal in life in open competition against all contenders.

Most 'successful' men would readily admit this in their hearts of hearts, but the conditioning over the years is so powerful that they would not dare to admit it openly that over the years it had been a futile experience to seek a goal in life. Ever more difficult to admit would be their experience that the achievement of such a goal had not really brought them any deep sense of fulfilment that their hearts had craved for. As soon as a goal is conceived, spontaneity is destroyed and the self-conscious sense of personal doership is taken over. From then on, vision has become pinpointed on the goal, thus missing everything really worthwhile in life.

The 'purposeful' life indeed misses the beauty of daily living: to enjoy the unicity of the Noumenon in the duality and multiplicity of the phenomenal living. It is only when the ego clearly realizes this fact that there springs into action the total freedom and then arises the floodlight of true vision which misses nothing and takes in everything. Then, spontaneous action, not being in conflict with the natural course of events, enables the man of understanding to be fully receptive to the entirety of the universe, and to a true feeling of fulfilment. Relaxed and free of tension, he lets life flow without being self-conscious either of the effort or the result.

An important point for the seeker to understand clearly, in order to avoid any confusion, is that the acceptance of the What-is in any moment does not shut out the phenomenal world as an illusion because then he would be making a false distinction between the real and the unreal, between the substance and the shadow, between the Noumenon and the phenomena. As the

Buddha has put it so vividly: samsara (life) is *dukkha* (suffering), Nirvana (the Source) is shanti (peace) – *and they are not two.*

The basic understanding has to be that any appearance, any shadow, cannot but be a reflection of that very Reality, which is all there is. Illusion cannot have an independent existence: Noumenality is at once both transcendent to, and immanent in, phenomenality, and any distinction is seen to be void. Thus, with this basic understanding, a certain amount of dispassion gets cultivated through the realization that any distinction between the attractive and the unattractive can only mean egoic involvement, and therefore suffering. Both the attractive and the un-attractive are interconnected polaric counterparts: the very basis of the phenomenal manifestation, and its functioning that we call 'life'.

A really important aspect of this basic understanding is that, in practical living, the usual rivalry and competition genuinely becomes more of a game – *lila* – rather than a strife and conflict, leading to guilt and shame for one's actions, and hatred and malice, jealousy and envy for the other's actions. In other words, the immediate result of the deep understanding clearly shows the absurdity of a strife between 'me' and the 'other', both being merely instruments through which the Primal Energy functions. Any situation in life – how could it have been otherwise?! Does it really matter?! The illusory distinctions merely constitute the diversity in the course of day-to-day living, which otherwise would have been an unbearable bore. There is the case of the famous actor of yesteryears, George Sanders, who committed suicide and left a note to say that he was taking his own life because he had everything life had to offer – good health, money, fame – and he was too bored to go on living!

The man of understanding does not withdraw and hide himself from the natural world of people and events: that would itself mean a judgement on life and living. He continues to remain in society, playing the game of daily living according to the regular rules, but his mind is empty of futile ambition, cunning, desire and artifice. He wanders through life witnessing and participating in all experiences without getting involved through attachments, either positively to the delights or negatively to the pains in the moment. Therefore, he is seen by the 'other' as extending virtue and kindness to the whole world of the 'other', without contending with anyone. Even an apparent contention becomes a joke when he is not keen at all on winning any argument.

In order to prevent any confusion from arising, it is necessary to clarify one point: it is not that thoughts, feelings, desires do not arise in the body-mind organism of the man of understanding, as a natural biological function. The arising of thoughts, feelings, desires in the mind is as natural and spontaneous as the arising of waves on an expanse of water. Any attempt to suppress this natural happening can only result in failure and frustration. What does happen after the dawning of the understanding is that the thoughts, feelings, desires that have arisen *are not pursued by the ego*. The understanding results in mere witnessing the natural process of the arising and the disappearing of the desires without any involvement, and then, when they do not get any sustenance from the involvement of the ego, they can only disappear in the course of time. In other words, in the absence of sustenance, the arising of the desires itself grows less and less both in its intensity and frequency.

The human mind is somehow accustomed to think of change in terms of lateral or horizontal growth, but our experience would seem to be that the change is more in the nature of a cycle: in the cycle of birth and death, creation and dissolution, rise and fall of political systems and civilizations, and in the inevitable cycles of happiness and unhappiness by way of gains and losses in the lives of individual entities. Yet the mind refuses to accept the inevitability of such cycles, and this refusal means frustration and misery. It is this kind of frustration and misery – and not the actual pain or pleasure in the moment – that the Buddha referred to as the *dukkha* of samsara, the suffering in life.

Acceptance of the existence of these cycles simply means accepting an inevitable fact of life and not a 'fatalistic' attitude. Such acceptance simply means witnessing them as an inevitable part of life and living, and thus not getting mentally involved in them. 'This too shall pass' is an excellent attitude in life that would prevent unnecessary frustration. Even one's physical energy is subject to these cycles. It is everyone's experience that the level of physical energy and mental zest is sometimes highly active and creative, while at other times, for no apparent reason, one feels stagnant, and physically and mentally rather depressed. Not accepting this inevitable fact – not going with the flow of life – means unnecessary frustration.

Going with the flow of life does not mean being indifferent to what the moment has brought. It does not mean 'detachment'. This is a specific area in which there is considerable confusion for the spiritual seeker. 'Going with the flow' simply means *fully* enjoying the pleasure of the moment for the very reason that it will not last; it also means dealing with the pain of the moment as best as one can, again knowing that too will pass. 'Going with the flow of life' means not pursuing the pleasure, nor unduly trying to avoid the inevitable pains. The astonishing noticeable fact is that this attitude makes the pleasures bring more pleasure and the pains bring less pain. In other words, 'going with the flow of life' brings an inner state of peace and harmony, grace and ease. Perhaps this is what is meant by the words 'Peace of God': the sheer joy of being.

There need be no confusion about non-resistance to the present moment. Non-resistance does not mean doing nothing. Indeed, it is the very basis of the Eastern martial arts: yield in order to overcome. In Taoism, there is a term '*wu wei*' which is pregnant with wisdom. It means 'activity without individual doership' – totally different from inactivity, arising from indecision, fear, inertia. It means 'non-action' in which there is no involvement of the ego. It means truly a natural action happening in the present moment, not action by the thinking mind and a tense body. As Jesus has put it: 'Consider the lilies of the field, how they grow; they neither toil nor do they spin.'

There have been recorded cases of prisoners waiting for execution on death row, when suddenly, inexplicably they realized the deepest joy and peace of true surrender. There have been recorded cases of prisoners in Hitler's extermination camps, while standing in a row waiting to be led to the gas chambers, suddenly laughing loud and hard, joking with the armed guards who of course, thought that tension had driven them to insanity, yet deeply recognizing the miracle of surrender to the present moment. They were no longer afraid of death because they had died to the present moment; Consciousness had released itself from the confines of a three-dimensional human object.

There is always a persistent curiosity, especially among spiritual seekers, coupled with considerable confusion, about what actually happens in the daily living of the one who has awakened to the Reality. Witnessing the lives of several sages, over quite a long period, a common thread has been seen among the several sages:

1　The sage seems to live his life with the total understanding that life lives itself through all the human and other bodies, including his own.

2　The sage seems to live his life with the total conviction that all the separate entities are separate only as waves, but in fact rise and fall on the one great ocean of Being. He *knows* that when the mind is still, the Reality that is experienced is totally devoid of all separations. Going with the flow of life, he is usually seen to be wholly free from anxiety and frustration.

3 The sage responds when his name is called, but *knows* that 'That' which responds *in all cases*, is the Primal Consciousness that is all there is. He is quite happy to be forgotten and ignored by the world. He truly appreciates the privilege of being anonymous.

4 The sage lives his life, witnessing life as it happens through the various separate entities with the constant awareness that the past and the future are abstractions and that this moment is the only Reality. Thus, the sage lives his life to the full, accepting all experiences, from moment to moment, unrestrained by the thinking mind, like 'piling fresh fruit in a basket without a bottom'.

5 The sage is seen to be helping anyone in any way he can in the moment, but people seem to be barely aware of his existence. He truly seems to extend virtue and kindness to the whole world without contending with anyone.

6 The sage lives his life letting spiritual practices, as such, happen when they do, fully aware that they may stop at the appropriate time: he has never been doing any spiritual practice.

In short, the sage lives his life outwardly in the world of good and evil, beauty and ugliness, yet without judging anyone. He is kind to the kind and the unkind alike; he is faithful to the faithful and the unfaithful alike. The sage seems to live his life, being a conscious but passive witness of the miracle of the unfolding of phenomenal existence in all its divergent unicity and ordinariness.

An area in which there is considerable confusion among spiritual seekers is the concept of 'duality' and separation. The seeker has been told in no uncertain terms that everything is Unicity and there is only one Source; and at the same time he is told to surrender to God. Such a situation must necessarily cause great confusion. This confusion is worse confounded with a distinction being made between 'duality' and 'dualism'.

The basic cause of human conflict and unhappiness is 'dualism' as distinct from 'duality'. It is absolutely necessary to clearly understand the basic difference between the two terms. In fact such a clear understanding could itself be the solution for human unhappiness because it would relieve the human being from the double bind in which he finds himself in his relentless pursuit of unalloyed happiness.

The fact of the matter is that 'duality' is polaric, interrelated, and therefore, not really separate; whereas 'dualism' means opposition, separation, and therefore, conflict. Phenomenal manifestation is a process of objectivization that basically requires an *apparent* dichotomy into a subject that perceives and object that is perceived. This is the process known as 'duality': all phenomena that are sensorially perceivable are the correlation of a subject (*object* cognizer) and the object (*object* cognized). This process of duality makes it clear that without such a process there cannot exist any phenomena, and that neither of the two phenomenal objects (neither the *cognizer* object nor the *cognized* object) has any independent existence of its own: *the existence of the one depends upon the existence of the other.*

When the basis of 'duality' is thus clearly apperceived, there cannot remain any question of either any samsara (phenomenal day-to-day living) or any 'bondage' for any conceptual individual for the simple reason that the 'individual' concerned does not have an independent existence but is merely the psychosomatic apparatus, the instrument through which the process of perceiving and cognizing happens. Our unhappiness, our conflict, our 'bondage' arises essentially because of the identification of What-we-are (Consciousness) with the object-cognizer element in the necessary dichotomy of the whole mind (Consciousness) into subject and object (both are only objects) in the process of the functioning of the manifestation, as duality.

This identification or entitification as a *separate*, independent entity (as the pseudo-subject) is the 'dualism' – the maya – which results as the practical application, in day-to-day living, of the original principle of 'duality', that is polaric, interrelated, and therefore, *not separate*. It is *this illusory entitification with doership that causes all the conflict*, all the suffering, all the unhappiness that is collectively termed 'bondage'. The very instantaneous apperception of this fact of the pseudo-subject as an independent entity-doer means the freedom from this bondage.

The one seemingly insurmountable difficulty for the average spiritual seeker regarding Self-realization, in his day-to-day living, is the concept of 'separation'. He has heard it said, time and time again, from different masters, that Self-realization cannot happen so long as he harbours the notion that he is separate from the other human beings. He has thus taken it for granted that Self-realization means the absence of separation. And yet, he finds it almost impossible to accept, even intellectually, that he himself as an independent entity-doer can ever possibly not be separate from every other ego-doer. And, to add to the confusion, in the many teachings, various methods are prescribed for the seeker to practise, several disciplines to be undertaken so that 'he' may convince himself that he is not a separate entity. The result is that there are hundreds of seekers who find themselves mired in frustration so deeply that some have even contemplated suicide. And the pity of it all is that the solution is truly so very simple!

And what is this simple principle that a separate entity is supposed to know that would make him accept totally that there is really no separation between the billions of separate human beings? This principle is that every human being is a *separate* uniquely designed instrument, through which the *same* Primal

Energy (or Source, or Consciousness or God) functions, and brings about whatever is supposed to happen through each separate human instrument, every moment, according to a Cosmic Law. In other words, the separation as such is only in regard to the outer appearance of the human instrument, but the functioning element is the same: the Source, the Primal Energy-Consciousness. The Primal Energy functions through each uniquely programmed human gadget precisely as electricity, an aspect of the same energy, functions through each electrical gadget, producing precisely what each electrical gadget is designed to produce. This is the way 'separation' both exists and does not exist in our day-to-day living. There is really no room at all for any confusion.

It is only the mind that is free from the restrictive preoccupation of doership that can be receptive to peace and tranquillity in the phenomenal day-to-day living. Also, it is only such a mind, not fragmented by the sense of personal doership – either for oneself or the other – that can be receptive to the experience of expanded Consciousness in the inner space, generally known as a mystical experience. And it is only such a mind which is free from any sense of real separation. And absence of separation means love.

In our day-to-day living, what happens is that our education extends to knowledge about our society in such a way that we can continue to be slaves to the mind rather than the masters. We cater to the endless desires and demands of a turbulent psyche that seeks security in life through material gains and rewards. A change can happen only when the human being realizes that material wealth and social status do not, by themselves, bring what the human being truly wants, deep down: to be anchored in peace and harmony, to be comfortable with oneself and comfortable with others all the time, while facing life and accepting whatever the moment brings.

The basic concept of Advaita is that human beings are not individual separate entities with free will and personal doership, but programmed body-mind instruments through which the One Consciousness or Primal Energy functions. Therefore, there is truly no individual entity responsible for any action. All actions – and their consequences or results – happen according to God's will or the Cosmic Law. Therefore, no one need blame himself or anyone else for any happening. Therefore, there is no question of any load of guilt or shame for one's actions, nor any jealousy or envy or hatred towards anyone else. This is what spiritual seeking is all about.

CHAPTER TWO

SIN AND GUILT

The wheel of life

Logic and reason of the West think of life as being linear. The East understands life and existence as being circular: the circle means returning to the starting point. Life begins with the first breath, and ends with the last breath. Samsara means the wheel of life, whether it is the seasons of the year or the rotation of the planets. It is curious – perhaps significant – that the East paid little attention to chronological history, only to the relationship of forces and events, the cause-effect relationship, which is the basis of life and living.

The circle has its own logic, magic, mystery: hardly any movement in the universe is linear. All movements seem to be circular, returning to the beginning and starting again, apparently endlessly: the movement of the stars or the planets including Earth, or the life of man. The manifestation has appeared with what science calls 'the Big Bang' or what mysticism calls 'the Awareness of Consciousness', the burst of the Potential Energy into its activization and finally going back into the nucleus when the burst of energy exhausts itself. When the new moon attains its fullness, the reverse movement starts.

Perhaps it is for this reason that Lao Tzu says, 'When the work is done, and when one's name is becoming to be known, it is wisdom to withdraw into obscurity.' Change is the very basis of life and living, yet it is the peculiarity, the nature of the mind, to want more and more of an acceptable fact and experience, and not to understand the significance of the circle. If you keep feeling a point that has been sharpened, if you insist on security all the time, the point cannot preserve its sharpness, the experience cannot preserve its freshness and vigour.

A child does not recognize the opposites as irreconcilable, like an adult, because the ego does not develop until the child is about three years old, when it begins to think in terms of the first person singular as the 'me'. There is no basic difference between the child and the sage. Neither recognizes the opposites: of course, the child because of ignorance, and the sage because of wisdom. Indeed, ignorance and knowledge are themselves the interconnected opposites, and wisdom transcends both.

A child has no conception of 'mine' and 'not-mine', and cannot understand the concept of theft. Nor does the child have any conception of Truth and untruth because it cannot differentiate between dream and Reality. It is only the ego that distinguishes between dream and Reality. The sage understands this 'Reality' as only a dream. This is the reason a precocious, intuitive child could say, 'We are all dreaming, and we shall wake up when we are dead.' Life and death are part of the flowing that is phenomenality.

Until the ego is born, when Consciousness identifies itself with the individual organism, there is no dualism in the infant. As Traherne has put it, 'All the world was his, the skies, the stars, the sun and the moon, and he was the only spectator and enjoyer of it, without any proprieties or fragmentations, until he was corrupted and made to learn the dirty devices of this world.' There is an indivisible innocence in the infant, but it is an ignorant innocence. The same innocence arises in the sage at the end of the process of evolution whereby the ego-doer arises and gets extinguished through the dawn of wisdom and realization. As Jesus has said, 'Only those who have become like children can enter the Kingdom of God.'

There is another aspect of similarity between the infant and the sage. If you observe an infant sleeping in his cot, you will notice that the infant breathes not through his chest but through his abdomen. The breathing of an adult is usually through the chest because, as has been established, the breathing moves from the abdomen towards the chest when the gradual building up of tensions in life brings about a separateness between the animal organism of the infant and the intellectual organism of the human adult. With wisdom, and the healing of the separation between 'me' and the 'other', the sage regains the normal abdominal breathing.

It is clearly noticed that the breathing in the average individual adult in deep sleep is much more through the abdomen than through the chest, but that when the sleep is restless or the individual is dreaming, there is a shift of the breathing upwards towards the chest. This simply means the more tense you are, the higher is the centre of your breathing.

There is a Japanese word – no other language would seem to have its equivalent – for the initial source of breath: *tanden*, supposedly located two inches below the navel. The further a person is away from natural existence, the further the breath moves away from *tanden*. (This has nothing to do with the breathing as seen or considered purely from the viewpoint of the athlete or physical culturist.)

According to Tao, there are three centres in the human organism: (1) the *tanden*, the natural or the spiritual centre; (2) the centre of the heart where resides the emotional person or the devotional seeker, and (3) the centre of the head, where resides the intellectual philosopher, the rationalist. The intellectual, the rationalist lives on the surface, where everything is cut and dried, logical and reasonable. The emotional devotee lives in the heart, where arise not only love and desire, but also devotion. But, as Lao Tzu says, the heart is not the ultimate depth; it is necessary to go to the deepest level of existence, the natural state of the *tanden* where the individual is in harmony with the totality of phenomenal existence.

The basics

When visitors come to see me, the first thing I tell them is that whatever I say is a 'concept' – not the truth. I add that anything any sage has ever said at any time in history is a concept, that whatever any scripture of any religion has ever said is a concept. A 'concept' is something that is liable to interpretation and there-fore acceptable to some people and not acceptable to others. The 'truth' is that which no one can deny.

Most visitors, when asked if they think there is something they know which is the truth and not a concept, have no reply. My answer then is that there indeed is ONE truth that no one can deny. An atheist may come to me and assert that he has studied the subject deeply for twenty years, and has a doctorate in Com-parative Religions, and he is totally convinced that 'God' does not exist. I would tell him that he is entitled to his view because 'God' is a concept. I would then ask him: God may or may not exist, but can you deny that you yourself do exist? This *impersonal* aware-ness of BEING, of existing, which no one can deny, is the only TRUTH. It is not capable of any interpretation. In other words, 'I AM' is the only truth. 'I am Tom, Dick or Harry' is not the truth. The truth 'I AM' is covered or hidden by the personal ego of the individual.

It is this individual ego who is the spiritual seeker. And the 'ego' really does not exist. When someone tells me that he has come to me in order to have his ego destroyed so that he can be 'Self-realized' or 'enlightened', I would ask him to produce his ego and I would smash him out of existence before his very eyes!

What then is the 'ego'? When I ask this question – what do you understand by the word 'ego'? – the answer from most people is that the ego is the 'identification with a body as an entity separate from the other people, and that this separation is what makes people unhappy'. But mere identification with a name and form (*naama, roopa*) cannot really constitute the ego because even a sage who is supposed to have had his ego destroyed also responds to his name being called exactly like the ordinary person. In other words, the ordinary person considers himself as an entity with a body and name, *separate from others*, exactly as the sage does! Then what is it that distinguishes the sage from the ordinary person? What is it that makes a sage a sage? The answer is that the sage has the total understanding without the slightest doubt that, in the words of the Buddha, '*Events happen, deeds are done, but there is no individual doer thereof.*' In other words, the ordinary person considers that he or she is the doer of his or her actions and is responsible for those actions; and that, similarly, every person is responsible for his or her actions. On the other hand, the sage has the total, absolute conviction that neither he nor anyone else is the doer of any action, that all action is the divine happening through some body-mind organism and not anything 'done' by anyone.

At this stage, the question arises: if no one is the 'doer' of any action, who lives his life in this world? Who is it that experiences happiness or unhappiness? Who is it that seeks 'Self-realization' or 'enlightenment' or whatever? The straight answer is that we think we live our lives, but in reality, life is being lived through the billions of body-mind organisms. It is the ego who thinks he is the doer, and experiences happiness or unhappiness. So, in this matter, the basic concept is that ever since a baby is born and seeks its mother's breast instinctively, life has been nothing but seeking, and it is the ego who thinks he is the seeker, the doer, responsible for his actions.

The basis of this concept is that the human being is really nothing more than a uniquely programmed instrument or computer through which the Source or Primal Energy or Consciousness or God (or whatever label you give to the Source – the ONE without a second) functions and brings about actions. In other words, the Source uses the billions of uniquely programmed human computers exactly as you use your computer. You put in an input in your programmed computer and the computer has no choice but to produce the output for which it has been programmed. You could, of course, say that the computer has the 'right' to produce the output just as you think it is your 'right' to produce your action!

So, what is the programming in 'your' body-mind organism, and how does the Source (or God) use the human computer? You had no choice about your parents and therefore about the genes or the unique DNA in your body-mind organism; nor did you have any choice about the environment in which you were born and in which your body-mind organism has been receiving its conditioning from day one. The unique DNA and the environmental conditioning together form the 'programming' in your body-mind computer.

It may seem shocking that the human being, who is supposed to have been created 'in the image of God', is being reduced to a programmed computer. But let us not forget that the human being is basically an object – a species of object that, together with thousands of other species of objects, form the totality of manifestation. And what functions through the billions of human computers is the Source or God or Primal Energy, producing through each human computer exactly that output or action that is supposed to happen according to the will of God (or Source) or according to, let us say, Natural Law or Cosmic Law. This is not unlike the fact that electricity, an aspect of the Primal Energy, functioning through each electrical gadget produces that which the particular gadget has been designed to produce.

How does the Source (or God) use the human computer? According to my concept, the input is a thought that comes from Consciousness, the Source; the brain responds to this input and out comes the output in the form of a reaction in the human body-mind organism. Research has proved that the thought input occurs half a second before the ego's reaction. It is therefore obvious that the individual ego has no control over the input, and, of course, the ego has had no control over the programming in the body-mind organism. In other words, the ego has no control over the input and has certainly had no control over the programming that dictates the reaction, which is obviously a biological or mechanical reaction. And yet the ego calls this reaction its own action! Thought is one input; the other inputs are based on the objects to which the senses respond – what is seen or heard or tasted or smelt or touched – over which the ego also has no control. In other words, what happens is that the brain reacts to an input in the body-mind organism strictly according to the programming over neither of which the ego has no control. *And yet the ego says that this mechanical reaction is his action!*

An important point is that the biological or mechanical reaction in the body-mind computer is exactly the same whether it is that of an ordinary person or of a sage. If the input is the same and the programming is similar, then the output is most likely to be the same. If the two persons see the same thing or hear the same thing, the output will be the same, e.g. anger or amusement or fear or pity or whatever. There is a great misconception that Self-realization or enlightenment brings about such a tremendous transformation that the sage becomes a perfect human being: no anger, no frustration, and no fear. Then the question arises: if the reaction in the programmed computer of the body-mind organism is more or less the same, what is the difference between a sage and an ordinary man? The answer lies in what happens after the initial reaction happens.

In the case of the ordinary person when a negative reaction happens – anger arises – the ego takes over the situation. The ego says, 'I am angry; I should not be angry, I am told by the doctor that if I do not control my anger, I shall have high blood pressure and that could lead to a heart attack or a stroke.' This is the involvement of the ego in horizontal time whereas the reaction in the body-mind computer is only in the present moment. In the case of a sage, anger arises and may take the form of shouting against the person who caused it. But there the reaction ends and the sage is open to whatever might happen in the next moment. I remember a particular incident when I was visiting my guru, Nisargadatta Maharaj. Someone asked a question, and anger arose. Maharaj shouted at him, 'You have been coming here for six years and you ask a stupid question like that?' The visitor concerned knew Maharaj well enough and he gave a witty answer; everyone laughed and Maharaj's laughter was the loudest: one moment anger, the next moment 'amusement'! In the case of the ordinary person, there would have been the identification of the ego with that anger as 'I am angry and that man made me angry; therefore, I shall not laugh at that man's wit'. In other words, in the case of the ordinary man, the involvement of the ego would have taken place horizontally in time and he would not have been open to what happened in the next moment. The sage lives from moment to moment, the body-mind organism responding to whatever happens from moment to moment, whereas the ego of the ordinary man reacts to the natural, biological reaction of the body-mind organism, and gets involved in horizontal time and is not open to what happens from moment to moment. The ego of the ordinary man is therefore sometimes happy and most times unhappy because of the involvement in horizontal time.

What does the spiritual seeker seek?

Consciousness not aware of itself suddenly becomes aware of itself – Potential Primal Energy suddenly activizes itself, and in that instant (the Big Bang!) the entire universe with its infinite variety is born. Consciousness is immanent in each atom and sub-atom, and at the same time transcends all manifestation and everything therein.

Noumenon and phenomena – unmanifest and manifest – are in essence ONE, which has divided itself in a sort of mirage or illusion in order to enjoy this duality as life and living. At the end of this apparent expression, when the activized energy has exhausted itself, the entire manifestation goes back into the Source, the Unmanifest:

> As the spider weaves its thread out of its own mouth, plays with it and then withdraws it again into itself, so the eternal unchangeable Lord, who is without form, without attributes, who is absolute knowledge and absolute bliss, evolves the whole universe out of Himself, plays with it for a while, and again withdraws it into Himself.
>
> *Bhagavatam*

From the point of view of this very basic concept, there can be no questioner to ask any questions. But questions can and do arise from the apparent ego who must live his life in this manifested world.

To my usual question, the visitor surprisingly often answers that he or she has been a 'spiritual seeker' for many years and that this constant questioning has been a cause of much misery. My usual reaction to such a statement is that the misery is perhaps the result of confusion about what the seeker is seeking and how that is to be achieved. It is, again, surprising how quickly this suggestion of mine is accepted with a sense of relief!

What are you really seeking? The usual answer is an embarrassed 'I really don't know'. Then I suggest that perhaps the reason he does not know what he is seeking is that he did not start the seeking! That really stuns the visitor because, deep down, he *knows* that the seeking happened and he did not ever deliberately start the seeking.

What does a spiritual seeker really seek? The answer often is contained in certain words he has come across in some books or in conversation with some spiritual seekers – such as 'I am seeking myself', or 'I am seeking the God within me', or 'I am seeking Truth' or something like that which is very vague. Sometimes I am surprised by a simple, honest answer like, 'I want to be comfortable with myself, and I know that I cannot be comfortable with myself unless I am comfortable with others.' My suggestion usually is that perhaps what he is looking for is THAT which transcends both the happiness in material things and the unhappiness in the lack of material things in life – perhaps we could call that PEACE. The actual experience of this peace happens in deep sleep and, also, during certain moments in the waking state when the thinking mind of expectation happens to be still.

What, therefore, the seeker is really seeking is the peace of deep sleep to prevail even in the waking state when the thinking mind is not dormant as in the sleeping state. Inner peace prevails in deep sleep because the ego is not active – the sense of personal doership accompanied by the sense of expectation is absent. The same inner peace can prevail even in the waking state only if this sense of personal doership is absent while participating in life. In other words, while activity is happening in the waking state in life and living, inner peace can prevail only if there is the total, unconditional conviction that there is no individual doer behind any action happening through any body-mind organism. This means in effect total unconditional acceptance of 'What-is' at any moment for the simple reason that there is no individual capable of doing anything, that everything that happens is a divine happening through some body-mind organism which simply had to happen, at the moment at the place where it happened, according to the will of the Source (or God), or, if you so prefer it, according to the 'Cosmic Law'.

What really brings about the inner peace which the seeker is seeking is the total absolute conviction that God's will prevails every moment, and, therefore, there is no question of any guilt or sin for any individual person. What prevents or obstructs the prevailing inner peace is the constant irritant: 'I should not have done what I did' or 'I should have done what I did not do.' The *total* acceptance of the four simple words 'Thy will be done' brings about this inner peace because the significance of those four simple words – which truly need no interpretation – is that if something has happened, or not happened, it could only be because that was God's will, and not because someone did or did not do something. In other words, being able to accept God's will (which itself depends on God's will!) means enormous relief from the monstrous load of sin and guilt on the mind.

In this regard, it is interesting to note a report from London, quoted in an Indian newspaper in 1998:

Bangladeshis are World's Happiest People
London, 9 December:

Would you believe it, Bangladesh is the happiest nation in the world. The United States, on the other hand, is a sad story. It ranks only 46th in the World Happiness Survey. That's way behind India, the 5th happiest place in the world, and others including Ghana and Latvia, Croatia and Estonia. Research led by London School of Economics professors into the link between personal spending power and the perceived quality of life has conclusively proved that money can buy everything but happiness. The study revealed that people in Bangladesh, one of the poorest countries in the world, derive far more happiness from their small incomes than, for example, the British (32nd on the list) do from their relatively large bank balances. In fact, people in most rich countries including Austria, the Netherlands, Switzerland, Canada, Japan and others are much unhappier than their poorer counterparts in countries like the Dominican Republic and Armenia.

Most unfortunate, however, are Russians and some other parts of the former Soviet Union. They are neither rich nor happy, indicates the World Happiness Survey. Slovenia, Lithuania, Slovakia, Russia, Ukraine, Belarus, Bulgaria, and Moldova follow the United States in the list to bring up the rear.

The study shows that although the British have twice as much more to spend in real terms compared with 40 years ago, their perceived quality of life has not improved. Earlier surveys revealed that many Britons thought money could bring happiness. The new study shows that such a link still exists in some countries because a small increase in income can mean large improvements in lifestyle.

However, beyond a certain income level, that direct relationship breaks down. According to the research, happiness in rich countries now is far more dependent on close personal relationships, good health and job satisfaction.

God's will and man's free will

My experience has been that most visitors are able to accept the concept of God's will prevailing *most of the time* because they not only see the logic of it but, more importantly, they experience a feeling of tremendous relief and freedom: freedom from guilt and responsibility. But the problem arises because the concept of personal doership and the corresponding responsibility for their actions is so deeply ingrained that they feel that the spirit of relief and freedom which they have felt may not be practical.

' "Thy will be done" is a very fine concept, but I have to live my life in a society which in practice does not accept this concept and holds me responsible for my actions. How do I live my life? What do I do every moment that I have to make a decision?' This is a very valid argument. My answer to this problem is simple: do whatever you feel like doing; do whatever you think you should do according to your own standards of what is right and wrong. In other words, you have the free will to do whatever you choose to decide. Having decided to do whatever you choose to do, thereafter what is your own personal experience? Have all your decisions turned into actual actions? Supposing some of your decisions have indeed turned into actions, have all those actions always produced the results that you have anticipated and for which you have held yourself responsible? The answer is obvious: some of your decisions have turned into actions, some have not; some of your actions have produced the anticipated results, some have not; indeed quite a few of 'your' actions have produced results quite contrary to your expectations. Therefore, it is your own experience that your free will extends merely to making a decision. What happens thereafter is, from your own experience, not in your control because various other factors come into play over which you have no control.

Now, let us investigate the supposed free will you have to make a decision. What is 'your' decision based on? If you investigate this point you will find out that you always base your decision on your 'programming', i.e. the genes or DNA and your conditioning which includes your education and practical experience, over which you truly have had no control. Recent research has brought out the fact that many of your actions – both good and bad, positive and negative – can be traced to your genes. So consider for yourself: how genuine is my 'free will'?!

Now, let us consider the question of your responsibility for your actions. Responsibility is essentially concerned with the results or consequences of what you consider to be your actions. But what we have found is that you can only make what you consider a responsible decision. The rest will depend upon God's will. In other words, an action happens because it is God's will, and the results or consequences are also God's will; the action and the consequences go together as God's will. Your responsibility, therefore, really gets restricted to your making a decision. No person would normally make an irresponsible decision! As a matter of fact, a normal person has usually a reputation of being either a responsible person or not one. Therefore, making a responsible decision is considered part of the 'nature' of a particular person; similarly, a person may have the reputation of generally being an irresponsible person. What is ordinarily considered the 'nature' of a person is essentially what we have been considering as the 'programming' of a body-mind organism. So, whether a person makes a responsible decision or not would generally depend on the programming of the concerned body-mind organism. And, it is everyone's experience in life that not every responsible person is a success in life; nor is a usually irresponsible person necessarily a failure. In other words, what kind of a life a person would have, depends not necessarily on the programming of the body-mind organism but entirely on the will of God or the destiny of the body-mind organism concerned.

Let me add a word about what I mean by the 'destiny' of a body-mind organism, according to my concept: the will of God is stamped as the destiny of a conception. If it is the destiny of a conception not to be born at all, that conception will be aborted. If it is the destiny of a conception to be born as a human object, the destiny of that born body-mind organism would be stamped at the moment of conception, for the entirety of the lifespan of that organism: what happens to it every moment of its life, when and how that organism will die. A baby may be born in a particular environment in certain circumstances, but it may be the destiny of that baby to have the environment completely changed and therefore its very life. I know of two instances that could be of considerable interest:

1   In Santa Barbara, California, I was introduced to a judge who was also a professor of law at the local university. He and his wife did not have any children even after twelve years of marriage, and they were vaguely thinking of adopting a child. Then a young lady student of his came to him for advice. Her problem was that she was pregnant and while her boyfriend wanted her to go in for an abortion, she herself very much wanted to have the baby. The idea of abortion was abhorrent to her. The judge asked her to see him again the next day, giving her the hope of a very acceptable solution. That night he discussed the matter with his wife: both the parents came from very good families, were handsome in looks, and brilliant in their studies – would she be agreeable to let the girl have the baby and they could adopt it? The wife was delighted. The next day, the judge informed the pregnant girl of the decision. And everything went well. I saw the baby boy in Santa Barbara. So it was the destiny of that particular conception not only not to be aborted but also to have a very good environment in which to grow up.

2   The other case concerns a middle-aged couple, good friends of mine, in New Jersey. They were childless after two abortions, and they were told that the wife could not have any children. One day they read about a baby in Guatemala, a lovely baby, three years old, whose mother was looking for a family who would adopt it. There was also a photograph. To make a long story short, the baby, who had a very bleak future in Guatemala, was adopted by this very nice American couple who were exceedingly happy to have that child. A couple of years later, the same mother wrote to this family saying that she was expecting another baby and asked if they would like to adopt it, too. The American couple agreed, and they now have two sisters as their adopted children and are very happy. I recently received a photograph of the parents with their two lovely young daughters.

39

The question of responsibility has another aspect: crime and punishment. Life is not necessarily logical according to man's judgement. Life is based on God's will or Cosmic Law, and it is impossible for the human intellect to understand the basis on which God's will works. So, a question arises in the human mind about the action and the consequences, when it is found either that a crime has not been detected and the criminal not punished, or that an innocent person has been punished for a crime he did not commit. The question concerns God's will. How could God allow this to happen? Or, perhaps, the question could be: why does God allow disease and war to happen; or, why does God create handicapped children?

When such questions arise, the matter must be considered from two aspects. One, who wants to know? The one who wants to know is, basically and essentially, an object in the manifestation who wants to know the basis on which the pure Subjectivity operates. How can an object ever know the pure Subject? So when the intellect asks this question, what has actually happened is that the intellect – the ego – has usurped the subjectivity of God, and, worse still, turned pure subjectivity into an object which this pseudo-subject wants to know! I am tempted to call this 'the original sin'! Another way in which to look at this problem is to perceive it as the petty human intellect trying to understand God's eternity: a school student would find it very much easier to understand the Theory of Relativity!

From all this, it would be clear that the culprit who creates problems and becomes unhappy is the intellect, the thinking mind, the EGO. Why did the Source (or God) create the ego so that the human being becomes unhappy? This is a valid question from the seeker and needs to be investigated. The answer is that the ego is the very basis of life as we know it, or the functioning of the manifestation, or the *lila* as the Hindu terminology uses the term. The very basis of life as we know it is twofold:

1 The functioning of manifestation – the *lila* – is based on the existence of the interconnected opposites; male and female, good and evil, beauty and ugliness. There never was a moment in the history of mankind when the interconnected opposites did not exist at the same time.

2 The basis of life as we know it is based on interhuman relationships: friendship and enmity, love and hate, likes and dislikes. These interhuman relationships can happen only when there are egos choosing one against the other, interacting with one another. Therefore, the Source (or God) had to create egos attached to every human body-mind organism so that the choosing between the interconnected opposites could happen and provide the basis for life as we know it, through interhuman relationships.

According to my concept, having created the ego for the interhuman relationships to happen, God also started the process of destroying the sense of personal doership in a limited number of cases in which Self-realization or enlightenment could happen. It is, of course, the sense of personal doership in the ego that is the cause of unhappiness in the ego. And in those instances where this process started, the relevant body-mind organisms were provided with appropriate programming for this process to happen. The significance of this concept is that spiritual seeking happens because the particular body-mind organism has been so programmed and not owing to the fact that any individual has *decided* to seek Self-realization or enlightenment.

As a matter of fact, ever since a baby is born and seeks its mother's breast intuitively, life is nothing but seeking. What kind of seeking happens depends upon the programming in each body-mind organism. The seeker is only the illusion of the ego with the sense of personal doership, created by God through divine hypnosis so that life as we know it could happen. Just this *total* realization that the personal doership is nothing more than a hypnosis and that all action is a divine happening through some human body-mind organism is what is generally known as Self-realization.

The question that remains is: how does this absolute, total, unconditional acceptance, that no action is an individual action, bring about the peace of Self-realization? The sage is a sage only because of this total, unconditional acceptance that all action through any body-mind organism is a divine happening, that, in the words of the Buddha, 'Events happen, deeds are done but there is no individual doer thereof.' Actions – physical and mental – keep on happening through every body-mind organism through the reaction of the brain to the input (a thought, something seen or heard, or tasted or smelt or touched) over which the ego had no control, according to the programming over which he also has had no control. Suppose an action happens through the organism of a sage. The sage has to live his life in a society that does not have the sage's understanding, and therefore considers the sage, like any other individual, to be responsible for his action. A particular action is judged by the society as a 'good' action; the approval of the society becomes an input in the body-mind computer of the sage, and the output is a sense of pleasure. But the sage's *total* understanding is that the action which has evoked the society's applause is not his action; therefore, while a sense of pleasure may arise, what will not arise is a sense of pride. On the other hand, if an action happening through the body-mind organism of a sage hurts someone unwittingly or is in any way disapproved by society, a sense of regret will arise, but, knowing that it was not his action, there cannot be a sense of guilt. Similarly, if someone else's action hurts a sage, the hurt will be accepted as the will of God or his own destiny, but, knowing that it was not anyone's action, while the hurt will be accepted as the will of God, the sage cannot hate anyone. Similarly, the sage cannot be jealous or envious of anyone: whatever is, could only be God's will.

In other words, the sage lives his life in society – participates in life just as actively as an ordinary person – enjoys the pleasures of life and suffers the pains and hurts of life like any ordinary person. The important point, however, is that, unlike the ordinary person, the sage participates in life without the load of pride or guilt, or hatred or jealousy or envy against anyone. Put another way, in the words of the Buddha, the sage participates in the life that is sorrow ('samsara is *dukkha*') but enjoys the peace (shanti) of Nirvana, at the same time. He thus proves the words of the Buddha: 'Samsara is *dukkha*, Nirvana is shanti, but they are not two!'

The final question that remains at this stage is: how does one acquire this total unconditional acceptance that all action is a divine happening and not the action of any individual person? The obvious answer is that no one can acquire or achieve this kind of acceptance about God's will unless that itself is God's will! But one can take considerable solace from the fact that seeking this peace of mind has already happened in one's case through God's grace and it is truly God's responsibility to further promote the process. In the words of Ramana Maharshi, 'Your head is already in the tiger's mouth, and there is no escape.' But, as has been said before, this fact that nothing can happen unless it is God's will does not prevent you from doing whatever you think you should do. You do have that *apparent* free will.

The only spiritual practice I usually recommend for the intellectual acceptance to go deeper into its finality is to experience the truth of this concept from personal experience. The ego may accept this concept of God's will intellectually, but the acceptance cannot reach the stage of finality unless the ego finds from its own investigation of its own personal experience that this concept is the truth as far as he or she is concerned. If only one thinks of one's own past experience, one is bound to come to the conclusion that all of the more significant events in one's life were not one's own actions, but happenings over which one had hardly any control and which were the result of circumstances over which one had no control. But that is not enough to convert the concept into actual fact. This must be proved from personal experience from day to day.

There must be an honest and thorough investigation into what you think are 'your' actions from day to day. This investigation is really one step further from Ramana Maharshi's famous 'Who am I?' This investigation that I suggest is based on the query: *'Am I the doer of what I think are my actions?'*

At the end of the day sit alone, quietly, for about twenty to thirty minutes, and think of one or more actions during the day which you were convinced were 'your' actions. Find out if you decided, out of the blue, to do that action; or, was it some thought or event which started that action over which you had absolutely no control? Then, investigate the course or process of that action and find out how much real control you had over it. If your investi-gation has been thorough and honest, you will come to the conclusion *in every case* that every action which you thought was 'your' action turns out to depend on several factors over which you had truly no control. In other words, you come to the conclusion that no action was truly your action. Of course, it is needless to say that your doing this investigation – and how honest and thorough it is – itself depends upon God's will!

Once this investigation begins – and proceeds, day after day – you may find that it has become an obsession which could be termed 'the dark night of the soul'! But this need not necessarily be so. How smooth or difficult the process of this investigation becomes, would itself be the will of God. The important point is that when the ego is finally convinced that he cannot truly call any action 'his' action, the ego is faced with the significant question: if no action is my action, and actions actually happen without any necessity of a 'me', then who is this 'me' I am so concerned about? *Is there a 'me' at all?!* The question becomes an unbearable pain, arising from the gut, from the Source, and the answer finally comes from the Source: 'My dear child, there never was a "me" who suffer the pain of life and all there has ever been is "I", the Source from which the manifestation has emerged, and it is "I" alone who has been functioning through the billions of human beings.'

An action happens because that is the will of God; the results or consequences, whatever they are, are also the will of God. The human object cannot know the results or consequences of any action – the same action need not produce the same consequences every time. And what is more, the consequences of any action will not be restricted to only the individual organism through which it happens – it could affect many others who had nothing to do with the original action. Thus, for instance, a decision made by the head of a large business enterprise could affect, for better or worse, not only the one who made that decision but many others: the many other businesses connected with the large enterprise and the many employees of the business concerned.

The concept of karma

The concept of karma (action or deed) is basically the concept of causation: an event has its consequences; a deed has its result; a cause has its effect. The chain of causation means a cause has its effect, the effect becomes the cause of a further effect, and so on. $A \rightarrow B \rightarrow C \rightarrow D$ and so on. If causation is seen from the concept of God's will, it can be seen that the cause and effect are interrelated. You can say either that A led to B or that in order for B to happen, according to God's will, A had to happen too. Viewed in this perspective, all actions in eternity are seen as the interrelated causation: cause led to effect, but for the effect to happen, the cause had to happen too! In other words, the chain of causation is seen as $A \leftrightarrow B \leftrightarrow C \leftrightarrow D$ ... and so on. The whole series of events in eternity is thus seen as a long chain of interconnected cause and effect stretching into eternity, almost without beginning and without end, happening according to God's will.

The concept of karma based on the individual's action

When the theory of karma is based not on any event or deed as such, but the action of an individual – not on 'Thy will be done' but the 'free will' of the human being – the theory gets an entirely different twist. The theory gets based on 'as you sow, so you reap'. The experience of life over a very long period has proved that this concept of sowing and reaping has not worked. Life proves again and again that someone sows and someone else reaps! Indeed, someone reaps when that someone has not sown anything at all! Not all crimes are detected, not all criminals are punished. Indeed in many cases, innocent people have been found guilty and punished.

However, the theory of karma based on individual actions proceeds to elaborate that the process of sowing and reaping is not restricted to one life, but extends from one life to another of the same individual 'soul'. Therefore, says the theory, if you have been suffering in this life, that is because 'you' did some bad actions in 'your' previous life. Therefore, further, you make sure that your actions in this life are good and pure, so that you do not suffer in your next life! The real problem that this theory does not face is the one the individual asks himself: who is suffering in this life because of whose actions in his or her previous life? It is the individual ego who suffers. For example, I am Robert in this life who is suffering; if in a previous life, some William did some bad deeds, why should I, Robert, suffer in this life? Again, why should I, Robert, do good actions and renounce a lot of fun in this life, so that some Dennis should enjoy a good life in the next life?! I am only concerned with Robert in this life, and I know nothing about any of my past lives.

According to my concept, according to Advaita or Non-duality – I would only repeat Lord Buddha's words: 'Events happen, deeds are done, but there is no individual doer thereof.' The events and the deeds will have their consequences, both according to the will of God; and since there are no individual doers, and the ego-doer is merely a fiction created by divine hypnosis, there is truly no Robert to suffer because of any William's bad actions. How much each body-mind organism suffers or enjoys in life is God's will, and no human object could ever possibly know on what basis God's will functions in life. Scientists may be able to create conditions immediately *after* the 'Big Bang', but could they ever create conditions immediately *before* the 'Big Bang'?!

The concept of sin and guilt

The basic principle of every religion happens to be the same.
    The Bible says: *Thy will be done.*
    The Hindu scriptures say:

1 *Twameva karta, twameva bhokta (Thou art the doer, Thou art the experiencer).*

2 *Twameva shrota, twameva vakta (Thou art the listener, Thou art the speaker).*

The Muslim religion says: *La'illaha il'Allahu (There is no Reality but God; there is only God).*

And yet there have been religious wars over hundreds of years. It certainly cannot be denied that whatever has happened – wars, natural disasters, diseases or whatever – could not have happened unless it was God's will. But the apparent cause, I think, is the fact that this basic principle, common to all religions, which is so simple and direct, needs no interpretation. Yet this common principle has been interpreted by successive generations of interpreters (by whatever name and authority called) in such a way that each religion has its own dogmas, mainly concerned with behaviour in daily life. And it is these interpretations – or rather misinterpretations – that are the cause of dissention among the followers of various religions: rites and rituals based on concepts of 'dos and don'ts', which have no foundation.

The interpretations of the various religions take the form of lists of 'dos and don'ts' which an individual is supposed to follow. If he does not follow those religious practices, he commits a sin which is deemed to have varyingly horrible consequences in this life and beyond! And, in these various daily routines, the basic principle of God's will in every religion is totally forgotten.

Let us now consider the problem of 'sin'. The dictionary defines 'sin' as 'a transgression against divine law or principles of morality; offence against good taste, propriety, etc.'. Obviously this is necessarily a vague description because the basis of sin differs from culture to culture. The dictionary further enumerates seven deadly sins, which are pride, lechery, envy, anger, covetousness, gluttony and sloth. One can only wonder, on this basis, if there could be any person who is not continuously committing one of these sins all the time!

Another interesting aspect of sin is food. The non-vegetarian human being would consider killing an animal for food as his natural right whilst a vegetarian would consider it a deadly sin. It is interesting to note that a brahmin on the west coast of India would consider it perfectly natural for him to eat fish – the vegetable from the ocean – whilst it would be a sin to eat eggs or animal flesh; on the other hand the brahmin in Kashmir, an area in India with a very cold climate, would consider it perfectly correct to eat goat flesh, but eating even eggs and fish would be a sin!

It is, therefore, apparent that there is no clear definition what 'sin' is. It is obviously decided by a group of influential people of the time what constitutes a sin, depending upon the circumstances of the time. For example, until a few years ago, abortion would have been considered a sin and a crime in almost every country and community in the world and yet today, almost every developing country is sponsoring abortion with clinics where women can have abortions without having to pay anything.

It is interesting to know what the *Bhagavad Gita* says about sin and guilt:

> *Naadatte kasyachit paapam na*
> *Chaiva sukritam vibhuhu /*
> *Adnyanevritam dnyaanam*
> *Tena muyhanti jantavaha //*
>
> V.15

You cannot commit a sin, nor a meritorious deed, of which the Lord takes note. The light of the basic knowledge is covered by the darkness of the ego's delusion, and thus the individual thinks in terms of sin and merit.

This verse firmly demolishes the concept of a God sitting somewhere in the clouds, peeping down and keeping a perfect account of every sin and every good deed done by every single human being, so that an individual may be punished or rewarded in due course. It should be clear that such a concept is steeped in ignorance. Such a concept cannot prevail if one is totally convinced that no action can happen except by God's will. If God's will is totally accepted, one's personal will cannot exist, and therefore, there cannot be any question of any sin or merit.

Before we can consider the relevance of God's will in our life, we must first be very clear about what we understand by the word 'God'. To me, God is the Source, Consciousness, the Supreme Power, Noumenon, Unicity or whatever other label may be used: the ONE Source from which has emerged the manifestation, the universe, the basis of which is the existence in the same moment of interconnected opposites. The Source, or God, transcends the interconnected opposites: the ONE without a second, the Unmanifest from which has emerged the duality of the manifested appearance.

In some philosophies, God is seen as an entity connected with the manifested appearance: the ruler of the manifested universe, the representative of the 'good'. So far so good. But the confusion arises when in the duality of manifestation they accept the Devil, as the representative of evil, the interconnected opposite, and yet consider 'God' as the 'Creator' of the universe – omnipresent, omnipotent and omniscient.

'God' cannot at the same time be the Source – ONE without the second – from which the duality of manifestation has emerged as an illusion, and also only one part of the interconnected opposites of God (the good) and Devil (the evil) within the manifestation. Herein lies the great confusion.

The need for interpreting God's will arises because the human intellect cannot accept what it considers as 'evil' happening with God's will. According to the human ego, God's will should not be applied to what the human intellect considers 'evil' because evil is represented by the Devil, as the representative of the evil forces.

Here is an instance described by a learned Christian preacher. The wife of a doctor died in spite of every possible device provided by modern science, in spite of the most modern devices provided by medical authorities from all over the world, which were available to the doctor. The preacher asked: when the doctor was doing his best to cure the wife of the disease from which she was suffering, was he fighting *against* the will of God? He then considered, if she had recovered, would the recovery not also have been called the will of God? He concluded that both ways cannot be possible for the will of God. However, is it so difficult to believe that whatever happened to the woman – whether she recovered or died – would be the will of God? Is it also so difficult to accept that the efforts of the husband, the influential doctor, were also the will of God at the moment?

The real problem for the thinking mind of the individual – whether the clergy or the laity – is the misconception that God is concerned only with what the individual person in authority considers at the moment, in the prevailing circumstances, to be the 'good' happening. In other words, the thinking mind of the human being cannot accept that *all* happening at any moment – 'What-is' at the present moment – to be God's will. That is because the word 'God' is not accepted as the 'Source', the ONE without a second, from which the entire manifestation has emerged. Thus the thinking mind, the ego, of both the clergy and the laity (in most cases) cannot accept that God's will concerns everything that exists at any moment: God's will does not depend upon what the human being considers as 'good' and 'evil'. For instance, a woman whose son was killed in one of the raids on Berlin in World War II, had the understanding to accept God's will for the happenings. But the clergyman questioned how that could possibly be the will of God. To him, it would seem more like the will of the enemy, of Hitler, of the evil forces that England was fighting.

And yet we are told: 'I am Alpha and Omega, the beginning and the end, the first and the last.' Does it mean 'I' am not in the middle? This reminds me of a verse in the *Bhagavad Gita*:

> *Aham atma gudakesha*
> *Sarva bhootashaya sthitah /*
> *Aham adishcha madhyam cha*
> *Bhootanam anta eva cha //*
>
> X.20

I am the ATMAN (pure Subjectivity) that dwells in the heart of every mortal creature: I am the beginning, I am the lifespan, and I am the end of all beings.

This is the central theme of the *Bhagavad Gita*; the meaning is very clear.

I would consider the will of God to prevail every moment. Suppose a killing happens. My interpretation of that event would be that the event was the will of God, or the destiny of the body-mind organisms concerned. The destiny of one, according to the will of God, was to die by being killed, the destiny of the other to do the killing. Whether the killer would be identified and executed or whether he would not be identified and therefore go free and unpunished would again be the destiny of the killer. Whether an innocent man would be punished is also God's will and the destiny of the man concerned. The fact of the matter is that it is impossible for the human being – an object in the totality of manifestation – to ever know and understand the basis on which God's will functions. As the German mystic, Meister Eckhart, has put it, all that the human being can do is to wonder and marvel at the magnificence and variety of God's creation and functioning: we cannot even begin to understand it.

If God's will is not accepted as prevailing every moment, an awful misconception will result which could make the learned clergyman assert that:

1 He could not possibly identify the will of God as something for which a man could be killed, jailed or put in a lunatic asylum; or

2 The ultimate meaning of the universe was LOVE and that God would never fail anyone unless that one opposed Him forever; or

3 Evil could do terrible things and that the more he read and thought, the more he would believe in the Devil.

If God is indeed in competition with the Devil, then this 'God' and the Devil have both been emanations from another SOURCE. Therefore, according to the view of the clergyman, 'God' cannot be the One Reality, the ONE whose will prevails every moment as the Cosmic Law or Universal Law.

52

Surrender to God's will has to be absolutely total and unconditional. It is not total surrender to God's will if it is interpreted conditionally. One hymn says:

> *Though dark my path and sad my lot*
> *Let me be still and murmur not,*
> *But breathe the prayer divinely taught,*
> *'Thy will be done'.*

This hymn has been called a 'bad hymn' by the clergyman. He says that undeserved misery, unhappiness, frustration, bereavement, calamity, ill health and so on can only occur through circumstances thrust into life by ignorance, folly or sin, and not through God's will or intention. He says that all evil that is temporarily successful, temporarily defeats God. He feels that the time to say 'Thy will be done' is only when the good prevails. And, of course, the 'good' is to be interpreted by him and not by his enemies!

This is what one articulate clergyman has said. On the other hand, there is the record of a Christian missionary called Staines and his two sons being locked in a car and the car being set on fire by a gang of extremist terrorists in Orissa in India, towards the end of the last century. The true understanding of the bereaved widow and mother was outstandingly clear when, totally contrary to the preaching of the clergyman as mentioned earlier, the wonderful lady declared that her husband and sons died because the lifespans allotted to her husband and sons by God were over! This is true surrender to the will of God, not the conditional surrender to the will of God only when it satisfies one's selfish ends.

The basis of the total acceptance of the will of God can only mean that all action is a divine happening through some human object or the other, that it is not something done by anyone. This concept raises two main objections by the thinking mind of the human being, which is what is generally known as the ego with a sense of personal doership.

1   The ego asks: if there is no personal doership, what happens to motivation, which is so important for personal achievement? To accept that all action happens only according to God's will would lead to fatalism. My reaction to this objection is the question, 'What do you really mean by "fatalism"?' It is surprising how loosely this word is used as an argument. So I try to supply the explanation. I say what you really mean by 'fatalism' is: 'If I am not the doer of any action, why should I get up in the morning and busy myself with whatever I have to do?' It is quickly agreed that this is what is meant by 'fatalism'. I proceed: 'Have you ever tried to do that? Can you really do that? Can you really stay in bed so that no action happens? – no action, physical or mental? What you probably mean by action is only physical action, but will not there be a multitude of questions arising in your mind which could make you get out of your bed?'

2   The other objection the ego raises is this: 'If I do not do any action and all action happens because it is God's will, what is to prevent me from taking a machine gun, going out and killing people aimlessly?' The answer to this objection is that a normal person with normal programming would simply not be able to do this. It is only a psychopathic organism that is so programmed that would be able to do it. Then the argument continues: 'All right, I accept that I may not be able to do this, but the psychopath could do it. And, if that action is God's will, why should the psychopath be punished?' The answer to this question is again, simple. The 'psychopath' is not going to be punished. It was the destiny of a body-mind organism to do the killing and it would be the destiny, also according to God's will for that object, that body-mind organism to be punished according to its destiny.

Why a body-mind organism is programmed the way it is, is a question raised by a human object – a species of object, which together with thousands of other objects constitutes the totality of manifestation which has emerged from the pure subjectivity of the Source. And it would obviously be impossible for an object ever to know the basis on which the pure Subjectivity works!

It is only when one is not able to accept the will of God with absolute totality that the problem arises about the will of God and man's freedom or free will. If one is able to accept totally and unconditionally that God's will prevails every single moment then one can accept that all action is a divine happening through some human body-mind organism and not the personal doing by any human being as sin or merit. When one is not able to accept the will of God in its entirety – and that itself will be the will of God – then there arises the need to interpret the will of God so that man's supposed freedom of will is not impaired.

One such misguided clergyman felt it necessary to divide the will of God into three parts:

1 The *intentional* will of God.

2 The *circumstantial* will of God.

3 The *ultimate* will of God.

This scholarly clergyman considers that such a distinction becomes necessary when one looks at the cross of Christ. He suggests that it was not God's intention from the beginning that Jesus should go to the cross. Yet, he gives no basis for such a presumption! He considers that Jesus came with the *intention* that men should follow him, not kill him. Therefore, says the clergyman, the phrase, 'The will of God', should be restricted to the intentional will of God, or God's ideal purpose. It was only in the circumstances wrought by men's evil that Christ was compelled to die and it was in this sense that Christ said, 'Nevertheless not what I will, but what Thou wilt.' This, of course, assumes that God has no control over what circumstances prevail at what time!

Then comes the third part: the ultimate will of God. This means that God cannot be *finally* defeated. And, this is also what the clergyman understands by God's omnipotence – that nothing can happen which *finally* defeats his will, not that everything that happens is his will.

The clergyman does not say when the ultimate becomes the ultimate. According to him, obviously the present moment is not the ultimate of something that has been happening for some time in circumstances over which evil – the Devil – had control, and not God. In other words, says the clergyman, God's 'intentional plan', in the case of the cross, had to be postponed to the 'ultimate will of God' because it was frustrated by the forces of evil; therefore, God obviously had no control over the evil forces causing the intermediate frustration!

Speaking of the circumstantial will of God, the clergyman says that there is an intentional purpose of God for every man's life, but man's free will creates circumstances of evil which interfere with God's plans. The cross was the symbol of the triumphant use of evil over God's holy purpose. However, by doing the circumstantial will of God we open the way for God's *ultimate* triumph.

The only trouble with *doing* the circumstantial will of God is that one does not know what the circumstantial will of God is whenever we have to make a decision. In other words, a man says, 'I am a God-fearing man and would want to do the circumstantial will of God at this moment, but how do I know the will of God in these present circumstances? Whatever anyone tells me would be his concept of God's circumstantial will. I really cannot know God's circumstantial will.' The only answer to this dilemma of the common man is that he may do whatever he thinks he should do according to his 'own nature' (which can only have been fashioned by God) and he would do precisely what God wanted him to do. In this way, he would not be burdened by the load of sin and guilt on his mind whatever the result of his action.

The very same insight regarding a man's actions has been expressed in a very bold way even around four hundred years ago by Gora, a potter saint from Maharashtra, India. These are the words of Gora in one of the *abhangas* sung every day after my talk with visitors:

Deha prapanchaachaa daasa /
Suke karo kaama //
Dehadhaari jo jo tyaache /
Vihita nitya karma /
Sadaachaara sanmaargaachaa aagalaa na dharma //

The body is subject to the laws of phenomenality,
Let it enjoy the work assigned to it by God or
   Nature.
Body-mind organisms do things which they are
   supposed to do.
There is no good path or good conduct for the instrument
Other than the way it is designed and programmed.

The unconditional acceptance of 'Thy will be done' is quite clear. There is no need for some superimposed rule of conduct or basis for making a decision other than what you think you should do.

The clergyman takes up another example: the case of the unmarried woman in middle age who has almost accepted the probability of remaining unmarried, with hopes becoming dimmer and dimmer. The clergyman cannot accept that the destiny of the woman, according to God's intentional will, could very well be that she remains unmarried. He considers that it cannot be the divine *intention* that any woman should remain unmarried because the body of every woman, her creative centres in the brain and her maternal impulse and sex instinct are sufficient evidence of this. However, what is she to do if she remains unmarried? She cannot have sex without sin. The clergyman says that it is evil and not God which has thrust this situation upon her. By a positive and creative attitude to the situation, she has to find out the circumstantial will of God in it, and contribute to her own inner harmony and to the final purpose of God.

The clergyman, of course, has no answer to two practical questions; in fact, he does not even think of them! First, how is the poor woman to know the 'circumstantial' will of God? And second, what is the poor woman to do if she has not been naturally gifted with the grit and determination to overcome biological drives by taking up some altruistic tasks which could achieve some similar or even more effective satisfaction?

Then the well-versed clergyman takes up the matter of disease. He explains that the Christian minister, as he does his visiting, is continually confronted by the question as to whether the onset of disease is the will of God. The clergyman says, '*The important answer is NO. The will of God for man is perfect health.*' Has the clergyman got that answer directly from God? Then there are those diseases that are owing to the invasion of germs. The clergyman cannot deny that God is also responsible for the creation of those germs that cause disease in man. Then he has the magnanimity to confess that he does not know why God has created the germs that can cause disease among 'His beloved children'. He adds that nobody can know the answer to such questions.

If the knowledgeable clergyman would only remember this same point – that no human object could possibly know the basis on which the will of God works – and also the point that God has not created the universe only for the benefit of His beloved human children, he would not make so many assertions with such confidence as if he were the personal confidant of God. The clergyman does not seem to remember that God has created the universe which includes not just one species of object called the human being, but thousands of other species of objects as well, which together form the totality of manifestation!

The question of sin and guilt arises only on the basis that it is the will of man which works and not the will of God. If 'Thy will be done' is totally accepted without the slightest reservation, and one does whatever one is programmed to do without the slightest sense of personal doership, the sense of sin or merit cannot arise. And it is, therefore, only if one is able to participate in life, and accept whatever happens as the will of God *at that moment* – pleasure or pain, happiness or unhappiness, success or failure – then that is Self-realization. And this way a sage participates in life without any load of sin and guilt on the mind.

Once Ramana Maharshi was asked a question by a young man with much sincerity and humility: 'I am carried away by the sight of the breasts of a young woman neighbour and I am often tempted to commit adultery with her. What should I do?'

The answer from Ramana Maharshi was: 'You are always pure. It is your senses and body which tempt you and which you confuse with your real Self. So first know who is there to be tempted? But even if adultery happens, do not think about it afterwards because you are yourself always pure. *You are not the sinner.*'

With his total ignorance of the significance of the straight and simple four words, 'Thy will be done', one can imagine the shock and disgust on the face of our clergyman if he heard these words of the sage! The sage says 'you are not the sinner' simply because if 'Thy will' is done *every time* how can there be a sinner?

It is from this point of view that the *Bhagavad Gita* boldly asserts:

You cannot commit a sin, nor a meritorious deed of which the Lord takes note. The light of the basic knowledge is covered by the darkness of the ego's delusion, and thus the individual thinks in terms of sin and merit.

v. 15

This verse is self-explanatory and needs no elaboration.

When Ramana Maharshi says, 'You are always pure,' he obviously does not refer to the fictitious ego with its sense of personal doership. The ego's sense of personal doership is indeed the delusion of the ego referred to by Ramana Maharshi. When something happens – what the society calls a good deed or an evil deed – whatever has happened could not have happened unless it was God's will. Unless this were so, God or Consciousness or Source – the ONE without a second – could not possibly be omnipotent in this life as we know it. In other words, 'Thy will be done' must apply to every moment, and not only to some 'ultimate' time.

In his novel, *The Razor's Edge*, the well-known novelist Somerset Maugham describes an incident concerning the central character called Larry, a young man who has been to see Ramana Maharshi, and has done a lot of reading and thinking about 'Who am I?' His understanding is quite deep. At one point when his money is all gone, he decides to go back to his native New York to earn a living. He gets a job as a cab driver, and lives in a small room rented from a woman in a small house. One night, as Larry was reading a book in bed, the middle-aged landlady walks into his room, takes off her clothes, and gets into Larry's bed. Larry puts his book aside and they have sex. Later on, the landlady puts on her clothes and leaves Larry's room. And Larry picks up the book and starts reading from where he has left off! In other words, sex has happened, and Larry, in Ramana Maharshi's words, 'does not think about it afterwards'! Something happened in one moment and that moment was not carried forward in horizontal time.

So the question arises: what do I do when I do not know the will of God? The practical answer is very simple: do what your 'nature' tells you to do. Your 'nature' is the programming in your body-mind organism which has been created by God. You can do what you think you should do, according to your programming. If it happens, it has happened because it was the will of God, whatever the consequences. If it has not happened, that too was the will of God. Truly you cannot go against God's will: the action is the will of God, and the consequences are also the will of God.

This is what Dante probably had in mind when he said, 'In His will is our peace.' This means, of course, that we accept whatever happens as His will – and not that something which hurts a certain group of people cannot be the will of God because God would certainly not want to hurt His beloved children. The acceptance of His will – in which is our peace – must include everything: we cannot sit in judgement over God. We must accept that the happening of Hitler, which led to the killing of millions of Jews, was as much a matter of His will as the happening of Jesus Christ and hundreds of Mother Teresas. In other words, a Mother Teresa and a psychopathic organism are created by the same Source or God. Similarly, it goes without saying that we, the objects God has created as human beings, have been created by the same Source or God who has created the smallpox germs and other germs. Whatever happens in the interactions between the different species of objects is the will of God: and man cannot sit in judgement over God. In other words, only in the total acceptance of His will shall lie our peace.

Meister Eckhart, the well-known German mystic, wrote:

> But God does not subdue the (individual) will – He sets it at liberty so that it does not want something different from what God Himself wants, and that means freedom. The mind, however, cannot want something different than what God wants – and that is not its bondage but its own freedom.

Meister Eckhart's writings were at first ignored by the Church, but when it found that the Meister Eckhart teachings were becoming more and more popular, the Church found themselves compelled to make a decision. Meister Eckhart was excommunicated – which in those days meant a death penalty – but before the decision could be conveyed to him, Meister Eckhart died a natural death.

Conclusion: the nature of the manifest world

The basic difficulty about providing an example or illustration or comparison to explain a metaphysical principle is that any such illustration would necessarily be at relative level and therefore unable to explain anything at absolute level.

Consciousness-at-rest is unaware of its existence until there is a *natural but sudden movement within itself* – known by various names in Vedic literature such as *Omkar* (the primeval sound), and perhaps as the 'Big Bang' in modern astronomy! The spontaneous arising of this movement is the sense of existence, the sense of Presence – I AM – which brings about spontaneously, simultaneously and concurrently the appearance in Consciousness of the phenomenal manifestation. The phenomenal manifestation necessitates certain presupposed phenomenal conditions without which such manifestation would not be possible: the creation of the twin concepts of 'space' and 'time'.

As objective phenomena there is no apparent difference between animate and inanimate objects, but subjectively it is sentience that is responsible for enabling the sentient beings to *perceive* the phenomenal manifestation. Sentience is an aspect of Consciousness – the primeval totality of energy – but it has nothing to do with the arising of the apparent manifestation. Although sentience enables the human being to perceive other objects – and intellect, another aspect of Consciousness, which enables him to discriminate – the human being is not different from any other phenomenon, made of the same five basic elements, and is an object, a species of object. Sentience brings about the identification with the body as an individual entity in the animal, including the human being. This is the ego. The big difference between the ego of the animal and the ego of the human being is that the ego of the human being is infused with the sense of personal doership. What the Source brings out of the human body-mind organism is seen by the human being as

62

his/her action. This sense of personal doership brings out pride of achievement, frustration of failure, guilt and sin for certain actions happening through his own body. Moreover, this same sense of personal doership brings out hatred, jealousy and envy for actions happening through the 'other' person. It is this load on the mind of pride, guilt, frustration, hatred, jealousy and envy that makes an individual basically feel the bondage of individuality.

With the total understanding – which means the annihilation of this load of sin and guilt and hatred through the sense of personal doership – the ego continues to participate in life, enjoys pleasure, suffers pain and hurt as the will of God, and not the doing of any individual person. The total understanding, therefore, means that all action is a divine happening and not the doing by any individual. Thus the total understanding – known as Self-realization or enlightenment – means participating in life along with the peace that results from the removal of the load of pride, sin, guilt, hatred and jealousy or envy.

Some time ago, I was watching the National Geographic channel on the television. I saw on the screen a tiny little fish merrily swimming along. Suddenly an enormous fish – perhaps fifty times its size – came in from behind and just gobbled up the tiny one. I thought: *that is the meaning of life* – life happens and life ends. No one need be concerned about sin and guilt, past and future: no regrets about the past, no expectations for the future. This is enjoying the shanti of Nirvana while participating in the samsara of *dukkha*. Whatever happens is God's will.

CHAPTER THREE

THE INFAMOUS EGO

ALL THERE IS IS Consciousness. In that original state – call it Reality, call it God, call it Absolute, call it Nothingness – there is no reason to be aware of anything. So Consciousness-at-rest is not aware of itself. It becomes aware of itself only when this sudden feeling, I AM, arises. I AM is the impersonal sense of being aware. And that is when Consciousness-at-rest becomes Consciousness-in-movement, when Potential Energy becomes manifested energy. They are not two. Nothing separate comes out of Potential Energy.

It is Consciousness alone that exists. It creates the illusion of the world-appearance and the ego-sense and perceives the illusion of diversity in what is truly pure Unicity. It seems difficult to comprehend how the universe could exist in the infinite Consciousness that is supposed to be transcendental. Truly there is nothing other than Consciousness, and therefore Consciousness cannot but be immanent in everything that appears to exist. And yet no phenomenal manifestation can have any kind of relationship with Consciousness because a relationship can exist only between two different entities. It is in this sense that Consciousness is transcendental to the manifested universe. The universe exists in Consciousness like future waves in a calm sea – only *apparently* different in potentiality.

Every thing or object in the manifested universe is a product of Consciousness, both during the illusion when the manifestation appeared to be 'real' and after the realization of the Truth. We are nothing but Consciousness, and never have been anything else. Perhaps it would be easier to 'understand' the Truth if it is conceived that there never has been any 'we' at any time, and that all there is – and has ever been – is Consciousness. 'We' think of ourselves, consciously or unconsciously, as sentient beings and therefore as separate from the manifestation: 'we' are the subject and the rest of the manifestation is the object. The reality is that 'we', as manifested phenomena, are actually nothing but a part of the one manifested universe. What makes us think of ourselves as separate is the fact that the apparent universe becomes known to us, as sentient beings, by sentience operating through cognitive faculties. This 'sentience' is an aspect of Consciousness in itself. And it is for this reason that we cannot get rid of the deepest feeling that 'I' am other than the manifested appearance. And so indeed we are, but the illusion (the maya) consists in the fact that instead of collectively considering ourselves as sentience which enables us to cognize the manifestation (including sentient beings) which has appeared in Consciousness, we consider ourselves as *separate* individual entities. And therein lies our suffering and bondage. As soon as there is realization (awakening to the fact) that we are not separate entities but Consciousness itself (with sentience acting as the means for cognizing the manifestation), the illusion of separateness – the cause of our suffering and bondage – disappears. There is then the clear apperception that unmanifested, we are Noumenon, and while manifested, we are appearance – no more separate than substance and its form (gold and the gold ornament). Manifestation arises from the Unmanifest and in due course sinks back into the Unmanifest. The human beings as individuals are really quite irrelevant except, of course, as illusory characters in a dream play which is known as 'life'.

People are told by masters that they should fight the ego, kill the ego, but what I'm saying is to *accept* the ego. Is that not unique? Don't fight the ego. Accept the ego. Why, because 'you' didn't create the ego. The Source has created the ego, and the Source is in the process of destroying the ego in some cases. That's why your head is in the tiger's mouth. There's no escape. There is no escape if you fight the ego. That's my point. If you keep on fighting the ego, the tiger will have its mouth open for ages and ages. You accept the ego, and the tiger will snap its jaws quickly.

RAMESH The resistance is the ego, and the ego, I'm not joking, will not easily give up.

ROBERT *But the desire to have the ego annihiliated is the very thing that keeps the ego alive.*

RAMESH You see, that is the joke. That is the divine joke. The ego is divine hypnosis. Where did the ego come from? That is the question, isn't it? Everybody says the ego is the problem. All you have to do is simply give up 'your' ego. But nobody tells you how to give up 'your' ego. 'You' are the ego! The 'me' is the ego, and the ego is not going to commit suicide. The ego could only have come from the same Source from which everything has come. The physical manifestation has come from the Source. The fictional 'me' has come from the Source.

Why did the Source create the fictional 'me'? Without the 'me' interhuman relationships would not happen. Without inter-human relationships, life as we know it could not happen. So for life as we know it to happen – for God's *lila*, or game, to happen – interhuman relationships have to happen. And for interhuman relationships to happen the ego has to be there. Ego simply means the creation of a feeling through divine hypnosis that 'I' am a doer and a separate being in control of this body. But all that really exists is the body-mind organism and the energy flowing through it.

That is the basis, exactly like there is an electrical gadget and electricity functioning through that gadget. But if the electrical gadget were hypnotized then the electrical gadget would think in terms of '*me*' producing the toast, '*me*' producing the mixture, '*me*' producing the light. Basically it is only the electricity and the gadget. Here it is only the same thing – Source, God or Energy, and the body-mind organism through which the Energy, or God, is functioning. So God has created the ego, and it is God who starts the gradual process of annihilation of the ego in some cases.

The individual 'doer' is the thinking mind wanting to know: after the work is done, what is going to happen to me? The 'me' is the thinking mind, the ego. The ego, according to my concept, is the identification with the name and form as an individual with the sense of doership – whatever happens to this body 'I' am doing it, and 'I' am the one who is going to suffer the consequences.

It is always the 'me' – the ego, the 'doer' – who says, 'I am doing the work.' According to my concept, the only way the thinking mind – the monkey mind, the conceptualizing mind – can be stilled is if there is *total unconditional acceptance* that there is no *individual doer*. Everything just happens. As long as there is an individual doer who thinks 'he' is doing it, then 'he' is bound to think and be concerned about responsibility and consequences. This is the thinking mind. But attention can be given to the work at hand without 'you' feeling 'you' are the doer. That is the working mind.

The real problem is how to arrive at the *total, unconditional acceptance* that 'you' are *never* the doer, that the doing is just happening. The answer is through practical and personal experience. All the doing that you think is 'my' doing is not because of you but in spite of you! And you know that because you have not been getting what you wanted all the time. What *happens* is never in your control, and that you know from practical experience, personal experience. When will you not feel the burden of responsibility and consequences? Only when you are totally convinced that you were not the doer of any action that happened. You are never the doer, and not only you but no one is ever the doer. No human being is a doer.

The 'one' who has come to this conclusion in the beginning is the ego, the 'one' who thought 'he' or 'she' was the doer. Gradually what will happen is the 'me', the ego, which came to the conclusion that 'he' or 'she' doesn't exist will then, over a period of time, find more and more from personal experience that 'he' or 'she' does nothing. Then the ego becomes weaker and weaker, and if it is the will of the Source, the ego collapses.

If the ego collapses, how does the body-mind organism function? The answer is – the body-mind organism will continue to function exactly as it was functioning before. Before, it was the Source that was functioning through the body-mind organism, and in the future the Source will continue to function through the body-mind organism.

That which takes care of itself is the working mind. The working mind continues to do what is necessary in the circumstances. Therefore, you still continue as someone accepted by society as responsible for his actions. So what happens? A deed happens, an action happens, and the deed or action is the will of God, or the Source. The will of God with respect to each body-mind object is what I call the destiny of that body-mind object stamped at the moment of conception.

So what is life? According to my concept life is just a multitude of body-mind objects through which the Source is functioning. We can only accept what is happening. We can never know *why* the Source is doing what it is doing. Why? Because if you want to know why God is doing what he is doing, then what is really happening is the created object wanting to know the will of the creator Subject. How is it possible? So the created object which has been endowed with the dubious gift of ego – the sense of doership, the thinking mind – can only accept the magnificence of God's creation. The object and the ego *cannot* even try to understand why God has done what God has done, because the created object can *never know* the will of the creator Subject.

To paraphrase a well-known researcher of the mind and its functioning: it is the ego which is the mechanism in the human mechanism that prevents the human mechanism from seeing its mechanistic nature.

ASHIKA When you speak about how our lives are determined, using the concepts of the robot or the computer, it sounds like it's very limiting – there's no choice, no freedom. But my experience is that I feel filled up with a sense of freedom.

RAMESH Sure, that's the whole point. So what is that sense of freedom which arises? What kind of freedom is it?

ASHIKA I am not that computer or the robot.

RAMESH *Exactly!* That is the whole point. So, freedom from what? Freedom from that which earlier identified itself with the computer. It means freedom from the computer itself, freedom from the identification with the computer. The feeling Ashika has now is that earlier you thought 'you' were the computer, and now you know that you are not the computer. That computer is being used by the Source, or God, to bring about such actions as are supposed to happen through that body-mind organism. Isn't that right?

ASHIKA I used to think that freedom was freedom of choice, to do what I want ...

RAMESH Free will.

ASHIKA Yes. That all seems to die ...

RAMESH So there is no free will. It does not bring a sense of constriction or freedom.

ASHIKA There is a totally different freedom – freedom of not being involved at all.

RAMESH Yes. Freedom from involvement. Your experience has been that involvement is what causes unhappiness – if there is no involvement there is no unhappiness. So really what you're saying is that the freedom is from unhappiness because the freedom is from involvement. And 'who' gets involved? The ego gets involved. *The freedom is the freedom from the ego.* And the ego is the sense of personal doership. So the freedom is ultimately the freedom from the sense of personal doership – both for this body-mind organism and other body-mind organisms.

This is remarkable as far as you are concerned. Others may not accept this, but as far as you're concerned the freedom extends to *everybody*. No one has free will. All that happens is that actions happen through the billions of body-mind computers. So there is no need for Ashika to feel guilty or proud or hate anybody. Is that acceptable?

ASHIKA Yes.

RAMESH This is the freedom that is reflected in your under-standing – freedom from guilt, freedom from pride, freedom from hate and envy – which means what? Freedom from involve-ment. It is the involvement which causes unhappiness – a little bit of happiness, a lot of unhappiness. So accepting what *happens* as something with which Ashika *cannot* be involved *and* over which Ashika has no control at all – this is the freedom that whatever is happening is beyond the control of *anyone*. Therefore whatever is happening is just accepted as something which is supposed to happen – and not by the will of any individual.

ASHIKA I was feeling confused because there was this tremen-dous sense of freedom, but it wasn't a sense of freedom from or a freedom to do. It was just this freedom to be.

RAMESH You see, the freedom from involvement is freedom from the bondage of the ego. The ego is restricted. So the ego who thought earlier that 'he' was free to do whatever 'he' liked now finds there is no 'Ashika' to do what anybody wants. This is the freedom from responsibility, freedom from the sense of personal doership, and freedom from guilt or pride.

This same freedom is translated by the ego as the loss of 'its' own personal free will. You see? So really this freedom is itself freedom from the ego, but the ego can't feel this freedom. Ego feels 'it' has lost the free will to do whatever it wants to do – which 'it' thought 'it' had. This was the confusion you felt – the freedom which arose from the loss of the sense of personal doership meant the loss of freedom for the ego. Does that make sense?

ASHIKA Yes.

RAMESH I repeat: freedom from the sense of personal doership means loss of freedom for the ego. And that is the confusion, because there is still this identification of the ego with this body-mind organism called Ashika. The ego still remains and feels terribly restricted.

RAMESH I say, 'Thy will be done,' which means the human being has no free will. *And yet* I tell you, 'Do whatever you like. What more freedom do you want?' Do you have a problem with these apparently contradictory statements? Can you explain why there is no problem for you, Nazneen? If there is no problem, it means they are not truly contradictory statements. Can you explain this? Some people may say they are obviously contradictory.

NAZNEEN For me it doesn't present a contradiction because whatever has been happening has been happening anyway. 'I' haven't been doing anything. So there really is no individual doer, and there never has been an individual doer. So when you say, 'Do whatever you like,' it means that whatever is going to happen is going to happen.

RAMESH Wait a minute. To 'whom' do I tell 'Do whatever you like'?

NAZNEEN You're telling the ego.

RAMESH I'm still telling the ego which exists. What you just said was that if there is an *understanding* that there is truly no ego, then there is no problem. That's correct. But that is not my point.
My question is – does the ego have a problem when I say, 'Do whatever you like. What more freedom do you want?' and yet to the same ego I'm saying, 'Thy will be done,' meaning you have no free will? Is there a contradiction? The ego asks the question, 'How do I live in society if I have no control over my actions?' And

my answer to the ego is, 'Do whatever you like. What more freedom can you want?'

NAZNEEN Yes, but your answer is that whatever you want and whatever you like is what God wants and God likes.

RAMESH *That is the point!* But why is it not a problem? That is the issue. And the problem is always, always for the intellect. Any problem is always for the intellect. The intellect says, 'You tell me that nothing happens unless it is the will of God; therefore, I have no free will. And yet you tell me to do what I like. What more freedom do I want?' So the intellect says that these two concepts are contradictory. How do you explain to the intellect – which is the ego, the thinking mind – that these are not contradictory?

The answer is you may do what you like, but what you like to do is exactly what God wants you to like to do at that moment in the given circumstance. Therefore, there is no contradiction. Do whatever you think you like. And how does God manage that? Through the programming. What you think you like is based on the programming – genes plus conditioning. God acts through the programming.

What use is that total freedom to do what you like to do if what happens is not in your control? To that extent you have no free will.

JAMES And therefore the freedom is useless.

RAMESH Ah! That is the point. That is the conclusion the ego has to come to – the impression of freedom, which it has been under for so many years – is useless.

REINA But then, nothing really matters.

RAMESH That is the final conclusion you come to! Nothing really matters. What is the final effect of Self-realization, of enlightenment? – whatever happens, what does it matter? The intellect will say, 'How can you tell me nothing matters? Of course it matters.' To the intellect everything matters. So 'nothing matters' is for the conclusion, the answer, the feeling that comes *from the heart*. What the sage feels every moment is – whatever is happening – what does it matter? But the ego says, 'Of course it matters.'

When the answer finally comes from the heart – nothing that happens really matters – what is the meaning of this? What is the significance of the heart coming to this conclusion? The significance is that whatever the ego perceives as happening – and that it matters – is really an illusion.

So only after the total final understanding is it that *nothing happens*. And if nothing happens what can matter? To 'whom'? So you go back to the first line of the saying by Ramana Maharshi as the final Truth – 'There is no creation, there is no destruction.' If there is no creation, there is no dissolution. If there is no creation, to 'whom' can anything matter? You see? So it is not the ego which says, 'What does it matter?' Of course it matters to the ego. But when the ego is demolished and the total, final understanding happens, then the real feeling comes up – what does anything that appears, matter? Because whatever appears is just that, only an appearance! What does an appearance matter? What does it matter? What is 'it'? The 'it' is an appearance. Nothing really happens. Nothing is created. The ultimate understanding is, it really doesn't matter.

LARA So when a sage talks about serenity and peace ...

RAMESH You see, the 'peace' is given as a bait to the ego who seeks enlightenment. In other words, the ego says, 'What do I get out of it?' What 'you' get out of it is nothing, and getting that 'nothing' means what? You are not seeking anything. What you are getting is the absence of seeking, and the absence of seeking means the absence of the seeker. So what does the seeker get? His own absence – which is peace. You have to use a word.

You see, in the beginning the seeker is questioning, 'What will I get out of it?' He or she is concerned with what happens in life. So in life, in Buddhist terms, what does the seeker find from experience? That samsara or life is *dukkha*. Life is misery. Having said this, what will the seeker want? He will want to leave the misery and go somewhere where there is no misery. The Buddha also gave that a name, and he called it Nirvana. So in the beginning of the seeking what the Buddha tempted the seeker with was that life is misery, and that misery will stop only if you get Nirvana. Then to make the joke a tragic joke, he said that samsara and Nirvana are one! Meaning, you cannot go from one place called life, or samsara, to another place called Nirvana. They are the same.

The significance of this, which very few accept, is that you have to find Nirvana – or what Nirvana represents, the peace – while being in samsara. You cannot escape samsara. You cannot escape life that is misery. All you can find, if that is the will of God and the destiny of the body-mind organism, is the peace, which represents Nirvana, while being in life. So the final point is you cannot escape life. You have to accept life as it happens, and accepting life as it happens means the peace of Nirvana.

How does the acceptance of life as it happens come about? How can it happen? Only if the ego-doer – 'I' live my life, 'I' am responsible for my life – gets removed. And that is God's will and the destiny of the body-mind organism.

But if the sense of personal doership gets removed, there is still a Lara. This point I must make clear. The sense of personal doership, when that is removed, the ego is removed, and when the ego is removed, Lara as the ego-doer is removed, but Lara is not removed. Ramana Maharshi lived for fifty years after Self-realization, so for fifty years he lived as Ramana Maharshi. If someone called him by name – Swami or Ramana or Bhagavan – he responded. That Ramana Maharshi responded to a name being called means there was identification with a name and form. So identification with a name and form continued with only one difference – there was no sense of personal doership. So when enlightenment happens, Lara does not disappear. Lara continues with the identification of this body and name. Lara's reactions continue more or less as before because they are based on the programming. And the programming more or less continues as long as the body continues.

RAMESH The bhakti turns into *jnana*. The devotion towards God as an entity turns into knowledge that all there is is the Source. So that is exactly what you're saying, you went in search of God and returned being God.

LARA Who was so peaceful and happy and not touching the ground anymore, like floating?

RAMESH No one. The peace prevailed, and the peace was experienced by that identification with a name and form – that identification with the name and form which responds to the name Lara being called.

LARA So that's okay?

RAMESH Certainly. That is part of what happens. So there is a Lara.

LARA There is a Lara?

RAMESH That is why I say that Lara need not fear that Lara disappears. Even after realization Lara will be pretty much there to respond to her name being called, but with this big difference: Lara who responds to her name being called knows that Lara doesn't do anything, nor does anyone else. So how does that peace happen? That peace happens because Lara, the identification with a name and form, realizes that she is not the doer nor is anyone else a doer. A sense of pleasure or a sense of regret may arise in that body-mind organism, but what will not arise, Lara, knowing that it is not 'your' action which has produced the appreciation or denouncement, is pride or guilt.

LARA The original reaction is impersonal in a way.

RAMESH It is impersonal, Lara. That is exactly the point I'm making. The reaction that arises in that body-mind organism because of that unique programming is impersonal. The ego comes in only when the ego reacts to that impersonal feeling.

LARA If there is no one who enjoys it, what's the point? Impersonal is just ...

RAMESH Yes, but therefore I said that Lara does not go away. So long as the body-mind organism is there – the identification with name and form – there is a Lara. Don't be misled, Lara will be still there saying, 'That was a good meal.' You see? 'I enjoyed that meal.' Lara will still be there to say, 'I enjoyed that meal.'

Lara, make no mistake. Enlightenment means the annihilation of Lara as the doer, the sense of personal doership. That goes and what remains is really harmless. What remains after enlightenment is harmless – in the terms of Ramana Maharshi – like the remnants of a burned rope. A burned rope will still leave a shape. Enlightenment will still leave identification with a name and form. Inputs, events which happen in the body-mind, continue to raise reactions, even fear and anger. So it does not mean that after enlightenment the sage is never angry. Of course, that is untrue. In that body-mind organism if the programming is such that anger is to arise, anger will arise. Even fear will arise. Compassion will arise almost all the time. A sense of gratitude will arise every time the thought occurs. You see, the thought would occur, 'How lucky I am. I've had a good life, and on top of it God has been kind enough to give the understanding.' A sense of gratitude arises.

LARA The confusion is from when I read the *Ashtavakra Samhita*. Because of my little understanding when I read it, there was the implication that there is no pleasure and no pain.

RAMESH That is right. Therefore, the written word has infinite limitation. That is the advantage of a *satsang* like this. If there is any clarity required, I can provide the clarity. But a book that is written, the author cannot anticipate all the different kinds of mis-understandings and try to solve them. For example, the feelings of pain and pleasure you mention. The pain and pleasure occur, but in the sage there is no 'one' to say, ' "I" am in pain' or ' "I" am in great pleasure.' So the absence of 'I' as the individual experiencer is what Ashtavakra meant. Pain and pleasure will be there, but there will be no individual experiencer of that pain or pleasure.

Let me put it this way. There are two body-mind organisms, one is an ordinary person and the other is a sage. Both are pro-grammed in such a way that it is easy to feel pain. And, for ex-ample, the ordinary person thinks 'he' is enlightened and when pain occurs will do his best not to shout because 'he' thinks 'he' is not supposed to. In the case of a sage if there is pain there is no 'he' to think what 'he' should or should not do. But will 'he' shout? No. The body-mind organism will shout. And that is what happened in the case of Ramakrishna Paramahamsa and in the case of Jesus. 'Oh, Father, why hast Thou forsaken me?' Who said that? Not Jesus. The body cried out in pain. Jesus didn't. You see? Then promptly the understanding comes, 'Thy will be done' – meaning, this is your will and the destiny of the body-mind to suffer the pain of being on the cross. It is happening. So let the body shout. Ramakrishna Paramahamsa was suffering from cancer and said, 'Mother, why are you making me suffer like this?' That 'me' is the identification with the body-mind organism. So the body shouts in pain. Or the body may laugh at some amusement, which is really the reaction of the brain to an event, the input, with laughter the output. The output is the shouting in pain or being timid or terrified or grateful. Any of those things can happen, but in the happening of any of these the ego is not involved.

RAMESH If a sage and an ordinary person see compassion arising in another person, the sage will witness the compassion arising in that body-mind organism. But the ordinary person will say, 'He's a compassionate person. Why am I not that compassionate? I would also like to be that compassionate.' That is the ego. In the case of a sage the happening of compassion, whether it arises in some other body-mind organism or in his own body-mind organism, makes no difference. The compassion arising, in whichever body-mind organism, is merely witnessed.

LARA It's all the same play really. It's just one play.

RAMESH That is the point! It is the same play; it is the same Energy; it is the same Source; it is the same God producing whatever is produced through whatever body-mind organism. Thinking, doing, experiencing – whatever happens through whichever body-mind organism, there is no individual doer. It is the same Source or Energy or God. That is the understanding of the sage. And therefore the sage does not see separation. In what sense does the sage not see separation? In this sense – *nobody does anything*. It is the same Energy functioning through every body-mind organism.

Therefore, there is truly no separation between body-mind organisms except in appearance. Whatever is seen is an appearance. The differences – the separation – are only appearances, not real. What functions through those different appearances is the same Energy, the same Source, the same God. In that sense the sage does not see separation. It is not that the sage does not see differences in different people. Of course he sees the differences in people – tall, short, handsome. All those differences are seen, but the differences are seen in appearances, in created objects. But the understanding is that through all those created objects the same Energy functions, therefore there is no separation. Anger arises in one case. Anger doesn't arise in another case. Compassion arises

– it makes no difference, because what arises depends on the programming over which there is no one in control.

Ramesh What you are saying is, I think, that with this understanding there is a certain amount of loneliness.

Lara An enormous amount of loneliness.

Ramesh That loneliness is felt by the identification with the body-mind organism. That identification continues, and Lara continues to live without a sense of doership and feels loneliness because the body-mind organism is programmed to like company. If the body-mind organism is programmed to like company, then there will be a sense of loneliness. But if in some other organism in which the understanding happens and that body-mind organism prefers to be by itself, there is then no loneliness. There will be joy, the priviledge of being alone.

Now if that loneliness hurts and you say, 'I don't want this loneliness,' then that is the ego. Loneliness happens because that is the programming. But if there is 'I don't like this loneliness, I prefer to be in company', then that is the ego which is still lurking.

Lara I much prefer to be alone, but I feel just as lonely along with my friends. Perhaps even more.

Ramesh That is the programming, so you have to accept it. It's simple. You have to accept it. The final word is acceptance of whatever happens without wanting What-is to be changed. The final peace occurs because regardless of the actions happening through this body-mind – there is no pride, no guilt. With actions happening through some other body-mind organism affecting Lara the hurt or pleasure may be there, but there is also the understanding that no one does anything. If there is hurt, hurt will be there, but Lara cannot find herself hating anybody. Whom would she hate? When the understanding is no one has the power to do anything, how can Lara hate anybody? So understanding that no one is a doer – neither Lara nor anyone else – means no pride, no guilt, no hate, no envy, no jealousy, which is equivalent to peace. The peace of Nirvana which prevails in the waking state.

LARA So there is nothing to hang on to.

RAMESH Nothing to hang on to because there is no 'one' to hang onto anything. You see? But so long as there is the one who comes in occasionally and wants to hang onto something, that ego is still there. All right, accept it – ego is still there. Let it remain as long as it wants to or as long as it is God's will. So the final acceptance is the acceptance of the ego.

Conclusion

When the ego is supposed to 'die', only the sense of personal doership is annihilated. The identification with the body-mind organism as an individual, living entity continues.

The ego – as an individual entity – therefore need not be afraid of being annihilated through Self-realization.

The ego, *without the sense of personal doership*, remains merely as the identification with the body-mind organism, functioning as the mere witness of all the actions happening through all body-mind organisms as divine happenings without anyone 'doing' anything.

CHAPTER FOUR

WHO CARES?

E VERY MONTH THE disciple faithfully sent his master an account of his progress.

In the first month he wrote: 'I feel an expansion of Consciousness and experience my oneness with the universe.' The master glanced at the note and threw it away.

The following month, this is what he had to say: 'I have finally discovered that the Divine is present in all things.' The master seemed disappointed.

The third month the disciple's words enthusiastically exclaimed: 'The mystery of the One and the many have been revealed to my wondering gaze.' The master shook his head and again threw the letter away.

The next letter said: 'No one is born, no one lives, and no one dies, for the ego-self is not.' The master threw his hands up in utter despair.

After that a month passed by, then two, then five months – and finally a whole year without another letter. The master thought it was time to remind his disciple of his duty to keep him informed of his spiritual progress.

Then the disciple wrote back: 'Who cares?'

When the master read those words a look of great satisfaction spread over his face.

A seeker hearing the teaching for the first time

RAMESH A seeker hearing the teaching for the first time is often stunned, even if the seeking has been going on for twenty years.

RAMESH People are told by masters that they should fight the ego, kill the ego, but what I'm saying is to *accept* the ego. Is that not unique? Don't fight the ego. Accept the ego. Why, because 'you' didn't create the ego. The Source has created the ego, and the Source is in the process of destroying the ego in some cases. That's why your head is in the tiger's mouth. There's no escape. There is no escape if you fight the ego. That's my point. If you keep on fighting the ego, the tiger will have its mouth open for ages and ages. You accept the ego, and the tiger will snap its jaws quickly.

Forget the teaching

RAMESH This teaching in many ways is unique. Usually with a teaching, it is to make a note of it, study hard, use it in practice. What I'm telling you is, *forget the teaching*. Let it work by itself. Very important!

Forget the teaching because 'who' wants to remember the teaching? It's the ego that wants to remember the teaching and wants to use that teaching to achieve something. But if you forget the teaching, then the teaching leading to the understanding will work by itself. And if the teaching doesn't lead to the understanding, then it's not worth it. So either way, forget the teaching! It's either effective or not effective. If it's not effective then there's no question. If it is effective, let it be effective!

Will the ego want to contribute to its own annihilation? No. The ego wants the teaching only to be able to use it, to achieve something – not for its own annihilation. If the teaching is forgotten the ego is forgotten, and the teaching works by itself.

Your effort is the obstruction. That's why I say forget the teaching – don't try to use it. Let that understanding work at whatever level.

Bhakti begins the teaching

RAMESH People ask me if there is anything unique about what I am saying. I'd say yes. What is unique about what I am saying is that I begin with bhakti and end in understanding. What is bhakti? Thy will be done. The 'me' says, 'You are all there is – Thy will be done.'

WARRICK When you say, 'Thy will be done,' I understand you to mean that God's will is, in fact, always being done.

RAMESH That is correct. Was being done, is being done, and will be done!

WARRICK And it is impossible for anything but God's will to be done.

RAMESH That is correct. But, truly, that is not the relevant part. The relevant part is, *'I' am nothing*. That is the relevant part. You [God] are all there is. Your will prevails all the time. Therefore to think, 'I can do anything; I can do something; I can achieve something,' is ridiculous. That is the relevant part – the helplessness of a created object. Acceptance, total acceptance of the fact a created object is helpless, is the relevant part.

Whose will prevails – and you call that God – is a concept which is necessary because the individual finds himself or herself so helpless. So the mind-intellect creates an object which is all-powerful and then says everything happens according to Thy will – which means it is not 'my' will. So accepting that 'I' am nothing, that 'I' am merely an object at the will of God is basically nothing but pure devotion, or bhakti. So what I say strictly begins with bhakti – Thy will be done.

Life has no value

ALTA Why was all this initiated in the first place?

RAMESH You paint a picture with a figure in it, and the figure wants to know why you painted the picture. The only answer is that you felt like it.

You see, you take a child to the seashore, give it a spade and a bucket. Promptly it will begin digging sand and piling it up into a castle or a mountain. It will take a lot of trouble over it for some time. But when the parent says it's time to go home, the child will kick down the castle over which it had spent a lot of trouble building. If you ask the child, 'Why did you take the trouble to build it and now you have destroyed it?' the child will not understand your question. But if you insist he will say, 'I built the castle because I liked to build it. I destroyed the castle because I liked to destroy it.'

The whole point is that the mind-intellect, which is ego, is conditioned from the beginning that everything must have a purpose. Life must have a purpose. Why, because life is precious. All you have to do is watch the TV, National Geographic or the BBC channel. You watch *Nature* and you see that life is anything but precious. Life has no value. Don't you feel it? It has no value. A bird lays eggs, and another one eats them, and then something else eats it.

Find out if life really has any meaning or whether life is precious. It just happens. *It just happens.* The mind-intellect gives meaning and then wants to know the meaning. Life has no meaning. The real meaning of life is that *life has no meaning.* It just *happens.*

The meanest

PHILIPPE After meeting some of the upcoming Advaita teachers, I really appreciate the way you formulate things. You're the meanest of all. You're the one who puts it right there immediately with great honesty. I think we all appreciate that very much.

RAMESH You mean I'm the meanest of the lot because I don't hold out carrots. I'm saying there are no carrots to have. Most people would like to have some carrots offered. Those people who still want carrots will go to the place where they will get carrots, and having eaten the carrots, they'll find themselves still dissatisfied and will come here.

Clarity or confusion

PREM Ramesh, I also love to hear you. Somehow you have such a unique clarity of description.

RAMESH Did you say unique? How? The Truth is only One.

PREM The Truth is One, but it seems that every expression is unique, and although somehow the results are the same ...

RAMESH The result is either confusion or clarity. Every teacher is unique, producing either confusion or clarity. So if a teaching produces confusion, why does it? The teacher certainly didn't intend that you should be confused.

PREM Maybe the teachers themselves are confused, therefore ...

RAMESH Now, why are the teachers confused? Because it is God's will.

PREM Yes, of course!

RAMESH Why are the teachers confused? Because they should confuse others. And why does this happen? Because it is God's will. Do you know why it is God's will? There is a verse in the *Bhagavad Gita* which says: 'There is only one seeker among thousands of people, and among those who seek hardly one knows me in principle.' So the thousands of seekers have got to be confused. How can they be confused unless there are teachers who are confused? Even that is God's will – that is my point.

PRATIMA Or the teacher may not be confused, but the disciple isn't ready.

RAMESH Sure. Then that is God's will.

PRATIMA So we can't blame the poor teachers totally.

RAMESH *You can't blame anybody for anything.* That is why it is also said in the *Bhagavad Gita*: 'You can commit no sin nor can you do a meritorious deed. Your original understanding is clouded by ignorance. That is why you think in terms of sin and merit.' This is what Lord Krishna says in the early part of the *Gita* and ends up: 'Surrender to Me and I will save you from all sins that you cannot help think you are doing.' That you think you cannot not commit sins is also God's will. So if you think you are committing sins, 'surrender to Me' and I'll relieve you of all sins. Surrender. But the joke is even the surrendering is not in your control. Why? Because so long as there is an individual who says, 'I surrender,' there is a surrenderer – there is an individual ego.

PRATIMA That's reassuring, the *Bhagavad Gita* having the contrast there. It's saying this on one the hand and then later saying the other. This is very beautiful that there is a place for everything.

RAMESH Why does Lord Krishna say, 'I'll save you from sins'? Because he knows that Arjuna's understanding, which is based on the programming of that body-mind organism, prevents Arjuna from understanding the Truth at the highest level. So Lord Krishna comes down to Arjuna's level: at your level you think that you are committing sins, then surrender to Me and I'll save you. But what I'm saying is even the *surrendering* is not in Arjuna's hands.

PRATIMA So the contradiction is there …

RAMESH There is no contradiction at all. Why? The understanding is: 'I can commit no sin because I commit no action. I don't do any action, so how can I commit a sin?' If that understanding happens suddenly, if it is God's will, then the rest of it is not relevant. But if the body-mind organism is not programmed for the sudden understanding to happen, then Lord Krishna comes down to the lower and lower levels of the millions of Arjunas.

Destiny to come and listen

RAMESH It is the will of God and the destiny of a body-mind organism to be able to come and listen to what is said. Even being able to listen is really and truly the grace of God. And *total* listening is also God's will and the destiny of the body-mind organism through which seeking is happening. So many people come here and they don't truly listen. While they are hearing what is said, the thinking mind is very active, ready to put up objections – 'Yes, but!' and 'Ah, but!' That is what the thinking mind does. So being able to listen totally is the will of God and the grace of God.

If you are able to listen totally, then the consequences will be quite different from listening half-heartedly and with 'Yes, but!'

No 'one' can get enlightenment

RAMESH What is the significance of the statement 'no one can get enlightenment'? What does it mean? This is the very root of the teaching. It means that it's stupid for any so-called master to ask anyone to do anything to achieve or get enlightenment. The core of this simple statement means, according to my concept, that enlightenment is the *annihilation* of the 'one' who 'wants' enlightenment. If there is enlightenment – which can only *happen* because it is the will of God – then it means that the 'one' who had earlier wanted enlightenment has been annihilated. So no 'one' can achieve enlightenment, and therefore no 'one' can enjoy enlightenment.

Million dollars or enlightenment

RAMESH Getting enlightenment is not in your control. Getting a million dollars is also God's will and the destiny of the body-mind organism. So whether you want a million dollars or you want enlightenment and whether you get what you want are not in your control. If you think it is in your control, I suggest that you go after a million dollars instead of enlightenment, because if you get the million dollars then there will be someone to enjoy that million dollars. But if you go after enlightenment and enlightenment happens, there will be no 'one' to enjoy enlightenment.

Consciousness is all there is

AUGUSTE What is Consciousness, really?

RAMESH Consciousness is the One without the second – the Source of everything.

The 'who', the 'what', the 'where', and the 'when' are all conceptual images in Consciousness. They are all 'real' as any mirage or dream ... The totality of manifestation, and everything therein, is Consciousness itself, the Unicity. All there is is Consciousness, not aware of itself in its noumenal Subjectivity, but perceived by itself as phenomenal manifestation in its objective expression. If this is understood in depth, there is nothing more to be understood. Why? Because such understanding must comport the realization that there is no individual entity as such. What we think we are is merely an appearance, an insubstantial shadow, whereas what we really and truly are, is Consciousness itself, the formless Brahman.

All that exists is universal Consciousness. The universe as such is not the universal Consciousness, but Consciousness is the universe, just as the bracelet is made of gold but the gold is not made of the bracelet. Whether the manifested universe exists or not, Consciousness is there as the subjective Absolute ... There is no causal relationship between Consciousness and the universe. The truth is that Consciousness alone exists and is immanent in what appears as the universe. In other words, Consciousness and the universe are not two in which any sort of relationship could exist.

The simple situation is that the appearance of the universe exists in infinite Consciousness, just as the notion of distance or emptiness exists in space ... It is Consciousness alone that exists. It creates the illusion of the world-appearance and the ego-sense, and perceives the illusion of diversity in what is truly pure Unicity ... It seems difficult to comprehend how the universe could exist in the infinite Consciousness that is supposed to be transcendental.

Truly there is nothing other than Consciousness, and therefore Consciousness cannot but be immanent in everything that appears to exist. And yet no phenomenal manifestation can have any kind of relationship with Consciousness because a relationship can exist only between two different entities. It is in this sense that Consciousness is transcendental to the manifested universe. The universe exists in Consciousness like future waves in a calm sea – only *apparently* different in potentiality.

What appears within Consciousness as its own reflection – the manifestation of the universe – is not separate or different from Consciousness. While the shadow, *by itself*, has no existence and is therefore unreal, the shadow is not different from the substance *when seen together*. When there is no mind in operation, when there is no conceptualizing, it is clearly known, felt, experienced, that phenomenality is only the objective expression of the subjective Noumenon ... God is that formless Subjectivity, pure Potential, the Infinite, Universal Consciousness which alone exists even after the cosmic dissolution. It is only within this pure, Infinite Consciousness, the Potential Plenum, that phenomenal manifestation arose as a mere reflection of that Potentiality, as a mere objective expression of that pure Subjectivity. The phenomenal objectivization of this pure Subjectivity appears and functions in our *outer* world of Consciousness in the waking state, precisely like sentient and insentient objects seem to exist and function in the inner world of Consciousness in the dream state. Nothing really happens.

The final Truth, as Ramana Maharshi and Nisargadatta Maharaj and all the sages before them have clearly stated, is that there is neither creation nor destruction, neither birth nor death, neither destiny nor free will, neither any path nor any achievement.

Consciousness-at-rest, Consciousness-in-action, I AM

All there is is Consciousness. In that original state – call it Reality, call it Absolute, call it Nothingness – there is no reason to be aware of anything. So Consciousness-at-rest is not aware of itself. It becomes aware of itself only when this sudden feeling, I AM, arises. I AM is the impersonal sense of being aware. And that is when Consciousness-at-rest becomes Consciousness-in-movement, when Potential Energy becomes actual energy. They are not two. Nothing separate comes out of the Potential Energy.

Consciousness-in-movement is not separate from Consciousness-at-rest. Consciousness-at-rest becomes Consciousness-in-movement, and that moment that science calls the Big Bang, the mystic calls the sudden arising of awareness … When you talk of Reality, you have converted Reality into a concept. Reality, as a word, is a concept. Reality, as Reality, is not something that you can think of. When you are the Reality, you cannot talk of Reality. So the moment you talk or think of something, it is in phenomenality and therefore conceptual.

I-I, I AM

LANCE I am having problems with the I-I and the I AM.

RAMESH There is no problem because they are not two. They are not two. Consciousness-at-rest is I-I. When it is in movement it is I AM. So I-I is a concept with which you are not really concerned. It is just a concept. What you are really concerned with is I AM.

LANCE I AM is the totality of manifestation.

RAMESH That is correct.

LANCE So if you are in the sleeping state, what is it then?

RAMESH I AM, because there is a body there and because it is in phenomenality.

LANCE So when there is no manifestation there is just I-I?

RAMESH Correct.

LANCE In a book about Ramana Maharshi it says that when you take the enquiry 'Who am I?' backwards, there is nothingness.

RAMESH You see, Ramana Maharshi, therefore, does not really distinguish between I-I and I AM because it is useless. I-I is merely a concept about which he said why bother. You are only concerned with I AM and I am Lance. And when Lance is not there, I AM is there.

LANCE What is the dream state, then?

RAMESH The dream state is identified Consciousness-in-action. What is the living dream, then? The living dream is the dream of the I AM. Lance has a personal dream and I AM has the living dream. So what happens really is that you wake up from your personal dream into the living dream.

LANCE In deep sleep there is I-I?

RAMESH I AM! You are really not concerned with I-I.

LANCE But right now there is a need to know.

RAMESH Then where did I AM come from? That is a conceptual question. And for that conceptual question the conceptual answer is that I AM is the activized, impersonal Energy in manifestation, and I-I is the Potential Energy. The personal 'I' which Lance thinks 'he' is, is the impersonal Energy identifying as an ego which thinks it is a doer and needs to know. When there truly are no more questions, then there is no doer. When there is no doer, then there is no ego. And when there is no ego, then the I AM shines forth from a body-mind organism without personal identification. When the body-mind organism dies, then the I AM continues as I AM. And when the totality of manifestation ends, then I AM is I-I, Consciousness-at-rest. And all of this is a concept.

PETER You said the 'I' in I AM is not the ego. But what is it? I did not get it when you said the I-I.

RAMESH You see, Consciousness not aware of itself, Potential Energy, is a concept. Make no mistake! I-I, I AM, I am Peter – the whole thing is a concept in order to understand your true nature. So I-I is Potential Energy before the manifestation.

PETER The manifestation of me.

RAMESH No. The totality of manifestation.

PETER So this is totally non-individual, this I?

RAMESH Right. Well, actually, whether it is I-I, I AM – they are not two. I-I becomes I AM in manifestation. I-I becomes aware of itself as I AM. But it is the same one Consciousness.

PETER Is it a name for Consciousness? Is it a label for Consciousness?

RAMESH That is right. A concept. That is why I keep saying that I AM becomes a concept when you *talk* about it. This pure Awareness of Existence is the Truth, but the moment I *talk* about it, it becomes a concept.

PETER What is the relation between Consciousness and the word 'I'?

RAMESH It is just a name given to Consciousness.

Peter Oh! Yes. It is just what you call a label.

Ramesh Yes, it is. You see, even 'Consciousness' is a label. 'God' is a label.

Peter Yes, it's confusing using the 'I' that we use for our individuality in this context.

Ramesh Therefore I say I-I, I AM, and I am Peter.

Peter These are three different 'I's.

Ramesh Or it is the same Consciousness, but the relevance is to a different point?

Peter Yes. The last one for the ego.

Ramesh The last one for the ego.

Peter The middle one, I AM …

Ramesh Impersonal Consciousness.

Peter And the I-I …

Ramesh Is the impersonal Consciousness before …

Peter Potentialization, manifestation.

Ramesh Yes. Quite right. Again they are words to explain something. You see?

Peter Yes. Yes.

Durganan This Consciousness, or God, has no characteristics …

Ramesh It has no characteristics. Characteristics refer to an object, and *This* is pure Subjectivity. The Source of everything.

Concept, I AM, present moment

RAMESH You must have heard me say it one hundred times: whatever I say is a concept. Whatever any sage has said at any time is a concept. Whatever any scripture of any religion has said is a concept. That God is a concept and that there is no God are concepts. The only thing which is not a concept is that which no one can deny – that he or she exists – I AM, I exist. *Impersonally* there is existence. *Personally* there is no existence.

PHILIPPE Yes. That's tricky because that sense of existence as soon as it is captured, is a 'me' again.

RAMESH Sure. So you see, I AM is always the present moment. The I AM is the present moment. In the I AM there is no need for any one to say, 'I AM' – because there is no one who says, 'I'm not.' You see? That is why it is impersonal Awareness. It is impersonal Consciousness … I AM is Consciousness aware of itself … Then what is the Source of I AM? Consciousness not aware of itself. So Consciousness *not* aware of itself becomes aware of itself as I AM.

RAMESH Consciousness is all there is. When Consciousness-at-rest goes into movement, manifestation arises. The functioning of manifestation is LIFE as we know it. Nothing can *happen* in life unless it is the will of the Source, or Consciousness.

When faith in the will of God is lost – even that would be God's will! – kindness and compassion come in. When kindness and compassion are lost, there arise moral dos and don'ts. When morality is lost, religious dogmas come in. Religion being the husk and not the kernel of faith in God, religious wars begin.

Manifestation

RAMESH All there is is Consciousness. That is the Source from which the manifestation has come. The functioning of manifestation is life as we know it, and in the functioning of manifestation nothing happens because it is the individual's will. *Nothing can happen unless it is the will of God*, and by 'God', I mean the Source.

So first, all there is is the Source. Call it Consciousness, call it the Self, as Ramana Maharshi said, call it what you like, but understand that what is meant is the one Source – One without the second. All there is is the Source from which has come this manifestation and the manifestation is the totality of objects. The human being is a species of object with the additional, dubious gift of the sense of personal doership, which is the ego. I repeat, the human being is no more than an object, a species of object, along with all other objects that form the totality of the objects in the manifestation.

In the *functioning* of manifestation comes the second basic concept – no 'one' *does* anything. Nothing *happens* unless it is the will of the Source, the will of God. This means the ego is an illusion. The sense of personal doership is an illusion. This is the final understanding.

The final understanding is that *there is no ego* as something distinct from the Source that becomes one with the Source. As long as you say, 'I am That,' the personal 'I' is a separate one from the Source, and what I am saying is, there is no 'I' at all – the 'I' meaning the 'me'. The ego does not become one with the Source. The ego disappears into the Source when there is the *total unconditional acceptance* that there *never was the ego*.

A reflection

RAMESH ... where I AM is concerned, whether there is manifestation or not, makes no difference. The manifestation has come from the I AM. The functioning of the manifestation is in the I AM. It is like a reflection in the mirror. So what you accept is that whatever happens is merely a reflection in the I AM. All manifestation is a reflection in the Source – otherwise, there would be two.

PETER So it can't be a reflection of the Source, it's a reflection in the Source?

RAMESH It can only be in the Source. All this is a reflection in the Source because the Source is all there is. So whatever happens, you choose a concept. You can't do without concepts, otherwise you have to remain silent. And if the question 'Who am I?' arises, that is the very first thought which needs an answer. The answer is a concept, a concept being something which points to the Truth. The value or usefulness of the concept is only to the extent that it points to the Truth. You see? And this concept – that the totality of manifestation and the functioning of this manifest-ation is a reflection in the Source – is a pointer to the Truth, *which is the Source.*

> *Just as the surface of a mirror exists within and without the image reflected in the mirror, so also the supreme Self exists both within and without the physical body.*
>
> *Ashtavakra Gita (19)*

Ashtavakra points out in this important verse that what we Noumenally are is definitely not a thing nor an object, which the personal pronoun cannot help suggesting, but more of a process or a background, like the screen on which a movie is seen. In the absence of the background there could be no appearance at all, although in the case of the phenomenal manifestation, the 'background' – Consciousness – is itself responsible for and constitutes the appearance. The point is that unless there is total 'withdrawal' into impersonality, the consideration of 'who (or what) am I' may mean in effect too simple a transference from phenomenality to Noumenality. It would not have the strength to break the conditioning brought about by the notion of identity leading to the supposed bondage. It is only a direct withdrawal into impersonality that is more likely to bring about the startling transformation known as *metanoesis*, whereby there is a sudden and immediate conviction that the identification with a separate individual entity never did really exist and was essentially nothing but an illusion.

Perhaps it is for this reason that Ashtavakra suggests the mirror simile for Consciousness, which reflects everything, retains nothing, and in itself has no perceptible existence. That is to say, Consciousness is the background of what we appear to be as phenomenal objects, and yet it is not anything objective. Just as the reflection in the mirror is a mere appearance without any existence, and the mirror is the one which has existence but is not affected in any way by the reflection, so also the psychosomatic apparatus [body-mind organism], being only an appearance in Consciousness, has no independent existence. The Consciousness in which it appears is not affected in any way by the appearance of the objects therein.

Ashtavakra in this verse brings out the transcendent aspect of the unmanifest Absolute in relation to the image or appearance of the manifest phenomena.

RAMESH The Source, which has created this manifestation within itself as a reflection, is making that manifestation function. So the manifestation and its functioning, which we call life – all of it is a reflection in the Source ... First, there is the Source. The Source creates a reflection. The reflection is I AM ... Now, Ramana Maharshi says the Source is the I-I. He calls it I-I merely to distinguish it from I AM. I-I is the Potential Energy. The Potential Energy activates itself as manifestation as I AM and becomes aware of the manifestation. The I AM is the impersonal Awareness of the manifestation and its functioning. Then, for the functioning of the manifestation to occur, the Source – or God, or I AM – creates these body-mind organisms, and thus individual 'me's, by identifying itself with these body-mind organisms. So the Universal Energy, the Potential Energy, activates itself into this manifestation. I-I on actualization becomes I AM, and I AM becomes I am Markus. Why does I AM become Markus? Because without Markus and all the billions of other names, life as we know it would not happen.

Simultaneously both real and unreal

RAMESH ... Then, is the manifestation real? It is real and unreal. The question – is the manifestation real or not? – is *misconceived*. The manifestation is both real and unreal: real to the extent that it can be observed, unreal on the basis that it has no independent existence of its own without Consciousness. So the only thing that has independent existence of its own is Reality, and that Reality is Consciousness. Consciousness is the only Reality. Everything else is a reflection of that Reality within itself.

A Pot and Immanence:

> Just as the all-pervading space is both inside
> and outside the pot, so also the eternal and
> all-pervading Consciousness is immanent in
> all beings and objects.

The boundary of the pot may appear to condition and limit the space within the pot but in fact space, as such, cannot be conditioned by the pot which itself exists in space. Similarly, although the Universal Consciousness may appear to be conditioned by the individual psychosomatic apparatus, all phenomenal objects are merely appearances in Consciousness. All there is is Consciousness, immanent in everything phenomenal, inasmuch as there cannot be any phenomena without Consciousness. In this concluding verse, Ashtavakra brings out the importance of emphasizing the ground – the background and the immanence – rather than the personal element so that the final spotlight is not so much on the true nature of the Self but more on the withdrawal into impersonality. Instead of saying that 'your' true nature is Consciousness, he says that all there is, within and without all phenomena, is Consciousness.

A shadow and duality

RAMESH [*Speaking with Scott.*] Ramana Maharshi, as the final Truth, begins by saying there is no creation and no dissolution. So if there is no creation, 'who' can ask any questions? If it is accepted that there is no creation, then the creation that is seen is illusory. The basic point is this: Unicity – the Source (Non-duality) – is really a concept. Manifestation (duality), also a concept, is what we live in. Thus all questions will be in duality.

If there is no creation, obviously there cannot be any Scott. But there is a Scott. So is there a Scott or is there not a Scott? The answer is not yes or no. The answer is yes in certain circumstances, no in other circumstances.

For example, you go out into the sun. There is a shadow. Is the shadow real or unreal? The answer is the shadow is real in certain circumstances and unreal in other circumstances. When you go out into the sun, the shadow is very much real – you can see it. But when you come inside, when you are home, there is no shadow. Likewise, when you are in duality Scott exists. But when you are not in duality – when you are in deep sleep – there is no Scott. So Scott exists in the waking state, in duality, and Scott does not exist in deep sleep.

The intellect says, 'Tell me yes or no.' And the answer is you cannot have a yes or no – yes in certain circumstances and no in other circumstances. The question that is asked is always in duality – when 'Scott' exists. That has to be accepted. So long as 'Scott' exists as the ego, the 'me', there will be questions.

SCOTT How is it that you remain firmly seeded in That? It's in and out, for me. In and out.

RAMESH There is always a flip-flop – no questions then suddenly questions arise. Eventually, at a certain point the understanding comes on top that there is truly no 'one' to ask any questions. No questions. So this flip-flop, the understanding coming up and the understanding being covered by dualism, keeps on happening until there is the final unconditional acceptance that there is truly no ego as the doer.

Duality and dualism

The human being experiences this basic duality of the observed object and the observing object. But along with the basic split of duality, the human being functions in dualism, which is the mental split between the 'me' and the other. It is in the mind that the separation between 'me' and the other arises. That is where the separation from duality to dualism occurs.

The basic split of duality happens in Consciousness itself, as a part of the process of perceiving the manifestation. For any manifestation to exist, it has to be observed. For observing to happen an observed object and an observer object are required. This duality between the observer object and the observed object is the basic split. In the human, the split goes even deeper into the dualism of 'me' and the other. The observer object assumes the subjectivity of the Absolute or Totality or God, saying, 'I am the subject, the rest of the world is my object.' The moment the 'me' and the other come into play, duality gets further subdivided into dualism. The observer object considers himself the observer subject, the experiencer, the doer.

Enlightenment is merely the reverse process where the pseudo-subject realizes that there cannot be a separate entity and the body-mind can only function as an instrument in the manifestation of Totality. When the sense of doership is lost, dualism is restored to its basic duality. Duality is an essential mechanism in phenomenality. Enlightenment is thus nothing but the reverse process from dualism to duality, the end of the sense of personal doership. There is the deepest possible realization that the individual human being is not a separate entity, but merely an instrument through which Totality or God functions. That is all it really means, a transformation from oneself as doer to an absence of the sense of doership.

... right and wrong, happiness and sorrow are pairs of inter-dependent opposites without which there cannot be any life in this world. The mind, however, does not accept the polarity, the interdependence of the opposites like beautiful and ugly, good and evil, etc., and thereby creates a dualism and conflict between the opposites.

So long as the body-mind continues, duality is still there. What-ever the body-mind does in duration, in space-time, is in duality. What is absent in enlightenment is dualism, 'me' as a separate entity and 'you' as another separate entity.

There can be no manifestation unless it is observed through the body; there can be no observation unless there is the mind; there is no mind unless there is Consciousness in the body-mind organism; and where can the Consciousness in the body-mind organism come from except from CONSCIOUSNESS, or the SOURCE? There is, therefore, no duality – only UNICITY.

Duality and space-time

In fact, there has been neither creation nor destruction. Bondage lasts only as long as mind invests a perceived object with Reality. Once that notion disappears, with it goes the supposed bondage. Here, in this objectified creation, only that which is thus objectified grows and decays. It is in this conceptualization and objectification that the duality is conceived as the very basis of the manifestation. Duality is necessary so that manifested objects may be perceived and cognized in a framework of space and time in which the objects are extended. It is essential to bear in mind that while the manifestation thus created is of the nature of mere appearance or illusion, it is real enough in the sense that the manifestation is a reflection in Consciousness. The shadow has no substance or nature of its own, but without the substance the shadow cannot arise.

The dream and space-time

HOLLY My question is about time. Does time happen all at once, or is it actually a sequence like the body-mind tends to see it?

RAMESH What happens in a dream, your personal dream? The moment before the dream starts there is no time for Holly. The moment the dream starts there is space and time. Old men dying, rivers and mountains hundreds of thousands of years old – all that happens in the personal dream which a moment before was not there.

Exactly the same thing happens when you wake up – the manifestation is there, the space is there, and the time is there. Space and time are the basis for the manifestation to appear. The mystic has been saying for years and now the physicist is saying it – no object exists unless it is observed. For the three-dimensional object extended in space to be observed, the observation needs time. So unless there is space, the three-dimensional object cannot be extended, and a three-dimensional object extended in space doesn't exist unless it is observed in time. Space-time is the basis for the manifestation and its functioning. Space-time comes along with the manifestation. The dreamed manifestation, a moment before the dream starts, doesn't exist. When the dream starts, things exist.

Divine hypnosis

INDRANI There is confusion in my mind, Ramesh. Could you please help me? Now, if you say this world is a reflection in Consciousness ...

RAMESH Yes.

INDRANI Yes, but something can only reflect if there is something ...

RAMESH Yes, Consciousness is all there is.

INDRANI Yes, but how does it reflect a world then?

RAMESH Consciousness creates the reflection within itself.

INDRANI Oh! An illusory world is that which is being reflected.

RAMESH That is correct. When you stand before the mirror, what is seen in the mirror is illusion. It's not there. It can be there only if you are there. So this illusory world as manifestation cannot be there in the absence of Consciousness. The moving pictures cannot be there in the absence of the screen. So, the screen is real. The moving pictures are not real. Consciousness is Reality. Everything is the manifestation, the human beings are part of the manifestation. The functioning of the manifestation is like a dream.

ANNAN How do I get in touch with my Consciousness and maintain that contact?

RAMESH Now, we've just said it is not 'your' Consciousness.

ANNAN It is not mine.

RAMESH It is not 'your' Consciousness. Annan wants to get in touch with 'his' Consciousness. What is Annan? To me it is merely the name given to a body-mind organism. So what I see is a body-mind organism which is an object, which is part of the totality of manifestation. You see? And this body-mind organism, this object as part of the manifestation, is an instrument through which the impersonal Consciousness, or Energy, functions. There are various gadgets – fans, lamps, kitchen gadgets – through which electricity functions. So all human beings are merely programmed instruments through which Consciousness, or impersonal Energy, or God, functions.

ANNAN How do I get in touch with Consciousness?

RAMESH 'Who' gets in touch with Consciousness? Consciousness is all there is. If Consciousness is all there is, can there be anything else that can get in touch with Consciousness? Consciousness is the Source of the manifestation, and this body-mind organism which considers itself Annan is part of the manifestation ...

Now a clever hypnotist can make two thousand people believe something which is not there is there as a solid entity, can he not? So if a clever hypnotist can make two thousand people believe there is something solid when there isn't, then is it difficult for the

Divine through hypnosis to make each individual body-mind organism think that the world is real, solid?

> *We are constantly being misled by God –*
> *through divine hypnosis –*
> *so that life as we know it may go on.*

Destiny

RAMESH ... God's will in respect of each body-mind organism is what I call the destiny of that body-mind organism, stamped at the moment of conception. At the moment of conception the destiny of that conception is stamped.

MARKUS So you can switch these words, God's will and destiny?

RAMESH They are the same thing. God's will in respect of each body-mind organism is the destiny. The destiny of a body-mind organism is God's will.

MARKUS So this says actually 'you' can't do anything, just accept.

RAMESH That is correct, Markus. That is indeed what I am saying. So if a conception is not destined to fructify into a baby, then that conception will be aborted. The mother may decide to abort the conception. If it is born, how long that organism will live is part of the destiny, and during that lifespan, what will happen is also part of the destiny, which is God's will.

So if a murder happens, what has really happened? What has happened is that one body-mind organism has been killed and another body-mind organism is the instrument through which this killing has happened. The one which was killed – it was the destiny of that body-mind organism to be killed by a particular body-mind organism – that is destiny. Nobody knows how one is going to die. It may be a natural death, it may be an accident, it may be murder, it may be suicide. So which of these four ways will apply to a particular body-mind organism is its destiny, stamped at the moment of conception. If it is the destiny of a body-mind organism to be murdered, that body-mind organism will be murdered. That will be the way that body-mind organism is supposed to die. What happens to the body-mind organism which committed the murder will subsequently also be the destiny of that body-mind organism. Not all crimes are detected. Not all crimes detected are punished. So whether that body-mind organism will be punished or not for the murder which happened through it will be its destiny and the will of God.

There was a body-mind organism called Mother Teresa which was so programmed that only wonderful things happened. Those wonderful things which happened brought a lot of rewards: Nobel Peace Prize, many other awards and any number of acknowledgements. So what has happened? What I am saying is there was no Mother Teresa who received all those awards. Mother Teresa was only the name of the body-mind organism whose destiny it was to receive them.

On the other hand there is a psychopathic organism. The psychopath didn't choose to be a psychopath. But the psychopath has been programmed to do what society and the law call evil acts, perverted acts. So those acts will happen through that body-mind organism which is programmed to commit such acts. That will be the destiny of that body-mind organism of the psychopath. And the psychopathic organism may or may not be punished, according to its destiny. But my main point is that whether it is the body-mind organism of a Mother Teresa or the body-mind organism of a psychopath, both have been produced by the same Source. We can only accept God's will. We cannot try to understand God's will. Why can we not?

MARKUS We cannot try to understand God's will?

RAMESH You cannot even begin to try, Markus, for this reason: our intelligence is very limited; our intellect is very limited;

whereas God's intellect is all eternity. So how can we, who can only see in a limited way, understand God's will? We cannot.

MARKUS Nobody can?

RAMESH Nobody can, because everybody is merely a small part of the total manifestation which is a reflection of the Source. All you can do, as you just said a little while ago, is to accept things as they are. This is it!

MARKUS As soon as you accept this, there are no questions anymore.

RAMESH That is the point. Whether you call it acceptance or surrender makes no difference to me. People who are happier to think in terms of God prefer the word 'surrender'. Those who are more intellectual and prefer to use the word Energy or Source will say 'acceptance'. It means the same thing. And what is the acceptance and the surrender? What is the basis of this acceptance and surrender? That there is truly no 'me' who can do anything. What is the final bottom line of acceptance and surrender? *That there is truly no 'me' who can do anything.* There is really, truly no 'me'.

NINA What about these man-made structures of good and bad, wrong and right, that we spend our whole lives battling – if it is God's will then there is nothing right and there is nothing wrong. The psychopath is doing what is his destiny.

RAMESH That is correct.

NINA The right and the wrong is imposed by us on ourselves.

RAMESH That is correct. That is quite correct. And that imposition of right and wrong for a particular body-mind organism is God's will in respect of that body-mind organism – not an individual but a body-mind organism. You see? It is the destiny of that body-mind organism we call a psychopath for certain things to happen. It was the destiny of a body-mind organism called Mother Teresa for those kinds of actions to happen.

NINA And the way of a psychopath or a murderer, according to our rules, is to be put into prison or given the death sentence. That is in his destiny?

RAMESH That is the destiny of that body-mind organism. Quite correct. That is indeed what I am saying. The act that happens is the destiny. The consequences of that act are also destiny.

NINA So the one that gets away with a heinous crime or the one who gets penalized by his peers for the crime, that is also in his destiny?

RAMESH And why do you forget the innocent man who gets punished? See, that is also destiny. And how may crimes have there been where innocent people were executed and then later it was realized that they were wrongly executed? That was the destiny of the man to be wrongly accused and executed.

BRUCE Ramesh, I have a question about the concept of destiny. When you refer to destiny, is it the destiny of the body-mind organism?

RAMESH Yes. Indeed!

SINGH Does that include or is that similar to the destiny of the ego?

RAMESH No. The ego has nothing to do with it. It is the destiny of the body-mind organism. The destiny is always of the body-mind organism. The ego, frankly, doesn't exist! The ego does not have a destiny.

BRENDAN Then why isn't it that the ego has the destiny? This, the body-mind organism, is just a mechanical ...

RAMESH I know. So what happens to the body-mind organism is the destiny of the body-mind organism. Whatever happens in life to that body-mind organism happens only to the body-mind organism – it does not happen to the ego. The ego, because of this hypnosis, thinks, 'It is happening to me.'

BRENDAN I thought you said mind and ego are synonymous.

RAMESH Yes! The thinking mind and the ego are the same.

Programming, conditioning and programmed computer

By programming I mean certain natural characteristics which were stamped at the moment of conception: physical, mental, intuitive, and emotional. And this body-mind organism has been conditioned by the environment. You had no choice about your parents, you had no choice about the genes or DNA, you had no choice about the environment; therefore, you had no choice about the conditioning which this body-mind receives. And by programming, I mean genes and conditioning.

MARK My sense is that there is a relationship between *vasanas* and the ego, if there are a lot of *vasanas* there is a strong ego.

RAMESH What does *vasana* mean? *Vasana* means inherited tendency.

MARK Programming?

RAMESH Inherited tendencies are the programming. In some cases the programming is such that there is great resistance, and

111

in other cases the programming is such that it is wide open – there is great receptivity.

MARK As a body-mind organism moves through life, you mentioned that the conditioning …

RAMESH The conditioning happens all the time. And the new conditioning may alter the old conditioning. New concepts deleting old concepts. As Ramana Maharshi said, that is the only purpose of a concept – to be used as a thorn to remove another thorn embedded in your foot, and then you throw both thorns away.

RAMESH … The brain is part of the inert body-mind organism that cannot create anything. It can only receive and react. The brain is a reacting agent, an apparatus.

MARKUS So this body-mind is receiving and doing?

RAMESH That's right. So what I'm saying is, a thought comes, the brain reacts to that thought, and that reaction is what Markus calls 'his' action. Markus sees something or hears something, the brain reacts to it, and that reaction is what Markus calls 'his' action. But Markus has no control over what will happen. Markus has no control over what thought will arise. Markus has no control over what he is going to see, or hear, or touch, or smell, or taste. Therefore, Markus has no control over what thought will arise or what he will see. The brain reacts to something over which Markus has no control, and how does the brain react? According to the programming – genes plus conditioning.

If you have a personal computer, you put in an input. What will be the output, Markus? Exactly according to the way it is programmed. What can a personal computer do except bring out an output strictly according to the way it is programmed? And who puts in the input? Not the computer. You put in the input. So with the body-mind organism, which is a programmed instrument or computer, God puts in an input. He makes you hear something, see something. He sends a thought. That is the input.

MARKUS What if there is a body-mind organism identifying with its name and who doubts what he or she is going to do? Is it already clear what will happen?

RAMESH Be mindful of what happens, Markus. Find out what happens from your personal experience, not because of a concept. From your own personal experience find out whether what you think is 'your' action is really someone's action. Or is it merely the reaction of the brain to an input over which you have no control, according to the programming over which you have had no control?

ROBERT The question I have is about conditioning. What I've been telling people is that in order for them to experience some healing or change, they have to go against their conditioning. I understand, especially now, that intrinsically it's impossible to go against one's conditioning. It just can't happen. Yet in therapy it seems that in some cases people are able to do new things. It seems like change is the ability or the occurrence of something going on that is not in the conditioning.

RAMESH What you are really saying, Robert, is that in telling them to try and change their conditioning, you are giving them fresh conditioning. What are you getting by sitting here? It's conditioning! – which could change or amend Robert's existing conditioning.

ROBERT That's very clear.

RAMESH What is happening now? You are getting fresh conditioning. Make no mistake.

ROBERT So this is just conditioning?

RAMESH This additional conditioning changes the attitude.

ROBERT The conditioning isn't fixed, it's constantly being …

RAMESH You're a psychologist?

ROBERT Yes.

RAMESH The psychologists tell me that the earliest conditioning is the firmest conditioning and is the basis of the personality. But conditioning is happening all the time, every moment. Whatever you hear, whatever you see is part of the conditioning. And that conditioning can amend the earlier conditioning.

That you must fight the ego is prior conditioning. Now I'm telling you – don't fight the ego. It is useless. The ego will not commit suicide. It is only that Power which created the ego that can destroy the ego. So accept the ego and let it continue as long as it is destined to continue. This is the conditioning that will alter the existing conditioning of being told to fight your ego.

ROBERT There is no going against conditioning …

RAMESH This is fresh conditioning. That's what I'm saying.

ROBERT What a great relief that conditioning happens!

RAMESH Conditioning is happening all the time. So what you are really trying to do professionally is not to tell them to change their conditioning but to do something. Your telling them to do something may be against their existing conditioning, but you are not really trying to tell them to change their conditioning.

I'm not telling you to change your conditioning. All I'm saying is, according to my concept, accepting the ego means weakening the ego.

❈

RAMESH Two sages are walking along the road. The programming in one is timidity, and the programming in the other is physical courage. Both see a woman being molested. That is what is seen. That is an event over which neither sage had any control. Upon seeing the woman's desperate situation, the brain in one sage reacts according to the programming and he goes to rescue her. In the process he badly injures her assailant and is arrested and goes to jail. The other sage, because he is programmed to be timid, hesitates and does nothing. The one programmed to be brave accepts the consequences of his actions. Likewise, the timid one accepts the consequences of his action. He doesn't feel guilt or think that he too should have been courageous.

Now the ordinary person would react differently. If brave, he may have done the same thing, but he would also get involved in the consequences of being arrested: I should not have hit the attacker; I should not have even helped the woman. This is involvement. The sage would simply accept the consequences. An ordinary, timid person would feel guilt about not helping or wish he were braver. This too is involvement. The timid sage would not get involved, he would accept his timidity and the consequences – not wishing he was programmed otherwise or had acted differently.

It is the judging by the ego, the thinking mind, which is the involvement. The working mind just does what it is programmed to do and accepts the consequences.

LARRY Carrying this example further, let's say a sage is a homosexual and unenlightened.

RAMESH 'Sage is unenlightened,' you said?

LARRY To begin with.

RAMESH No, then he cannot be a sage. A sage is enlightened.

LARRY All right, then there is a person who is a homosexual and enlightenment has not happened. There is some evidence that homosexuality is genetic.

RAMESH Oh, a great deal of evidence I'm told.

LARRY Time passes and enlightenment happens in that body-mind which is genetically programmed towards homosexuality. So then, that body-mind could be a sage and a homosexual.

RAMESH Oh yes! Certainly. That would be the programming of that body-mind organism.

LARRY Okay, so that follows. He wouldn't feel guilt after enlightenment.

RAMESH That's the point. He wouldn't feel guilt. The destiny would be accepted.

What is the difference between anger arising in a sage and anger arising in an ordinary person? Anger arises because the brain reacts to what is heard or seen. The brain produces the anger, not the ego. Where does the ego come in? The ego reacts to the reaction of the brain. That is involvement. In the sage the anger arises as a reaction of the brain, but the sage witnesses it taking its course. The anger may result in an action. The sage watches the anger arise and take its action. The sage doesn't say it was 'I' who was angry and 'I' did this act.

The subsequent reaction to the basic reaction is the ego, the involvement. The original reaction is a physical reaction of the brain. The subsequent reaction is the ego. In the case of the ordinary person, he would say, ' "I" was angry. "I" shouldn't be angry. My doctor has told me not to be angry, so therefore "I" must do something not to get angry. "I" must find some way not to get angry. "I" must control myself.' This goes round and round and round. In the case of the sage, anger arises and simply takes its course with no involvement.

Here is a specific example in the case of Nisargadatta Maharaj. What happened was someone asked a question. Maharaj's ears heard the question. So hearing of the question happened. The brain reacted to that question and anger arose: 'You've been coming here for many years and you ask a stupid question like that?' Anger arose. But what happened? Almost immediately thereafter the same man made a statement that was very humorous, and Maharaj laughed the loudest. So one split second anger arose, and in the next minute laughter arose. In the case of an ordinary man what would have happened? He would have said that he was not going to laugh. But there was no Maharaj to get angry. Anger came and went and laughter took its place.

About fear, it too arises. For example, there are two ordinary people. Fear arises in the case of one, and fear does not arise in the case of the other. Arising of the fear has nothing to do with the ego, but the ego reacts to that fear. And as with anger so with fear, the ordinary person says, ' "I" was afraid. "I" get afraid. "I" wish "I" could be like my friend who doesn't become afraid.' So the involvement arises because of not being able to accept the programming.

In the case of a sage, fear may also arise. If so, he accepts that the body-mind organism is so programmed that in having a particular kind of experience, fear arises. The fear may make him run away, but in running away the sage will not say, ' "I" should not have run away. My friend did not run away. Why did "I" run away? "I" should not get afraid.' That would be the involvement of the ego – the ego's reaction to the fear.

So there is a basic reaction and also the reaction of the ego. In the case of the sage a basic reaction happens because it is a programmed reaction of the brain. But there is no ego, and therefore there is no involvement of the ego. There is no reaction to the basic reaction by the ego.

Don't forget, this is a concept. It is what I say. You have to find out from your own experience if this concept is acceptable or not. That will depend on God's will and your destiny. It is remarkable how confirmation of what I'm saying is found in the *Bhagavad Gita*. In the *Bhagavad Gita* it says that likes and dislikes arise when the senses come in contact with their respective objects, and that you should not get involved in the arising of the likes and dislikes. *That* is the problem. The involvement is the problem, not the arising of the likes and dislikes. The arising of the likes and dislikes is a natural thing – getting involved with them is the problem.

Ego

RAMESH What is the bondage? The bondage is – 'I' am a separate person with free will and responsible for my actions, and therefore 'I' must do good things. What is the bondage? The ego is the bondage. 'Who' is happy or 'who' is unhappy? The ego, the sense of doership. The body can't be happy or unhappy. So the 'one' who is happy or unhappy is the ego. And what is liberation? Liberation is the freedom from the alternating sense of happiness and unhappiness. Liberation is the total, final understanding in the heart that there is no doer, no experiencer.

Every religion tells you to get rid of your ego, but the 'one' to whom the religions tell to get rid of the ego – *is the ego!* The ego is told to get rid of the ego! But the ego is not going to commit suicide. Therefore the question really is, who created the ego? But who created the ego? You didn't create the ego. Where could the ego have come from? Where could it have come from except from the Source! Whether you call that Source, Consciousness or Primal Energy or God or Awareness makes no difference, so long as you understand that it is the Source – One without a second.

So the ego has also come from the Source. That is why I call the ego divine hypnosis. The hypnosis is – 'I' consider myself a separate being with a sense of doership. Why has the Source created the hypnosis of separation? Because without separation interhuman relationships won't happen. It is only because of this separation that we have friendship and enmity, love and hate. All that arises only because each individual considers himself or herself a separate being. And without interhuman relationships life as we know it would not happen.

Remember, the Source having created this ego, or divine hypnosis, is in the process of removing the hypnosis in a few cases, not in all cases. So the ego – the sense of separation, the divine hypnosis, the sense of personal doership – basically has been destroyed by the Source in the case of a few body-mind organisms called sages.

What remains in the case of a body-mind organism called a sage? The programming remains. That's why you may have ten sages, and in each case the sense of personal doership has been demolished, but they differ in life. Why, because the programming is different. In other words, even though the ego is destroyed, the Source continues to use those body-mind organisms of the sages in the same way the Source uses other body-mind organisms – to put in an input and bring out an output. So the body-mind organisms of the sages continue to function exactly like before but without the sense of doership.

If the body-mind organism of a sage has the programming to be quick of temper, then that sage before liberation happened got angry very quickly. And after enlightenment the sage continues to become angry very quickly. The programming is for anger to arise. The only difference is that earlier the sage used to say, 'I shouldn't get angry with my friends. My friends don't like it. And I'm told I must not get angry because my blood pressure will rise, therefore I'm told that I must control my anger.' All that was the *involvement* of the ego, which used to happen before the doership was destroyed. What happens after the doership has been destroyed? When anger arises the sage does not say, 'I am angry. I shouldn't get angry.' The anger that arises and the effect of it is merely witnessed, including the consequences. On the other hand, if something is happening and compassion arises, earlier the ego would have said, 'I am a compassionate man and people should respect me.' But now there is no such thinking. All he sees is compassion arising and taking its course.

The compassion of a sage may take any form. Finding someone hurt he may bandage them, or seeing someone in need he may reach into his pocket and give some money. So the compassion arises and takes its own course, but the sage is never involved in that action as 'his' action. That is the only difference according to my concept. The sense of personal doership has been erased forever. He just witnesses things happening not as 'my' action or someone else's action. If an action from some other body-mind organism hurts the sage, the hurt will be there. But knowing that no one does anything, the sage cannot hate anybody. Whom will he hate? All actions are God's actions. Or if you wish to put it another way, all actions are the impersonal functioning of Consciousness. So 'whom' will the sage hate? Consciousness? God?

With the doership having been destroyed the sage does not get proud; the sage does not feel guilty; the sage does not hate nor envy anybody. So the absence of guilt, pride, hate, envy makes life peaceful. And that is what the search has all been for – peace during the waking state which exists in the deep sleep state. My concept of all spiritual search is to have that peace which prevails during deep sleep even during the waking state, during your ordinary working life.

Every event, every thought, every feeling concerning any 'individual' is a movement in Consciousness, *brought about by Consciousness.*

Every thing or object in the manifested universe is a product of Consciousness, both during the illusion when the manifestation appeared to be 'real' and after the realization of the Truth ... We are nothing but Consciousness, and never have been anything else. Perhaps it would be easier to 'understand' the Truth if it is conceived that there never has been any 'we' at any time, and that all there is – and has ever been – is Consciousness. 'We' think of ourselves, consciously or unconsciously, as sentient beings and therefore as separate from the manifestation: 'we' are the subject and the rest of the manifestation is the object. The reality is that 'we', as manifested phenomena, are actually nothing but a part of the one manifested universe. What makes us think of ourselves as separate is the fact that the apparent universe becomes known to us, as sentient beings, through sentience operating through cognitive faculties. This 'sentience', as an aspect of Consciousness in *itself*, is a direct manifestation of the whole-mind. And it is for this reason that we cannot get rid of the deepest feeling that 'I' am other than the manifested appearance. And so indeed we are, but the illusion (the maya) consists in the fact that instead of *collectively* considering ourselves as sentience which enables us to cognize the manifestation (including sentient beings) which has appeared in Consciousness, we consider ourselves as *separate* individual entities. And therein lies our suffering and bondage. As soon as there is realization (awakening to the fact) that we are not separate entities but Consciousness itself (with sentience acting as the means for cognizing the manifestation), the illusion of separateness – the cause of our suffering and bondage – disappears. There is then the clear apperception that unmanifested, we

121

are Noumenon, and while manifested, we are appearance – no more separate than substance and its form (gold and the gold ornament). Manifestation arises from the Unmanifest and in due course sinks back into the Unmanifest. The human beings *as individuals* are *really* quite irrelevant, except, of course, as illusory characters in a dream play which is known as 'life', or as instruments through which everying happens.

Free will

RAMESH First you tell me what you mean by 'free will'.

RON The notion that 'I' can choose between one thing and another.

RAMESH Yes, but does that include the consequences of what you choose? Your free will is to choose one thing or the other. Does your free will include the actual happening of what you choose?

MARK No.

RAMESH What use is your apparent free will, Mark? So that free will which is of no use, you have! So what is the free will? To choose. Certainly you can choose, but whether what you choose happens or not is not in your control. That's why when people use these words, I usually stop them and have them tell me what they mean by 'free will'.

MARK The logic that you've laid out, which makes sense to me, is that there is a natural unfolding of creation, that once it's set in motion it unfolds in a very complex and determined pattern. And then there's this ego which thinks it can choose one way or the other.

RAMESH You see, what do you make your choice on? How do you make your choice?

MARK That would be my question, because I would ask the question, 'Who chooses?'

RAMESH 'Who' chooses? The ego chooses. But the ego chooses on what basis? My point is that the ego makes its 'choice' *on the programming it has received*, without any choice.

MARK And has no control over.

RAMESH The environmental conditioning over which the ego has no control.

MARK Or DNA, or whatever.

RAMESH That's right, so there is DNA, or the genes, over which you had no choice plus the environmental conditioning over which you have had no choice. It is these two things that I call the programming based on which you will make 'your' choice. You'll make your choice on what you have been conditioned to think is right or wrong. So if your free will is based on the programming over which you have had no control, then 'whose' free will are we talking about?

MARK So even the free will is a function of the absolute Subject, or the Source?

RAMESH That's right, or rather the free will that you value so much is based on something over which you have had no control.

MARK That's good. That's really good!

RAMESH I come back again to the valid question of the ego. The ego has a valid question: in living in society I'm expected to make a choice – do I not make a choice? I say, 'Of course you do.' But all I'm saying is that the choice you make, consider whether it is really 'your' choice or does the choice *happen*?

123

MIRABAI More and more my experience is that it's not 'me' making any decision anyway! Increasingly I have these flashes of the experience that it really is just Consciousness happening – when I say something, I do something, I make a decision. It feels more and more as if decisions are being made – moving my arm, it's predestined. Frequently it feels like that, and this is beginning to give me a sense of that freedom.

RAMESH Can you explain that a little bit, Mirabai, as you understand it? As you say, the question was asked of Ramana Maharshi: 'I raised my arm. Is that also predetermined?' And Ramana Maharshi said, 'Yes.' *Just one word*. How would you explain that, that even your raising your arm is predestined – predetermined?

EDDIE It would be a reaction to something at that moment. Even if I say to you or somebody says, 'You are raising your arm because you want to,' or whatever. I would be reacting to that or I would not react to that. So it is a reaction!

RAMESH That is *absolutely* correct, Eddie. In other words, why did the man raise his arm? The raising of the arm was the reaction of the brain to what was heard – that everything is predetermined. Just seconds before Ramana Maharshi had said, 'Everything is predetermined.' That was heard by the man – by that body-mind organism – and the brain reacted: 'I have no free will? I can raise my arm.' So the raising of the arm was the reaction of the brain to what was heard. It is as much a reaction as scratching when there is an itch.

EDDIE And even if you say, 'I have an itch. I'm not going to scratch. I'm not going to react.' That's a reaction.

RAMESH Correct. Absolutely.

RAMESH But make no mistake. I keep repeating it: all this is a concept. Make no mistake. It is a concept.

WENDELL But people seek the Truth through that.

RAMESH Yes.

CINDY So it's not the truth that there is no free will?

RAMESH No. I told you: the only Truth is I AM – I exist. That is the only Truth. Everything else is a concept. Rebirth is a concept. Your karma is a concept. 'There is no karma which is yours, all that happens is God's will' is a concept. But the concept that only God's will prevails – *that* concept gives rise to a simple life: no guilt, no pride, no hate. The concept 'I have free will' leads to frustration and pride and hate.

CRAIG Ramesh, though it is a concept, I find that most people who believe in free will have not really thought about the whole matter.

RAMESH That's correct. That is why I say if you believe that you have free will, find out from your own experience in the past six months or six years to what extent your free will has prevailed. From your own experience you'll find that really there's no free will.

WENDELL Ramesh, if we accept the concept that there's no individual entity, that solves a lot of problems, doesn't it?

RAMESH It makes life simple, Wendell. How does it make life simple? Because if I am not the doer then why should I feel guilty, why should I feel pride, and why should I hate people? So no guilt, no pride, no hate make life simple. I mean other than that, what does one really need in life? Forget about spirituality. Forget about seeking. Forget about enlightenment. What is it that one needs in life? No guilt, no pride, no hate, no envy make life simple. It means *peace*.

You're quite right. If you seek peace in this life, then the only thing to understand is that you are not the doer, that you're truly not responsible for anything that you do. But that doesn't mean that you have to be irresponsible. Because the answer ultimately is do whatever you like according to any standards of morality and responsibility you have. The standards of morality and responsibility are part of the *programming*, and you cannot act other than through your programming.

Thought, feeling and prayer

RAMESH The thought and the feeling – there is no difference! A thought arises. A feeling arises. No difference. Scientific research shows that what you consider 'your' thought arises half a second before you say it is 'your' thought, and therefore, you didn't bring about that thought. The thought occurs, and because of that thought the brain mechanically reacts to it as an input into the computer and brings out an output according to the programming. By 'programming' I mean you had no choice in being born to particular parents, therefore you had no choice about your genes, DNA. By the same token you had no choice about being born into a particular environment in which you received your conditioning. So this DNA plus environmental conditioning, over which you have had no control, is what I call the programming of this body-mind computer. And what you think is 'your' action is merely the Source, or God or Ishwara, putting in an input and the output comes according to the programming. So where is this 'Salome' who thinks and prays?

SALOME No. That is another thing, because when I pray I thank Him for these thoughts: 'I am extremely grateful that you give me this feeling. It is by your grace that I can think this way and feel this way. Nothing is mine. It is only by your grace that I feel this.' So even this prayer is a thank you that I can pray this way.

RAMESH So that is a prayer made by an individual 'me', isn't it? And what I'm saying, Salome, is that there is really no individual 'me'. Whatever Salome thinks 'she' does is merely the mechanical reaction of the brain to an input over which she had no control according to the programming over which she has had no control. But you think 'you' are doing this praying.

SALOME No. As soon as I think this I thank Him for giving me the thought because it is not my doing.

RAMESH So it is still Salome thanking God for giving her the thought and the feeling!

SALOME So where do you overcome that?

RAMESH You see, 'Where do "you" overcome that?' There is only one way – there is *no action which is Salome's action*, including the praying. Who did the praying? Salome thinks, 'I do the praying.' And what I'm saying is prayer *happens* as a purely mechanical reaction of the brain to an input. And what is the input? A thought. The brain reacts to that thought and prays. So the prayer *happens*.

JIM An enlightened being has no control over the thoughts that come?

RAMESH Are you saying that even the enlightened being – the body-mind organism in which enlightenment has happened – has no control over what thought will come? You are right! That is precisely what I'm saying.

JIM Is thought not ego?

RAMESH Thought is not the ego! Thinking is the ego!

Ramesh 'The choosing by Consciousness among the QM [Quantum Mechanics] possibilities is an unconscious process. A personal awareness of that choice comes about one half second later than a "readiness potential" that appears in the brainwave,' says brain surgeon Benjamin Libet. 'Thus, there can be no free will, that most precious "possession" in the West.' The Indian sage, Ramana Maharshi, said the same thing.

So as I understand it, Quantum Mechanics says that nobody can know what is going to happen in the next minute, in the next hour. The flight of a particle you don't know where it is going to end. You cannot predict it. That's what Niels Bohr says according to the Theory of Uncertainty. When this theory was explained to Albert Einstein, he said that he could find no fault with the Theory of Uncertainty, which says that you never know what is going to happen at any given time. Albert Einstein said that although he could find no fault with the theory, his conditioning and upbringing would not let him accept the Theory of Uncertainty. He said, 'I find no fault with this theory, but I cannot accept the implication that God is playing dice with the universe.' Then Niels Bohr replied to him, 'God is *not* playing dice with the universe. You think God is playing dice with the universe because you don't have all the information that God has.'

You see, God has the full information, He knows what is happening. He sees the whole picture. It's already there. But we don't possess God's knowledge so nothing is certain. From the wave of probability something happens at any moment to anyone. So when the wave collapses something happens. A thought arises, a desire arises, and it takes a split second for the brain to react to it and for the mind-ego to immediately take possession and say that it is 'my' thought, 'my' desire. So the desire arises when the quantum wave collapses. The ego accepts it as 'its' desire. Now, you tell me if the desire is of the ego or that of Consciousness.

Emotions

MAUNA Do you mean that for an enlightened person there are no emotions coming up?

RAMESH Sure the emotions come. But supposing an emotion came into this body-mind organism. What would I do? Merely notice it. Watch it arising. It is witnessed as if it is somebody else's, *not 'mine'*! You see, the emotion which arises is the reaction of the brain and its conditioning and subsequent memories to something which is seen, or smelled, or heard. So someone comes here and keeps asking questions, the brain reacts to that, and a feeling of great compassion arises. It arises, but it is also known that there is nothing I can do to help that person to get rid of those emotions which he is concerned with. The emotion of compassion arises because of the suffering of the other person who is not easily able to accept the teaching. So you see, compassion arises, but along with that compassion is also the understanding that what happens is the destiny of that body-mind organism.

The compassion which arises does not become a burden for me. The fear which may arise does not become an anxiety for me because there is no thinking mind thinking it is my responsibility to make him understand. An ordinary teacher would be very much concerned that it is his or her responsibility to make students understand. So there is the thinking mind which is the involvement!

Responsibility

RAMESH So even if you tentatively accept that any action which you call 'my' action is really not 'my' action – it is just happening according to God's will – then something which you think 'you' have done and, therefore, caused some harm or grief to someone else is not a reason to feel guilt. In fact, every human being carries an enormous load of guilt. Most of the thoughts that come are,

'I wish I hadn't done this, then so-and-so wouldn't have suffered', or 'I wouldn't have been frustrated'.

MARKUS Yes, but there is no guilt …

RAMESH So what I'm saying, Markus, is if you truly accept that it was not 'your' action anyway, why should you feel guilt? If you truly accept that it was not 'your' action and this action has been praised by others, then why should Markus feel proud? If it is not Markus's action at all, and it is only something which Markus *sees* as happening, then what I'm saying is there is no guilt, and there is no pride.

MARKUS There is no guilt. There is even no morality?

RAMESH Wait a minute, we'll come to that. There is no guilt, there is no pride, and more importantly, if Markus understands that nothing can happen unless it is God's will – it is not Markus's action – then Markus also knows that something which happens through another body-mind organism is not 'his' or 'her' action. Consequently, whatever action another body-mind organism might think is 'his' action affecting you, *you* know that it is not 'his' action. So how can you think of anybody as your enemy? How can you hate anybody? How can you envy anybody? Once you accept that no individual does *anything* – actions happen through each body-mind organism according to the way it is pro-grammed by God – then four beautiful things happen: no guilt, no pride, no hate, no envy. Life becomes simple.

Now, that must raise some questions. The main question at this time being: 'If I am not responsible for anything, and things just happen, why should I do anything at all? Why should I not remain in bed all day?'

MARKUS I was thinking this yesterday.

RAMESH You see, that is a valid question which the mind-intellect must ask. Who is this 'me'? It is the mind-intellect. The mind-intellect is the 'Markus'. So the mind-intellect, the ego, says, 'If I don't do anything, and I am not responsible for anything, why should I do anything at all? Why should I not lie in bed and do nothing?' The answer to that is very simple, Markus. Markus thought 'he' was functioning, but what was really functioning? – the *Energy*, the Universal Energy functioning through this body-mind organism. That is the One which produces actions. So that Universal Energy functioning or operating through this body-mind organism will continue to operate, and that Energy will not let Markus remain idle for any length of time. Some action will happen through this body-mind organism because the Energy will bring it about – physical *or mental*. So the Universal Energy inside this body-mind organism will continue to bring about actions because that is its nature. It is the nature of the Universal Energy to produce.

Markus It would also be a bit boring just to be in bed all day.

Ramesh That is what the mind-intellect says, and this is quite right. That is also another part of it. And what you have said, in fact, is exactly what I have said: it would be boring to lie in bed because of the Energy inside – you can't keep that Energy suppressed, controlled all the time. You see? So you cannot remain idle. That is one aspect. The second aspect is responsibility. Markus's mind-intellect asks, 'If I am not responsible for what I do, why should I not take a machine gun and go out and kill twenty people? If I am not responsible and everything that happens is God's will, why should I not take a machine gun and go out and kill people?'

Markus Yes, but why should I do it?

Ramesh No, why should you *not*? Why should you not do it since you are not responsible? The point is if you are not responsible for 'your' actions, why should you not do this? I'm taking an extreme case. You see, the answer to that, again, is that the basic misconception is you are saying why should 'you' not do this and kill people? But what actually happens is that there is *no* 'you' to do anything.

MARKUS If there is someone who is shooting twenty people, is this also God's will?

RAMESH It is, Markus. That is what I am saying. And therefore, what I am also saying is 'you' cannot do it because this body-mind organism is not programmed to kill twenty innocent people. So how can this body-mind do such a thing simply because the brain hears that 'you' are not responsible?

MARKUS So there is no question actually of you just sitting in bed and doing nothing, because anyway you can't do anything against God's will.

RAMESH That's right. So what remains is the question of responsibility. A murderer can say, 'Yes, the murder happened, but this teaching tells me that "I" have not committed the murder, God has committed the murder. Why should I be punished?' That is the next question. You see? The answer to that is very simple – God's will in respect of each body-mind organism is what I call the destiny of that body-mind organism, stamped at the moment of conception.

RAMESH Mitra, I noticed yesterday that there was considerable receptivity. There was no resistance. There was much acceptance of what was said.

MITRA My identity has always been based on what I know. I know this and I know that. Yesterday it went straight here [*points at the heart*] that I know nothing.

RAMESH How do you mean that you know nothing?

Mitra I do healing. Last night a cousin was not feeling well and she asked me to give a session. I put my hands out, and there was no longer this worry about trying to control the result. Usually there is this thing that 'Oh, I hope she'll do well. I hope she'll be fine', but that doesn't seem to happen any more.

Ramesh Underlying that feeling 'I hope she will be well', what is the real feeling?

Mitra I am the doer.

Ramesh I hope 'I' shall be able to cure her. Isn't it?

Mitra That wasn't there last night. It just wasn't there.

Ramesh So you had the feeling that whatever was happening was happening, and whether she got cured or not …

Mitra That was her destiny.

Ramesh That's right. It didn't depend on 'you'. It depended on her destiny.

Mitra It was so freeing.

Ramesh 'It was so freeing.' Yes! What was the freedom from? That freedom was from responsibility, that it was your responsibility to cure her.

Mitra And that can be so heavy.

Ramesh Ohhhh! Heavy!!

Mitra Terrible.

Ramesh So this freedom we're talking about is freedom from responsibility, freedom from guilt, and freedom from pride. But freedom from responsibility does *not mean* freedom from consequences. You understand what I'm saying?

Mitra Yes. But they are not connected, are they?

RAMESH They are not connected. You see there is freedom from responsibility – 'responsibility' refers to the person. Consequences are just *happening, over which you have no control.*

MITRA You said yesterday that events happen and deeds are done.

RAMESH Yes, and therefore I keep repeating that a deed has consequences, but the consequences cannot be predicted. A crime is committed, it is detected, the crime is punished. A crime happens, it is not detected, it is not punished. A crime is not done, and yet the person is punished. So what the consequences will be, no one really knows.

Death – God's will prevails

RAMESH God's will does prevail in *everything*, from the smallest thing to the biggest event. That is my concept. Yesterday, the Australian missionary and his two children were burned to death in a car. Did you read the widow's remarks? They moved me greatly. She said, 'Each human being has a lifespan given by God, no one can change it.' And she said this not when it happened to someone else but when it happened to her own husband and two children. I was astonished at the depth of the understanding from the heart. What she was saying is that the lifespan of each body-mind organism is God given, and no one can change it.

So what I'm saying is God's will prevails in the smallest thing and the biggest event. God's will prevailed when the manifestation happened, and it's God's will when the manifestation will disappear into nothingness again.

KAREN My question is what happens at death. What is death?

RAMESH What happens is that that which existed before the birth continues to exist after the death of a body-mind object. An object is created. An object is destroyed.

KAREN Is there Awareness before birth and after death?

RAMESH That Awareness is the Source. The Source has always been there.

KAREN I think what you are saying is that for you it wouldn't make any difference whether you are alive or dead.

RAMESH Yes. Exactly. No difference at all. Who is alive or dead makes no difference. An object is created and an object will be destroyed. The Source creates an object, and the Source destroys the object. The span of life of an object is determined by the Source.

KAREN This is tricky because for you it doesn't matter.

RAMESH Consciousness is all there is. And there is no 'you' – another – to be that Consciousness. All there is is Consciousness. The real problem is 'who' wants to know? All there is is the Source. So 'who' is this who wants to know anything? If the Source is all there is, 'who' is this who wants to know anything? It is only the ego, and the ego is a fiction, divine hypnosis. The ego is created by the Source through divine hypnosis so that between the egos interhuman relationships should happen and life as we know it, which is described as an illusion, should happen. All there is is the Source. Everything else is an appearance, an illusion. And this 'Karen' that wants to know is part of the illusion.

KAREN The Source has no desire to know ...

RAMESH For something to be known there has to be a subject and an object, and the Source is all there is. So where is the object for the Source, or whatever name you give it, to know?

RAMESH If you like deep sleep, why are you afraid of death? In deep sleep isn't Vimar dead?

VIMAR I have no memory of deep sleep so I can't ...

RAMESH So when you are dead you won't have any memory of being dead!

VIMAR It seems when I look at this fear, when the existence of identity is threatened, it brings tremendous turmoil.

RAMESH Sure! The ego doesn't want to be killed! But I tell you why you are not afraid of deep sleep, because *you think you know* that you are going to wake up. But you don't really know. Deep sleep by itself is enjoyable and is wanted so much because in deep sleep the ego is not there. It is not that the ego enjoys deep sleep. No, the ego does not enjoy deep sleep, because in deep sleep the *ego doesn't exist*. There is peace in deep sleep. There is no ego enjoying any peace in deep sleep. In fact, the peace you have in deep sleep really means the absence of the ego. The ego is absent in deep sleep, so why be afraid of the absence of the ego permanently?

All I'm saying is, there is no need to be afraid of death. Death is like deep sleep and means peace! That's what death really is – it means peace. But the ego doesn't know that, and that is why the ego is afraid. The ego thinks it is enjoying the peace in deep sleep, but the peace in deep sleep exists because there is absence of the ego. And death is simply a longer deep sleep. Oh, yes.

That is why I keep repeating: anything that any sage has said at any time, anything any scripture of any religion has said at any time is a concept. A concept being something some people will accept, some people will not.

RAMESH What you did not understand is that the ego can be annihilated and yet Catherine can live on. Is that what you are saying?

CATHERINE Yes.

RAMESH It was your understanding before coming here that if the ego was annihilated, then Catherine could no longer exist, that this body-mind organism could no longer function. It was your understanding that only when the body-mind died could the ego be annihilated.

CATHERINE Yes. And of course this caused a lot of fear. I believed that one day I had to let go of my ego, and at the same time I would be dead.

RAMESH You must have heard me say several times that after Self-realization happened in the body-mind organism called Ramana Maharshi it continued living for fifty years. And for the body-mind organism to continue living, identification with the name and form had to be there. Therefore, if someone called Ramana Maharshi 'Swami' or 'Bhagavan', he would respond. That he responded to his name being called obviously meant that there had to be identification not only with the body but with the name.

CATHERINE That makes it much simpler, and it's not so frightening any more.

RAMESH What was the fear about?

CATHERINE Of dying.

RAMESH Enlightenment may happen if it is God's will and the destiny of this body-mind organism, but Catherine would still continue to live as this body-mind organism. If somebody would call Catherine by name, Catherine would respond. So Catherine would still have to live her life in society very much alive. That's the understanding now, isn't it?

CATHERINE That's true. And probably with the same guilt feelings as before.

RAMESH That is not so. That's why you've not understood the point properly. If enlightenment happens, Catherine will live her life without the feeling of guilt – which there used to be before, because Catherine thought that she was the doer. So with the understanding that Catherine is not the doer, Catherine lives in this world without the sense of guilt, pride, hate, or envy. For enlightenment to happen, Catherine doesn't have to die.

Births – reincarnation

SCOTT In one aspect you say that there is nothing, it all comes from nothing, it goes back to nothing. And at another point in a book you say something about reincarnation, which I know is conceptual. But I didn't understand why you said this. It was contradictory to me because I know no individual ego or encapsulated ego continues – there is no continuation. It's all back to nothing.

RAMESH Again to use Buddha's words: 'There is no soul.' Therefore there is no soul to go into another [birth].

SCOTT I guess that is why people want to cling to life and want the idea of another life. This way there is some certainty for something uncertain.

RAMESH The intellect likes to think of rebirth because the ego does not want to die. The ego says, 'I know this body is going to die, but I don't want to die.'

SCOTT I appreciate your straightforwardness. It's really nice.

Ramesh My point is, what is rebirth based on? The theory of rebirth is based on the 'doing' by an individual. If the actions of an individual in a particular life are so good, he will have a very good next birth. If you are suffering in this birth that is because in your previous birth you did a lot of bad things. According to the theory of rebirth, the ego does not die, because the ego is the one who is 'doing' things.

Scott That's an illusion.

Ramesh Yes. But only *if* you accept the illusion! The intellects of many people don't accept it. In these cases the intellects are appeased – ah, at least there is some basis for my suffering. There is some basis for a child being born handicapped, for someone being born a millionaire. The intellect says, 'Now I know why there is a millionaire and I'm a pauper.' The intellect accepts it. But my question is this – 'who' enjoys the fruits of the good or bad actions? It's a different ego in a different body.

The future body's personality will be drawn from the totality of the Universal Consciousness which is the collection of all the 'clouds of images' that keep on getting generated. This total collection gets distributed among new bodies as they are being created, with certain given characteristics which will produce precisely those actions which are necessary to the script of the divine playwright. No individual is concerned as an individual with any previous entity.

In regard to 'I' and 'me', there is perhaps a certain misunderstanding. When the 'I' is spoken of as the real thing and the 'me' as an imposter, a wrong impression is likely to be created that each 'me' has a real 'I'. That is not so. There are billions of 'me's but only one 'I' – and even that is a concept! What a joke!!

Working mind and thinking mind

RAMESH Ramana Maharshi said, 'Mind is a collection of thoughts.' He must have been speaking in Tamil. In my case the concepts of a working mind and thinking mind arose, which people have found very useful for understanding. When Ramana Maharshi referred to the mind he was referring to the thinking mind. The thinking mind is a series of personal thoughts and what I call horizontal thinking. Ramana Maharshi said 'collection of thoughts', which is involvement in both cases. Horizontal thinking is involvement.

BRENDAN But Ramesh, Nisargadatta Maharaj said, 'Mind is the content of the Consciousness.'

RAMESH Yes. That is to say Consciousness is the source of the mind. Where does the mind arise? Where does thinking arise? Only if you are conscious.

BRENDAN How can you differentiate between ego and mind?

RAMESH You can't. They are the same. The thinking mind and the ego are the same. They are synonyms ...

SINGH So when you say body-mind organism, you include mind.

RAMESH In the body-mind organism mind can be both working mind and thinking mind. In the ordinary case it is both the working mind and the thinking mind. In the case of a sage it is only the working mind.

SINGH Is the body-mind organism like the programme in a data machine which produces thinking?

RAMESH The thinking happens according to the way that the body-mind organism has been programmed. The thought will arise as God's input into a particular body-mind organism. Why does a thought occur? Because that is supposed to produce an output. So the equation E=MC² was there all the time, but it was only that body-mind organism named Einstein which was programmed to receive the equation, that got that thought.

BRENDAN When you use the term 'body-mind organism', you don't mean mind?

RAMESH The term 'body-mind organism' means body and, in the case of an ordinary person, both the working mind and the thinking mind, but only the working mind in the case of a sage.

RAMESH The wanting to know is the individual sense of doership – 'I' want to know. Therefore Ramana Maharshi repeatedly said, 'If the question arises, do not try to answer the question. Find out who wants to know.' If you really go into 'who wants to know', the 'who' will disappear because there is truly no 'who'.

The arising of the question is not in your control, nor whether you take delivery of that question and get yourself horizontally involved. The arising of the question is a vertical happening. Getting involved in that question is a horizontal involvement. So the horizontal involvement is avoided with this question: 'Who wants to know?'

GAIL So going into who you are, is that a horizontal activity?

RAMESH You see, the asking the question 'Who wants to know?' is the working mind. The arising of the question is vertical, the involvement of the *thinking mind is horizontal*. The working mind is not horizontal. The working mind is in the present moment. So in the present moment the working mind asks the question 'Who wants to know?' and if the thinking mind doesn't come in and try to answer the question, then the 'who' disappears. That is the theory of it.

RAMESH What was the message which you think you got from *I Am That?*

FREDDIE Not to hold on to anything, but I can see that my mind acts like a monkey. It always needs to grasp, and if it lets go it grasps again. It's always busy.

RAMESH But did *I Am That* tell you to quieten the mind? Which as you say is like a monkey. I think what the book told you was that the problem is the monkey mind. It didn't tell you how to quieten it. You've come here five thousand miles, is there something you expect from me?

FREDDIE There are expectations that maybe you will turn my mind off.

RAMESH Press the button on the remote control and the monkey mind just stops. But tell me, Freddie, if I were able to do that, how will Freddie live his life without the mind?

FREDDIE I have the idea that life will become easier.

RAMESH Quite correct. Life will indeed become simpler without the monkey mind. So what you want turned off is not the mind as such but the monkey part of it. For this reason I have a concept which says there are two aspects to the mind. One is the monkey mind – the thinking mind. The mind which asks questions, provides answers, and asks further questions of those answers and goes on and on and on. That is the monkey mind, or what I call the *thinking mind*.

There is another aspect of the mind I call the *working mind*. It is the working mind that is necessary for Freddie to live his life. The working mind is only focused with doing what needs to be done *at the moment in the circumstances*. It is *not concerned*, not even with whether the work that is being done is necessary or not. Nor is it concerned with the consequences. It is only focused on doing the job that is being done, and it is not concerned with 'who' is doing the job.

It is the thinking mind which says, ' "I" am doing this work, and "I" must find out what the consequences are going to be.' So the thinking mind always thinks about the consequences in the future. The working mind is not concerned with the future.

Why is the working mind not concerned with the future? Because the 'one' who is concerned with the consequences of the future is the thinking mind, the ego. In the working mind *there is no individual*, no ego, who does the work. So in the working mind if there is no individual doing the work, then 'who' is to worry about the consequences? In the working mind there is no individual worker – the work is just being done.

The individual 'doer' is the thinking mind wanting to know: after the work is done, what is going to happen to me? The 'me' is the thinking mind, the ego. The ego, according to my concept, is the identification with the name and form as an individual with the sense of doership – whatever happens to this body 'I' am doing it, and 'I' am the one who is going to suffer the consequences.

FREDDIE There is always this longing to make the best decision and to get the best out of it – always, always, always.

RAMESH So it is always the 'me' – the ego, the 'doer' – who says, ' "I" am doing the work.' According to my concept, the only way the thinking mind – the monkey mind, the conceptualizing mind – can be stilled is if there is *total unconditional acceptance* that there is no *individual doer*. Everything just happens. As long as there is an individual doer who thinks 'he' is doing it, then 'he' is bound to think and be concerned about responsibility and consequences. This is the thinking mind. But attention can be given to the work at hand without 'you' feeling 'you' are the doer. That is the working mind.

The real problem is how does Freddie arrive at the *total, unconditional acceptance* that Freddie never is the doer, that the doing is just happening? Through practical and personal experience. All the doing that Freddie thinks is 'his' doing is not because of Freddie but in spite of Freddie! And you know that because Freddie has not been getting what he wanted all the time. So what *happens* is never in Freddie's control, and that you know from practical experience, personal experience. When will Freddie not feel the burden of responsibility and consequences? Only when Freddie is totally convinced that he was not the doer of any action that happened. Freddie is never the doer, and not only Freddie but no one is ever the doer. No human being is a doer.

FREDDIE Who has come to this conclusion?

RAMESH Quite right. The 'one' who has come to this conclusion in the beginning is the *ego*, the 'one' who thought 'he' was the doer. Gradually what will happen is the 'I', the ego, which came to the conclusion that 'he' doesn't exist will then, over a period of time, find more and more from personal experience that 'he' does nothing. Then the ego becomes weaker and weaker, and if it is the will of the Source, the ego collapses.

If the ego collapses, how does this body-mind organism function? The answer is – the body-mind organism will continue to function exactly as it was functioning before. Before it was the Source that was functioning through this body-mind organism, and in the future the Source will continue to function through this body-mind organism. Earlier Freddie thought 'he' was functioning. Now Freddie knows 'he' is not functioning. The functioning itself, as such, will continue in the future exactly as in the past.

FREDDIE There is this belief that I have to take care of myself.

RAMESH That's right. So that which takes care of itself is the working mind. The working mind continues to do what is necessary in the circumstances. Therefore, Freddie still continues as someone accepted by society as responsible for his actions. So what happens? A deed happens, an action happens, and the deed or action is the will of God, or the Source. The will of God in respect of each body-mind object is what I call the destiny of that body-mind object stamped at the moment of conception.

So what is life? According to my concept life is just a multitude of body-mind objects through which the Source is functioning. We can only accept what is happening. We can never know why the Source is doing what it is doing. Why? Because if you want to know why God is doing what he is doing, then what is really happening is the created object wanting to know the will of the creator Subject. How is it possible? So the created object which has been endowed with the dubious gift of the ego – the sense of doership, the thinking mind – can only accept the magnificence of God's creation. The object and the ego cannot even try to understand why God has done what God has done, because the created object can never know the will of the creator Subject.

SHEN Do you say that we should get rid of the thinking mind?

RAMESH No, I don't. This is where the confusion is. 'Who' is to get rid of the thinking mind? The 'one' who is supposed to get rid of the thinking mind is the ego. So if it is the will of God and the destiny of that body-mind organism the thinking mind *will be got rid of*! 'You' cannot get rid of the thinking mind. 'You' are the thinking mind. And the thinking mind goes when and if you are able to analyse your actions and come to the conclusion that 'you' are really not doing anything.

SHEN But sometimes its necessary to see ahead.

RAMESH Yes. You mean you have to plan things. Of course. Suppose the sage has to catch a plane at midnight. He will plan when it is best to leave for the airport, when to have dinner prior to leaving, when to arrange for the car. All this is the planning of the working mind. It's not the thinking mind. But the thinking mind is there in the case of the ordinary person doing the same planning. Where is the difference? The ordinary person says, 'I've done this planning; suppose the taxi has a flat tyre; suppose I'm not able to reach there; suppose the plane doesn't leave; suppose the plane crashes.' All that is the thinking mind, which doesn't happen in the case of a sage. He does what is supposed to be done and knows that whatever happens in the future is not in his control.

SHEN This sounds very reasonable and logical, but it really doesn't come inside.

RAMESH So it goes inside only when you do the *sadhana* or practice of analysing your actions and finding out whether it is 'Shen' who is doing the actions or whether the actions are just *happening*. And if the actions are happening and you come to the conclusion day after day that actions just *happen*, that 'Shen' has not been doing anything, then the question arises – if 'Shen' is not doing anything 'who' is 'Shen'? Who am I? The question arises and the answer arises from the same Source – there is no 'Shen'. The point is that actions are happening through the body-mind organism not according to 'Shen's' will but according to the will of the Source. So Shen merely watches whatever is happening not as 'Shen's' actions.

PREM I don't really have any questions. I have curiosity, I suppose, but no burning questions.

RAMESH Curiosity is the thinking mind. Thinking mind asks a question. Thinking mind provides an answer. Then the thinking mind provides further questions based on the answer, and the thinking mind provides further answers, and then further questions. You see?

❊

RAMESH The sage considers the consequences in making a judgement – *in making a plan!* The flight may be missed regardless of the working mind's planning. The sage is not concerned with the consequences of missing the flight. That is why the Sufi says, 'Trust in God, but tie up your camel!' It is the working mind that ties up the camel and makes sure that the rope is properly tied. After that it is the thinking mind that is concerned with what happens if somebody steals the camel.

Seeking

RAMESH My concept is this. Ever since a baby is born and seeks its mother's breast intuitively, life is nothing but seeking – but there has never been a seeker. What kind of seeking happens depends on the programming, over which you have no control. There are some people who consider themselves seekers of money. Some seek fame. Some seek power. And some seek, among other things, God. This kind of seeking, let's call it spirit--ual seeking, or seeking God, or seeking freedom from the ego – what you call it is immaterial – is happening to these body-mind organisms sitting here because they are programmed for this kind of seeking to happen.

The seeking begins with an individual ego – seeker – seeking enlightenment, or Self-realization, as an object which will give him or her more pleasure than he or she can ever imagine getting from the material world. That is where it starts. The seeking by the ego for enlightenment can end *not* with intellectual understanding but *only* with the *absolute understanding intuited in the heart* that there never was a seeker, a doer – there never was a seeker for any seeking. There is seeking but no individual seeker. There is doing but no individual doer thereof. That is the end of it! And the end of the seeking can be brought about only by that Power which started the seeking.

DINESH Can we interpret 'there never was a seeker' as a deception?

RAMESH Why use the word 'deception'? If you use the word 'deception', then I would say life and living are a deception which is what Ramana Maharshi has put in more respectable words: 'There is no creation. There is no dissolution.'

There never has been a creation, meaning 'the creation' is an illusion. The whole creation is an illusion. That is the final understanding you get to. Until then, life is very real. And if life is real then the human being is very real with responsibilities. But make no mistake, the human being is merely a programmed computer – billions of uniquely programmed computers through which the Source is functioning.

RAMESH Seeking *happens*. 'You' didn't start the seeking. Ramana Maharshi said it this way, 'Your head is already in the tiger's mouth.' You didn't put it there. The seeking has begun because it was God's will, or the will of the Source, that seeking should happen through a body-mind organism. And how that seeking progresses is obviously not in 'your' hands. It's in the hands of the Power that started the seeking. So leave God's business to God.

RAMESH Lord Krishna says: 'Out of thousands there is hardly one who seeks Me, and among those who are seeking, hardly one knows Me in principle.' Now, who decides, Markus, who will do the seeking? In fact, the seeking itself is God's will, God's grace.

You think 'you' are a seeker. Markus thinks 'he' is a seeker seeking God, but the seeking was not Markus's choice. Markus is, you can say, lucky or fortunate that the Source, or God, decided that the seeking would begin in this body-mind organism. So the seeking began not because Markus decided at some point, 'From tomorrow I will seek the truth.' In fact, the seeking has happened *in spite of Markus*. The seeking is really misery, isn't it? By and large?

MARKUS The seeking itself – it is, yes.

RAMESH The seeking itself is misery. Why should Markus choose to be miserable? So what I am saying is the seeking has begun. The seeking begins with a Markus thinking, 'I am seeking God, or enlightenment, or peace,' or whatever you call it. The seeking begins with Markus thinking 'he' is doing the seeking, and the seeking can end only when there is the realization that there never was a seeker. The seeking is God's grace and the realization is God's grace, or the will of the Source.

So the seeking begins with an individual thinking 'he' is the seeker and cannot end until there is the firm realization that there never was a seeker. Truly, there is no Markus other than a name given to a body-mind organism. In other words, the seeking ends only when there is the realization – there never was a thinker, thinking was happening; there never was a doer, doing was happening; there never was an experiencer, experiencing was happening. Thinking, doing, experiencing are all part of the functioning of manifestation which can only happen through a body-mind organism.

Why did the seeking for God happen in this body-mind organism, whereas in some other body-mind organism the seeking is for money? He only seeks money, and he thinks that Markus is crazy looking for something in the air, that Markus would be much happier if he sought money or power or fame. Now, why is seeking money happening through one body-mind organism, and why is seeking God or Truth happening through this body-mind organism called Markus?

MARKUS This is God's will.

RAMESH Exactly. This is what I call God's will or the intention of the Source.

What is enlightenment? Peace of deep sleep

RAMESH So what is the search for? The spiritual search is for that peace which exists in deep sleep and having it even in the waking state. What is the basis of that peace in deep sleep? It is the non-existence of Elaine as the doer. So how can that peace happen in the waking state? Only when Elaine disappears as a doer, as an individual doer who believes, ' "I" am in control of "my" life. "I" do things, everything that happens through this body-mind organism are "my" actions.'

ELAINE In deep sleep there's no personal awareness.

RAMESH The personal awareness is the sense of doership. You see? So the question really is: 'How can Elaine enjoy that peace which exists in deep sleep in the waking state?' And the answer is only when there is the total acceptance that what functions is the body-mind organism, and there is no Elaine doing anything. When this happens the sense of personal doership is annihilated.

When the understanding is that whatever happens through any body-mind organism is merely witnessed as the impersonal functioning of Consciousness, or the impersonal functioning of Totality; then the sense of a personal Elaine is not there, and the same peace exists in the waking state which exists in deep sleep. But this happens only when there is total, unconditional acceptance that there is no individual doer. And the happening of that acceptance is not in your control.

TIM Acceptance has nothing to do with your spiritual insight?

RAMESH 'Whose' spiritual insight? That is the confusion. 'Whose' spiritual insight is the problem.

Subject – pseudo-subject

RAMESH What is seeking? Seeking is 'you' wanting to know God. Whatever you know is an object, and you are the subject. So if you want to know God, what does it mean? You are the subject and God is the object, but what exists is the other way around. God is the Subject and you are the object. So how can an object know the Subject? In trying to know God, what the object has done is usurp the subjectivity of God, and what is worse – this pseudo-subject having usurped the subjectivity of God has turned God into an object that the pseudo-subject wants to know. Therefore, the more the seeker tries to seek God, the more frustrated he becomes.

After the talk there are some *bhajans* being sung, and one of the *bhajans* is by a sage who put it so easily and beautifully. He said, 'I went to know God and returned being God.' In other words, the object tried to know God, but what really happened was the object disappeared into pure Subjectivity. It is the thinking mind that wants to know God, and the thinking mind, the ego, disappears when there is the realization that there has never been a doer, a seeker. Confusion is no more.

The *total, unconditional, final acceptance* happens only when there is no individual acceptor who says, ' "I" accept that "I" am not the doer.' This personal acceptance is not what I'm talking about. The acceptance I'm speaking of is the impersonal acceptance in which there is no individual acceptor, or knower. And if the one who wanted to know God has disappeared, then what has happened? It was destiny and God's will that happened – the one who wanted to know God has become God, because God is all there is – the seeker and the seeking have been wiped out. Con-fusion has been wiped out. There are no more doubts, no more questions.

I repeat: the one observer is, of course, Consciousness – Universal Consciousness – in which has appeared, like a network of waves on the ocean, the totality of the phenomenal manifestation. Universal Consciousness (subjective Noumenon) is, therefore, the only observer (as pure Subjectivity) and everything else in the manifestation is an object. But in life, because of identification with the body, each human being forgets that he is as much of an object as the other objects which he observes. He assumes the subjectivity of the absolute Noumenon and considers himself the observer of the other observed object. By so usurping the subjectivity of the one absolute Subject, the human being commits the original sin and, therefore, comes under bondage. In other words, Universal Consciousness having conditioned itself as the personal or individual Consciousness by identification with a separate entity, considers the person, the limited ego, as the subject observer. As soon as this mistaken identity is realized and the true identity as the one Subject – or witness – is established, the bondage disappears, there is enlightenment. In brief, the 'me' (in opposition to the 'other') disappears, and in its place shines the 'I' as the one formless eternal observer Subject.

Ego is not God – never has been a seeker

MIRABAI And then the ego is God too, right? Is not the ego God as well?

RAMESH The ego *is not* God because the ego does not exist! But if you mean where could the ego have come from except from the Source or God, then yes, God created the ego. God created the ego through what I call divine hypnosis. God creates the ego and God is destroying the ego, not in each case but in some cases where the seeking is happening. That is why I say to the seeker, 'The most important thing that the seeker has to understand is that "he" or "she" has never been a seeker.' So I always say that the seeking begins with a seeker seeking enlightenment as something that will give him or her more happiness than anything in the world has given. That's how it begins.

EDDIE Is it the ego itself that thinks it exists, that thinks it is seeking?

RAMESH Of course! Of course! Therefore the ego says, ' "I" am doing things, "I" am in control of my life.'

PREM You say that in one moment there is the ordinary man and in the next moment there is a realized man?

RAMESH 'He' is *not* a realized man, Prem. Understand that 'he' is *not* a Self-realized man. And this is *most* important to understand. There is realization. This is the confusion.

Why ego asks questions

RAMESH The whole point is that any question is asked by the ego. Why does the ego ask the question? Because the ego wants to achieve enlightenment. Why does the ego ask the question? Because the ego is the seeker. So seeking is happening through a particular ego, and the ego – through whom the seeking is happening – didn't choose to do it. If he knew what misery the seeking is, he would have chosen not to seek. So the seeking is something that is happening, and you have not chosen to seek. That is the basis of what I am saying.

The 'one in a thousand' that Lord Krishna is speaking of, that 'one' didn't choose to be the seeker – the seeking *happened*. But instead of letting it happen, letting that Power which started the seeking carry on the seeking, the ego who thinks he or she is the seeker wants to know the best way to *achieve* enlightenment. Why do you want enlightenment? Because you are expecting it to give you the greatest pleasure this world has given you. So I always say that the seeking begins with an illusory seeker seeking enlightenment as an object which would give him great pleasure. The seeking ends only with the total realization – unquestioned, unconditional realization – that there never was a seeker. That's when it ends.

So when does it really end? It ends with the realization – what am 'I' doing? What am 'I' seeking? 'I' didn't choose to do any seeking. Will the seeking end in this body-mind organism? Who cares? So when the 'Who cares?' arises *from the depths of your being* – I don't really care a damn whether enlightenment happens or not; it's not my business; I'm not the seeker – then enlightenment is very, very close indeed.

Seeking is a process

RAMESH The Source started the seeking and in doing that has started the process of the ego being destroyed – which is what Ramana Maharshi said, 'Your head is already in the tiger's mouth. There is no escape.' Meaning, the Source has started the process of destroying the ego, and it's only the Source that can do it.

The main point to understand is that the ego will not destroy itself. *The ego is being destroyed.* And remember Ramana Maharshi's words, 'There is no escape.' The seeking was started by the Source, and the seeking will proceed at its own pace according to the will of the Source. So the only thing to understand is that nothing happens unless it is God's will, the will of the Source.

❋

RAMESH What is the seeking about? The seeking is *not seeking the Source*, but the seeking is the removal of that which hides the Source – the sense of personal doership, the ego. You are told that 'you' are to remove the ego. I ask 'who' is to remove 'whose' ego? Therefore I come to the conclusion that the ego which hides the Source – only that Power, or Source, which created the ego can remove it. Who created the ego? Where did the ego come from? The ego can only have come from the one Source, and the Source is in the process of destroying the ego – one in thousands. And that is the process which is happening.

GERRY So it is a process?

RAMESH Oh, indeed it is a process! There is a process. Certainly! In other words, enlightenment is a process. The usual concept I give is this, and whenever anybody uses a concept he has to use objects. What is a seeker doing? According to my concept a seeker is climbing a staircase. He doesn't know if there are thirty steps or three hundred thousand steps. All he knows is he cannot stop climbing! He didn't start the climbing. The climbing is *happening* and he keeps on climbing.

So in one particular case the final step may be the thirtieth step. The step from the twenty-ninth to the thirtieth is always sudden. But there is a process and all I'm saying is, 'You didn't start that process.' Therefore there is no 'you' to reach the thirtieth step. Twenty-ninth to thirtieth is sudden. That is why they say the awakening is always sudden.

The only way to deal with the ego is to understand what the ego is and how it has arisen: all there is is Consciousness, and it is the Consciousness which has *deliberately* identified itself with each individual body-mind mechanism in order to perceive the manifestation in the duality of observer/observed. So, the entire functioning of the totality of manifestation, the *lila*, is an impersonal affair of evolution concerning the process of initial identification; the identified existence covering a certain period; the mind turning inward; the beginning of the process of dis-identification; and the final understanding of this very impersonal process, or enlightenment, in which Consciousness has regained its original 'purity'.

Your statement that 'this belief that I was dependent on the Unknown for this boon (being in the I AM) occasionally engendered in me the egoic fear that this bounty might be withdrawn and I would be lost'. This is the core of the matter. This fear will disappear when you remember – or bring your attention to the fact – that a 'you' or a 'me' cannot have the bounty, that all there is is Consciousness which itself initiated the process of identification as a separate entity. The process of identification has continued for a while, and then the mind turned inwards and the process of disidentification has started and gone a long way forward. All that now remains is to witness the 'progress' of this process. Who witnesses this progress? Consciousness, of course.

Effort and self-improvement

This question of individual volition and personal effort is extremely subtle and difficult to understand. And yet it is absolutely necessary not only to understand it intellectually but to absorb it in our very being. Confusion arises because most masters seem to have taught predestination in theory but free will in practice! Jesus Christ affirmed that without the will of God not even a sparrow can fall, and that the very hairs on one's head are numbered. And the Koran very definitely affirms that all knowledge and power are with God and that He leads aright whom He will and leads astray whom He will. And yet both Christ and the Koran exhort men to right effort and both condemn sin. The *apparent* contradiction would easily be solved if one kept in mind the concept of spiritual evolution mentioned above. The absolute illusoriness of the individual human being – and his so-called effort – will be quickly understood by the one who is on the very brim of enlightenment, whereas someone who is much lower on the scale will more easily accept the concept of effort, determin-ation and concentration ... The type of human being who relies on his personal effort at one stage may, at a later stage, come to realize that such effort as is made is truly the effort of the Totality of functioning and not that of any illusory individual doer.

So long as a person considers effort as his personal effort, with the purpose of achieving something, he is rejecting the all-mightiness of the Almighty. So long as a person wants something from the Almighty, he is rejecting the fact of 'Thy will be done'. *True love of God means surrender to Him, wanting nothing, not even salvation.*

RAMESH So long as there is an 'Allan' wanting to be at one with God, being God cannot happen. Therefore, being God can happen only when there is no Allan wanting to be one with God. And that can only happen if it is God's will. That's it. That's the last word, Allan.

ALLAN That's the last word. Thank you, because when you look at me ...

RAMESH When I look at you, Allan, do you know what I feel? Deep compassion. That is what I feel. I feel deep compassion because Allan keeps on trying *to do*, which is impossible. That is why I keep on telling Allan, 'So long as there is an Allan wanting to be one with God, being God cannot happen.' It can only happen if it is God's will. Therefore, is there something that Allan can do? Yes! *Leave it to God.* That is the only thing you can do – leave it to God. In the meantime let life happen through this body-mind organism and merely witness what is happening.

ALLAN That is why I think I enjoy life more and more.

RAMESH Good, good.

It is not often realized that there cannot be the slightest trace of intention or planning in an action that is spontaneous and natural. What is more, spontaneity and naturalness cannot be 'achieved' either by trying or trying not to try! ... This may again seem to be an impossible impasse, but it is really not so. Effort (or an effort not to make an effort) is based on desire or volition, which itself is an aspect of the 'me-concept' or the ego. It is the split mind which sees the apparent impasse as such, while spontaneity is synonymous with the absence of the split mind.

All dualism is illusion, all action is spontaneous and all volition is an illusion. Once this is realized one ceases to try to be spontaneous. *Seeing the illusoriness of volition makes all action automatically spontaneous.* By the same token it must also be clear that it needs no effort as such through any disciplines or practices or devices, such as any repeated affirmations of any formulas or thoughts or words, in order to see something which is already there. The Chinese philosophy calls all effort to realize the Tao as 'putting legs on a snake' because 'everything is Tao'. It is interesting to note that Nisargadatta Maharaj referred to such efforts in similar terms.

It is extremely difficult for any ordinary man to grasp the fact that nothing more than a deep understanding, an unshakable conviction, of one's true nature is all that is necessary for the transformation to take place. It has been man's conditioning from the earliest day of his life that it is only personal effort that can bring him anything in life: even as a baby he had to cry before his hunger was satisfied. And now he is told that understanding is all that is necessary and, what is more, that any effort by a 'me' could well be counterproductive. This seems incredible, quite unacceptable …

The wise man is convinced, beyond a shadow of a doubt, that he cannot control the results or consequences of his actions, because they form part of the total actions taking place in Totality. All that he can do is to concentrate his attention – his working mind – on the work at hand. The result is that such work – done to the best of his ability, without being hampered by the thinking, conceptualizing, worrying mind – will naturally be at its best, performed with much less physical effort, and almost no nervous strain.

RAMESH If a person wants to improve himself, my answer to that is do whatever you want to do. What more freedom do you want?

PRATIMA But you know that it's not really the freedom of your own will, you know it's God's will.

RAMESH So that's why I tell him, do whatever you like. But I also tell him – having told him to do whatever he likes – what you think you like in the precise moment in the given circumstances is exactly what you are supposed to like according to God's will. But this does not prevent you from trying to do whatever you want to improve yourself. Which is what the person wants.

So I don't tell him all this is illusion, all this is maya. If you want to improve yourself, improve yourself. Fine. That's good.

PRATIMA But you do say that it's maya, this idea of personal will, that you can do what you want but know that it is God's will that is occurring.

RAMESH So my basis of this is 'Thy will be done'. He says, 'Does it mean that I have no free will?' So I say, 'Has your free will prevailed every time? Have you got what you wanted every time? No. Has anything that you didn't want, not happen? Yes, it has. What is your experience?' The experience is that you know what you want doesn't always happen. Therefore I say, 'What you want sometimes happens, sometimes doesn't happen, and whether it happens or not depends on God's will.'

NORMAN A major movement today in the world is what is called the 'New Age movement', and one of its philosophies is to improve yourself. So I deal with my anger or whatever I had with my parents which makes my life not so happy, then I do something which changes that behavior. So how does that relate …?

RAMESH Wait a minute. All you have told me so far is that you do something that you think you should do. You think you should improve yourself? Then do something to improve yourself. Fine! It fits in totally with what I have said. All I'm saying is do whatever you think you should do. That is one of my basic concepts.

NORMAN So it's unimportant whether you try to improve yourself as an individual or not.

RAMESH 'Unimportant' for 'whom', Norman? It is important for Norman to improve himself, so Norman improves himself. Where is the question of its being unimportant for whom?

Norman tries to improve himself because it is important to improve himself, and he tries it. My only point is, Norman, having tried to improve yourself, whether the improvement happens or not is not in your control. But it *does not prevent you from trying to do whatever you want to do* to improve yourself.

NORMAN My own experience over time is that self-improvement does not have an end in itself.

RAMESH It never ends, does it?

NORMAN No, and it doesn't bring about peace of mind.

RAMESH That's the point, it doesn't bring about peace of mind. You are in competition with yourself. Isn't that what it is? The fact that you want to improve yourself means you're not happy with What-is at that moment, and that keeps going on all the time. On the other hand, I'm not saying that this prevents you. Everything has a sense of reason in life.

MARTIN Can this divine hypnosis be removed?

RAMESH Sure. Certainly. How? Only that Power that created the hypnosis can remove the hypnosis. The hypnotized being cannot get rid of the hypnosis. And that is what the seeking is all about. The seeking is the hypnotized being wanting to remove the hypnosis and wanting to know how he or she can do it.

MARTIN And it's pointless trying?

RAMESH That is correct. That is precisely what I am saying. And yet the trying is happening, is it not, Martin?

MARTIN Yes.

RAMESH So why is the trying happening?

MARTIN Because divine hypnosis is also creating the trying.

RAMESH That is correct. That is precisely correct. That Power which has created the hypnosis is creating this effort to get rid of the hypnosis. That is why I keep saying that there is *no individual seeker seeking enlightenment*.

MARTIN Still it feels so much as if I was real. I continue getting involved with all this and ...

RAMESH That is itself the hypnosis. 'I' am Martin; 'I' am a separate being; 'I' am in control of my life; 'I' want to achieve enlightenment – that is the hypnosis. That is the confusion.

Analysis of actions – the only sadhana

RAMESH So how can identification with a name and form, which is harmless, be such a tremendous obstruction to your *being* God? The ego, as I use the concept, is not mere identification with a name and form, but identification with a name and form as a separate entity, as a *separate* doer of his or her actions. That is the real obstruction, not mere identification with a name and form – but identification with a name and form as a *separate individual doer* or as an individual doer *separate* from another *individual doer*. You see? That *separateness as a doer* is the real problem.

So how can you get rid of the idea that you are the doer of the actions which happen through this body-mind organism? My answer, my concept, is that you have to first understand intellectually, and then by personal experience come to the inevitable, unconditional acceptance that you are not an individual separate from others doing separate actions.

First comes the intellectual understanding that you are not a separate doer. Then from personal experience this concept becomes so deeply ingrained that it becomes an unconditional, totally acceptable understanding. Now how can that be?

TIM You said one could do the practice of analysing actions. You said that by doing this the ego could be weakened.

RAMESH The ego starts doing it, and in the process the ego gets weaker.

TIM Then you said that at some point the question is asked from the Source directly …

RAMESH The question *arises*! That means the ego is so weak that the ego cannot even ask that question. It could be that in certain practices the ego gets stronger and stronger. In this process which I suggest, the ego, according to my concept, will get weaker and weaker as there is greater and greater realization from personal experience that the ego is not doing anything – that the *ego cannot do* anything – the *doing happens*. Then the ego gets weaker and weaker and ultimately dies.

GARY I have a problem when you ask us to analyse these actions. The problem is that I no longer trust my sense of either intellect or feeling to be able to determine this. I watch my mind or my feelings and at one moment I seem to feel very strongly this way, and then I discover that no, actually my feeling was very different. Everything seems so confused and muddled inside of me. I don't think it's possible to determine whether you are the doer or not the doer.

RAMESH Gary, I'm not saying to watch your feelings. I'm not saying watch your thoughts. All I'm saying is some action happens during the day, does it not?

GARY But how can I determine …

RAMESH Easy! Take a simple action. You leave here and end up going to an unknown restaurant. At the end of the day, if you analyse this entire action as it happened, you will find that several thoughts came over which you had no control. What were they? 'I'm hungry. I want to eat something. I don't have much money with me so I want to find a clean restaurant where I will get reasonably good food at reasonable prices.' So you ask someone, 'Is there a place …' 'Sure, just around the corner.'

So what happened? There was a series of thoughts. The brain responded to those thoughts according to circumstances over which you had no control – hunger arose; you like good and clean food, due to your conditioning; you discovered you had left most of your money in your room. So the brain reacted to the existing situation and asked directions of someone, 'Is there a place here where I can go?' So how much was it 'your' action and how much was it a chain of circumstances and conditioning that lead you to go to that restaurant? And you come to the conclusion, 'It was not "my" action. "I" was suddenly hungry, and "I" was led to a restaurant by a set of circumstances over which "I" had no control.'

GARY My perception is that this changes in time. That's why I say that I don't trust my senses. When something is occurring or about to occur, it appears to me that I have control. When something has already occurred, it appears to me that I had no control. It doesn't matter what the thing is. So it's a question of time – how I see it through time.

RAMESH That's why I say, 'At the end of the day …'

GARY Then it will always appear that I had no control.

RAMESH That is exactly my point.

GARY But if I'm looking forward it always appears that I have control.

RAMESH Yes, 'it always appears'. You are one hundred per cent correct. 'It always *appears*' that 'you' have control.

GARY In both cases 'it appears'.

RAMESH No. At the end of the day when you analyse it, you come to the conclusion you had *no control*. A thought occurred, or you heard something, a suggestion, or you saw something. The brain reacted to what was seen or heard or thought. You can use this analysis for *any* action, and at the end of the day you'll find from personal experience that it was not 'your' action.

This analysing the action, any action, for me is the only *sadhana* or practice you need to do. That is my concept. Do this *sadhana* to the extent that is possible for you to do it – and this depends upon God's will and the destiny of the body-mind organism. So to the extent that it is possible for you to do this *sadhana*, you come to the conclusion that no action is really 'your' action. And if this happens day after day after day, then at some point – again, if it is the will of God and the destiny of the body-mind organism – the question will arise from the very depths of your being, 'If Gary doesn't do anything, who is Gary?' As Lord Buddha said, 'There is no doer thereof.' That is the conclusion that you come to from *personal* experience – if Gary doesn't do anything, who is Gary? Who am I?

This is Ramana Maharshi's question, 'Who am I?' It is most important to understand that it is not the intellect which asks. If the intellect asks, then the intellect provides the answer. And the answer the intellect provides, the intellect again questions. You keep on going in circles.

But when the question *arises* from the Source, if this is the will of the Source and the destiny of the body-mind organism, then the answer comes not from the intellect – the answer comes from the Source. There never has been a Gary other than a name given to a body-mind organism. So there never has been any doer. Gary, the ego, doesn't exist. If Gary doesn't exist then what exists? *Only the Source.* Source is all there is.

Gary, my basic concept is that every human being is a pro-grammed instrument or computer which the Source uses, and each human computer is unique. No two are alike because of the DNA and the conditioning each receives and over which there is no control. Together the DNA and the conditioning are what I call the programming. And what does the Source do in order to bring about an action that the Source wants? It puts in an input. What is an input? The Source sends you a thought, the brain reacts to that thought and brings out an output according to the programming. Gary says this output is 'his' action. But when you analyse each action you come to the conclusion that no action is 'your' action.

GARY But I don't know if it's impossible for somebody to gain more control over themselves.

RAMESH For 'whom'?

GARY I don't know.

RAMESH For whom? That is the whole point, Gary. The question – who is Gary? The answer – there is no Gary!

GARY You say the ego doesn't exist.

RAMESH Yes.

GARY The ego affects the body, the body exists from a certain point of view. If the ego is worrying and upset over what it's going to do, the body may become sick. So if that which exists is affected by that which does not exist, it's illogical.

RAMESH And that is why so long as the ego is there, it can affect the body and worry about the body being sick.

GARY So then the ego does exist.

RAMESH The ego exists. Now, you go out into the sun, Gary. There is a shadow. Is there a shadow or is there no shadow?

GARY Both. Yes and no.

RAMESH That's it! So does the ego exist? Yes and no. That is what you find out. If the ego doesn't *do* anything, the ego doesn't exist. 'Gary' *exists* because the ego exists. If 'Gary' doesn't *do* anything,

Gary doesn't exist. So the annihilation of the ego means there is no 'Gary' to say, 'I am now happy. I am now unhappy.'

Happiness and unhappiness exist because of the ego. So the final, total, intuited understanding and acceptance in the heart is that *there is no ego* – there never has been an ego. Happiness and unhappiness are merely something created by the ego. The ego never really exists just as a shadow never really exists – when you come into the house where is the shadow? So with this understanding that 'Gary' never *does* anything, you come into the house!

GARY I feel this ego, this sense of 'me' – almost like a physical thing.

RAMESH It is. Therefore the ego does considerable harm. Why is Gary unhappy? Because Gary thinks 'Gary' exists. Why does Gary think 'Gary' exists? Because he thinks 'he' *does* actions. If 'Gary' doesn't *do* anything – who is Gary?

GARY Even if I can't do anything, it seems to me that I exist.

RAMESH Ah, yes. But what is *That* which exists without doing anything? The Source, I AM, I Am That I Am. *That* is what exists when Gary is not the doer. And when you are in the I AM there is no happiness or unhappiness – which is peace.

JANINE It's more difficult to analyse the action as it's happening because you have to use your working mind, and the thinking mind is there. You have to make decisions. You have to do things. It's more obvious that you are not the doer when you look at the past.

RAMESH No, no. You misunderstand! I'm not saying you analyse your action when you're doing it. You can't. When you do something you should do it *as if* you have free will. You just do. If you

167

have to make a decision, you make a decision *as if* you have free will. That is the whole point. Later in the day, at the end of the day, you sit back and analyse some of your actions. *Make no mistake, it is still the ego which analyses them.* Let the ego analyse the actions at the end of the day, and find out 'whose' actions. Were they 'your' actions or did they originate with something over which 'you' had no control, and then the brain reacted to that over which you had no control, and an event happened – which you call 'your' action.

This misunderstanding, I'm glad it came up. I'm not suggesting that when an action is happening you find out whether it is your action or not. You can't do it.

JANINE It's impossible.

RAMESH At that moment you make a decision *as if* you had free will, *as if* it is your decision, based on facts and possible consequences. Later in the evening you analyse the action and how it happened.

That there is no doer is a concept, a theory. It can become truth for you *only from practical experience.* This is why you must try and analyse from your own personal experience whether it was 'your' action or if it *just happened.* Otherwise, it only remains theory.

So for the theory to become actual experience, you have to find out for yourself. And gradually what will happen is, as you analyse your actions at the end of each day, you will find that as the actions are happening there will be a *witnessing* of how they are *just happening.*

Over a course of time it will *so happen that,* while doing something, you will be aware that you are not doing whatever because such and such a thing *just happens.* This won't occur in the beginning. But when this does begin to happen, it will be at a stage when the ego is very, very weak.

But forget about it. This too can only happen. If you keep it in mind you'll be expecting it, and that will be an obstruction. In every effort to remember, the ego is present. The ego is absent only when the *understanding* brings about the *remembering*.

This is why Ramana Maharshi says Self-realization is the easiest thing. Then he says you must practise a lot. Practise what? Asking yourself, 'Who am I?' My point is that the question 'Who am I?' *arises* from this *sadhana* of analysis. When you come repeatedly to the point that nothing is 'my' action, day after day, then the question *just arises*. 'You', the ego, don't ask the question. The question comes from the depths of your being – if there is no action that 'I' do, who is this 'me'? So Ramana Maharshi's question *arises* only when the theory becomes practice, and you know that actions are not 'your' actions.

MARK From what you said about *sadhana*, the only *sadhana* that you recommend is the analysis of doership, and I would connect that with a way of lessening the grip of the ego.

RAMESH That's right – for the ego to get weaker. My only point about most *sadhana* is that there is an ego aware, all the time – 'I' am doing this *sadhana*; 'I' am making this effort; 'I' must get a reward. So at the end of twenty years the honest seeker says, 'I have meditated for twenty years and I have got nothing. This *sadhana* is useless. I must seek another *sadhana*. I must go to another ashram. I must go to another guru.'

My point is that most *sadhana* are based on the individual doer, the seeker, the ego doing something with the expectation of getting something. Therefore you are asked to meditate. Certainly. But so long as there is a meditator expecting to get something out of the meditation, then that meditation, according to my concept, is useless. True meditation is when, by the grace of God and the destiny of the individual, gradually the 'meditator' disappears into meditation so that at the end of the meditation there is no remnant of any ego doing meditation with expectation. Then meditation happens totally differently. According to my concept, only that is *true meditation* in which there is no individual meditator expecting to get anything out of it.

The whole purpose of this *sadhana* that I recommend is to get rid of the ego. Unfortunately, in most cases of *sadhana* meditation, the meditator is convinced into thinking that 'he' will get something. The ego is made to expect something. That is the unfortunate part, the cause of the confusion.

MARK I'm just wondering. If someone practises something with the notion that 'he' is doing and that 'he' will get something as a result of the practice, then isn't it also possible that the practice will subvert the expectation?

RAMESH Certainly! That's what I'm saying. In some cases, if it is the will of God, or the Source, then gradually the meditator may become merged in the meditation – or the ego could get stronger and stronger as the expectations get stronger and there is frustration after twenty and thirty years.

MARK I think the question in the back of my mind about all of this is the notion of judgement about other *sadhana*. If one or another *sadhana* is practised which ultimately leads to the enquiry 'Who am I?' and the understanding is deepening from this questioning, then whatever *sadhana* was practised was the right thing for that body-mind organism to go through.

RAMESH I wouldn't use the word 'right' or 'wrong', Mark. That was the destiny of that body-mind organism to go through whatever process. 'Right' or 'wrong' I wouldn't say.

Pleasure arising from successful analysis

RAMESH Having succeeded in the analysis, what is the input? The input is success in analysis. What has happened? Analysis has succeeded. The brain reacts to that event and brings about a sense of pleasure. Why not? Enjoy that pleasure.

The sense of pleasure is different from a sense of pride: 'I' have done it, not many are able to do it – that is pride. But you cannot prevent the brain reacting to the successful analysis and bringing about a sense of pleasure. Let the sense of pleasure arise. And on the contrary, if your analysis had not been so successful, then a sense of failure may have arisen. That is also merely a mechanical reaction of the brain. The answer is, I'll try again next time.

So the reaction of the brain to an event, a thought, or something seen or heard is a natural reaction. The personal reaction to the natural reaction is the ego. The natural reaction of the brain is not in your control.

TIM In a way I was thinking that if you get the message from the analysis, you hang up the phone.

RAMESH That is exactly it! I think that is a very good metaphor. 'I get the message.' What's the message? Nothing happens unless it is God's will. Put the phone down! You see? What's the message? Nothing happens unless it is God's will. Put the phone down.

JOHN We're all walking around with phones in our hands.

RAMESH That's the trouble – mobiles and all kinds of ...

Self-enquiry – Who am I?

RAMESH Does Ramana Maharshi have a basic? Yes indeed – the question, 'Who am I?' And when he says this, the 'I' is in the Tamil

171

language. What he means in English is not 'Who am I?' but 'Who is this me?' In other words, is there a 'me' at all? This is my interpretation. Who is this 'me'? Is there a 'me' at all?

If and when you come to the conclusion that no action is 'your' action, then the intellect doesn't ask the question – the question arises from the very depths of your being. If 'you' have not been doing anything, if no action is 'your' action, who is this 'me'? Does the 'me' exist? Who is this 'me' about whom I've been so concerned all this life? That is Ramana Maharshi's question.

If the intellect asks the question 'Who am I?' the intellect will provide an answer. Having provided the answer, the intellect will produce doubts. Having produced the doubts, the intellect will produce further answers that will raise further questions and doubts. And these answers and doubts will be like a dog chasing its tail.

When you come to this conclusion from personal experience – that no action is 'your' action – the intellect doesn't ask the question, the question *arises* from the very depths of your being – which is the Source, or God. It was God's will that the question arose. It was God's will that you are here listening to these concepts. It was God's will that you tried this concept of analysing actions from personal experience. So we can hope that it will also be God's will that the answer will arise – *there never has been a 'me' as the doer of any actions*. So if 'you' have never been the doer of any actions, then no one else has ever been the doer of any actions either.

If doubts arise, go back to the basic – nothing happens unless it is God's will – and the doubts will collapse.

Flip-flop and involvement

MITRA We talked yesterday about flip-flop, that there were moments of calm, and there were moments when I was watching my own attachment to the involvement. Even that, it's like what can 'I' do? And there was a sense of freedom with that too. It's like 'I' can't do anything, so if I'm getting attached, I'm getting attached.

RAMESH Involvement happens – knowing that you could have done nothing about the *happening* of the involvement. Even the *happening* of the involvement was a *happening* over which you have no control. With that understanding, the involvement is accepted.

MITRA It's just watched.

RAMESH The involvement in the involvement takes place when you wish that the involvement had not happened and hope the involvement will not happen in the future. That is the involvement in the involvement. But what the understanding produces is that you have no control over the involvement, which means all right there was involvement; there is involvement, but I could not have avoided it. That is what the understanding produces. So what the understanding leads to is that the involvement is merely *witnessed* as something which is happening without the wish that it had not happened – without the hope that it will not happen again.

MITRA That means you just stop projecting anything into the future.

RAMESH That is it! So you don't get involved in the involvement. 'Who' doesn't get involved in the involvement? It is the ego, the sense of personal doership which is involved – 'I' could have avoided the involvement; if 'I' had not done this 'I' wouldn't have been involved; so therefore, in order not to be involved in the future 'I' must take care not to do this or that.

When you've accepted the involvement, what have you really done? Accepting the involvement means, in effect, accepting the ego. Not accepting the ego means strengthening the ego.

MITRA The more you fight against it the more power you give it.

RAMESH That's *exactly* the point! The ego gets its nourishment from your opposition to it. It gets its nourishment from your fighting it. But if the ego keeps on getting no nourishment, the ego gets weaker and the understanding goes deeper. That is why I say, 'Don't fight the ego – accept the ego.'

Many people find this difficult to accept. Most of the books, most of the masters tell you the ego is the problem, that you must kill the ego. And that is the question.

MITRA And so you struggle.

RAMESH You struggle and say, 'I did this thing wrong. I really shouldn't have done it.' So don't fight the ego, accept the ego. Why? Because you didn't create the ego. The Source has created the ego, and the Source is in the process of destroying the ego. That's why your head is in the tiger's mouth. There's no escape. There is no escape if you fight the ego. That's my point. If you keep on fighting the ego, the tiger will have its mouth open for ages and ages. You accept the ego, and the tiger will snap its jaws quickly!

The point, of course, is that the individual is an illusion, deliverance and bondage are illusions, and the tiger's mouth is also an illusion.

CHRISTIAN The freedom which arises in the absence of personal doership, is this …?

RAMESH But that is what you have to remember …

CHRISTIAN No but, the first moment the absence is there, the freedom arises …

RAMESH No, no! Wait a minute. *That* is what you have to remember, what you have just said intuitively, 'The freedom that *arises*,' not freedom which 'I' am supposed to achieve. That is the whole point. The freedom can only arise. It is not something Christian can achieve.

CHRISTIAN Does it have a momentary existence? Does it fade again?

RAMESH Until the understanding is total, certainly there is a flip-flop – 'I think I've got it; I've lost it.'

CHRISTIAN But the bliss experience, the bliss experience which accompanies the sense of freedom. There is a sense of freedom from personal doership. Before there was bondage, then suddenly there is the realization there is no personal doership, and then a sense of freedom arises which is accompanied by bliss.

RAMESH You see, 'bliss' is the word. Is a sense of freedom a sense of bliss or peace? I prefer the word 'peace'. And if I use the word 'peace' I'll send a lot of seekers away – 'If all I'm going to get is peace, I'm not concerned. I want bliss.'

So the word 'peace' will send a lot of seekers away. That's why elsewhere the word 'peace' is not used very often. 'Bliss' is the word! 'Come to my ashram and I'll give you bliss.' One thousand, two thousand, ten thousand, five hundred million dollars, so that ashram is worth five hundred million dollars, another is worth three hundred million.

It so happened a millionaire having spent most of his life seeking money turned his attention to spiritual seeking. When his friends found this out, they immediately told him, 'Your attachment to money is the problem. It's your greatest obstacle.' One of them provided him with the number of a swami who might be able to help him. So the millionaire called the swami and asked, 'What am I to do? My friends have warned me that the greatest barrier to the success of my spiritual search is my attachment to money.' The swami immediately replied, 'Don't do anything until I get there. I'm leaving right away!'

Temporarily no ego, no doer

ROBERT At some point while you were talking I felt my heart opening, and I started to weep. And then this little voice inside of me which I know very well started questioning, doubting, and criticizing, and then an understanding came that even that is an expression of Consciousness. When that came I just melted away and there was this sense that everything is just happening: everything including my struggle with myself, including my doubt of myself, and my criticizing of myself. It's just happening. And something just dropped away.

RAMESH What dropped away do you think, Robert? 'Everything is just happening' and the total acceptance of that made what drop away, do you think?

ROBERT The doubting self, the me, the part of the me ...

RAMESH That's right, the sense of doership.

ROBERT That's what puts me down – 'You're wrong. You're going to fail.' That part just went.

RAMESH In fact what dropped off was 'Yes, but!' That dropped off and only the 'Yes' remained. So now what happens, Robert? Everything happens as used to happen before.

ROBERT It doesn't matter. That felt like such a burden was taken away. It doesn't matter what happens.

RAMESH You'd be astonished, Robert, how many have said those actual words – 'It doesn't matter.' You'd be amazed. At a certain point those are the words that come – 'It doesn't matter.' What does it mean? What do you think, as a psychologist, is the significance of, 'It doesn't matter'?

ROBERT There's no egoic involvement.

RAMESH I would say there is no one to 'whom' it can matter. What does, 'It does not matter' mean? It means there is no one to 'whom' it can matter – 'it' being whatever 'it' is. So your coming back again and again to all these things means the weakening of what is generally known as the ego which, according to my interpretation, is the sense of personal doership – the 'me'. So, 'It does not matter' means there is no longer any 'me', at least temporarily, to 'whom' whatever doesn't matter.

Witnessing and observing

RAMESH The opposite of witnessing is observing. In the observing there is an individual observer which is the ego, the 'me'. When there is an 'individual' observing something it is the nature of the programming of the body-mind organism, which the individual thinks he is, to judge it. So the observing by an observer is almost always accompanied by judgement. And the judgement means happiness or unhappiness. In witnessing there is no individual witnesser, therefore there is no judging.

A perfect example of witnessing is a baby, a baby who has just awakened. The baby witnesses everything and is interested. The stare of the baby is not blank, rather there is no judging. Witnessing is impersonal because there is no individual witnesser. Observing is personal and therefore there is judgement.

SALOME The word 'involvement', is there involvement in witnessing as there is in observing?

RAMESH Involvement is that of the observer – by judging. Witnessing is impersonal in which there is no individual witnesser, and, therefore, there is no involvement. The involvement is of the individual, the ego, the 'me', the thinking mind. In witnessing there is no individual.

So what is happening here and now? You think 'you' are talking and 'I' am listening, or 'I' am talking and 'you' are listening. But what is *happening* is the talking and listening are *just happening* between two body-mind organisms according to the will of God, and this is being witnessed.

WILLIAM You are speaking now and witnessing at the same time?

RAMESH That is correct.

WILLIAM So witnessing itself is not part of relative reality. It's an absolute thing because there is no 'one' who witnesses.

RAMESH That is exactly the point. The happening is impersonal, the talking and listening are impersonal, and the witnessing is also impersonal.

WILLIAM So Ramesh as the witnesser …

RAMESH Ramesh is *not* the witnesser. That is the whole point.

WILLIAM No, that's right, but it's difficult to phrase the question. Is there awareness of witnessing?

RAMESH There is impersonal awareness in witnessing. There is no 'someone' witnessing. In observing there is an observer. In other words, there is a 'someone' with personal awareness believing that 'he' or 'she' is doing the observing – and judging!

WILLIAM Okay. Witnessing just happens.

RAMESH Witnessing is Understanding-in-action.

Witnessing, non-witnessing samadhi

What witnessing does is to be disassociated from the ego while recognizing its validity as the operational element in the body-mind mechanism which must persist as a part of the psychic construct of the psychosomatic mechanism. Such an *operational element* must obviously continue to exist so long as the body continues to exist, but it is no longer confused with the *functional essence* in the body which is common to all sentient beings – the impersonal Consciousness.

VALERIA Does thinking in terms of images stop entirely during the witnessing state?

RAMESH In the witnessing state there is something to witness, and what is witnessed? The images.

VALERIA The image produces a reaction in the brain? That too?

RAMESH Then that reaction of the brain is also witnessed.

VALERIA So it's not like the brain goes totally blank.

RAMESH Let me give you an example. You sit in the reception lounge at the Taj. You are sitting there comfortably waiting for someone. What do you see? People coming in, registering. People coming down with their luggage. People talking. Now, all that is witnessed. There is no judgement. All that is just witnessed as a picture which is really a collection of images. When does the witnessing get interrupted?

VALERIA When you say that you like and don't like.

RAMESH That is one thing. It gets interrupted when suddenly you see someone coming and you say, 'I think I know him.' The impersonal witnessing gets obstructed by the personal recognition of someone. In the sage the witnessing being interrupted by the working mind does not lead to the involvement of the thinking mind. In the ordinary person the thinking mind may become involved, if not, then the moment you realize that it was not the person you thought it was, the personal observing may stop and the witnessing continue to happen. So sometimes witnessing happens, sometimes observing happens. Observing happens when there is judging. Let the judging happen.

VALERIA When a judgement happens, and it is the possibility to say a judgement has happened – you witness that too.

RAMESH That is correct. A judgement has happened because it was supposed to happen. So then that judgement gets cut off. But if you say, 'I should not have judged that. I am not supposed to judge.' Then it is more involvement. So if the involvement happens, then accept even the involvement, and the acceptance of the involvement at that stage gets cut off. If the involvement is not accepted then it goes on and on and on.

VALERIA But there is no blank?

RAMESH The blank happens this way. Again, for example, you are sitting in the reception lounge. You are physically a bit tired, mentally you have no interest in what is going on, you close your eyes and sit quietly. You are not asleep, Consciousness is still there, sounds of people coming and going, smells come, but there is nothing to witness because your eyes are closed. Then that state is the non-witnessing state – Consciousness is still there.

VALERIA And a thought may come in that state or not come.

RAMESH So if a thought comes, that thought is witnessed. From non-witnessing to witnessing of that thought and back to non-witnessing. Therefore non-witnessing to witnessing is an extremely easy movement, like the automatic change of gears. It does not require an effort. But if that non-witnessing state is not disturbed for a while and it goes deeper, then in the deeper state you may fall asleep or it may be a state of samadhi. So witnessing and non-witnessing are easy, one to the other. And it happens more often than one would imagine.

In the non-witnessing state there is nothing to witness. Your eyes are closed. Then a thought comes and it is witnessed, and the smells are smelled, and sounds are heard. If that state is not disturbed, it goes deeper, then the smells are no longer smelled, the sounds are no longer heard. And that state in which Consciousness is suspended is called the state of samadhi, and to move from that state into the witnessing or observing state again may be quite a stronger shake-up.

TAMARA In the case of a sage, witnessing is constant?

RAMESH It is, except when the working mind is going on. When the working mind is not happening, then the state of the sage varies between witnessing and non-witnessing.

Once, the very first man who took me to the States originally wrote me a letter saying that he was going to pass through Bombay for three or four days while on a world tour and asked if he could come and see me. I said yes. So he came for a few days and stayed for three months. We had a fixed arrangement that he would come in the mornings. One day I was in the rocking chair waiting for him; the street noise was not that loud and my eyes were closed. When he came in he saw me with my eyes closed so he entered quietly and took his seat. Then something happened and I looked up. I said, 'Henry, you are here.' And he said, 'Wait a minute. What state of mind were you in?' I replied that I hadn't thought about it. 'But now that you mention it, I might call it the non-witnessing state. Now you are here, we are talking, and this conversation that is taking place is being witnessed. You go away, nothing happens, the witnessing of our conversation has not been replaced by any other manifestation to be witnessed so I sit again with my eyes closed – witnessing is not occurring, it is non-witnessing.' There is really just a hairline between witnessing and non-witnessing. It is so easy – from one to the other happens spontaneously.

RAMESH As the witnessing and non-witnessing become more frequent what does this signify? It signifies less involvement. Less involvement means fewer thoughts, but more importantly it means less thinking. You see the difference? Fewer thoughts are not in your control. If the witnessing and non-witnessing become deeper, a thought arises, it's witnessed, and goes. But if the witnessing and non-witnessing are not at the deeper level, then that thought leads to thinking, horizontal thinking. A thought arises vertically and is prevented from leading to horizontal thinking because of the happening of witnessing. And the happening of witnessing and non-witnessing together is the Understanding-in-action.

When there is a realization that this is *happening* you cannot prevent a sense of pleasure, a sense of gratitude arising. It *arises*. You see? Until the ego is totally annihilated, a sense of gratitude arises that it is happening in 'you'. But this has nothing to do with 'you'. It has nothing to do with 'your' involvement. The *arising* of a sense of gratitude is *not* involvement. The involvement of the ego may happen later, if the ego reacts to the natural arising.

Guru

ALTA What's the meaning of the guru? That's what I don't know.

RAMESH You know, there is a meaning of the word 'guru': *gu-ru* is remover of darkness. Darkness is ignorance. So remover of darkness means giver of knowledge.

ROBERT And that knowledge can be given without words.

RAMESH In fact, Ramana Maharshi always said that is the strongest way.

ROBERT The first time I saw you, before you spoke a word, you were looking at me as you are looking at me now, and I received a deep understanding of all there is is Consciousness.

RAMESH But it doesn't happen in every case. Ramana Maharshi said that is the quickest way. But it can happen only in a few cases. In most cases some talking has to happen, some physical presence is necessary. Your having read the books and coming here and listening, have these made any difference, Robert?

ROBERT Yes.

The disciple is initially concerned with 'acquiring' knowledge as such at an intellectual level. The guru is fully aware that there is no such thing as ignorance which could be removed by the acquisition of knowledge. He knows that every individual is the Universal Consciousness which has identified itself with the individual body-mind organism, and that such identification is itself the ignorance that the disciple talks about. The disciple *thinks* that it is the acquisition of knowledge which will get rid of the ignorance while the guru *knows* that ignorance is itself the result of the positive action of identification.

TAAVI You very beautifully presented that the ego has really nothing to do with the truth-seeking, there is nothing the ego can do. You were also saying it is God's grace. But it also looks like the grace is flowing through gurus.

RAMESH The guru is merely a mechanism in phenomenality for this to happen. For the grace to flow, the guru is the mechanism.

TAAVI Then being in the presence of a guru or a saint is very good for the seeking to take place.

RAMESH For the seeking to *progress*. When the seeking begins, the guru is not necessary. For the seeking to progress the guru is necessary, and whether you get a guru or a suitable guru will depend on the destiny of the body-mind organism. If the destiny

183

is for a process to be long-winded, then the process will take you first to a place where rituals are done, then to some other place where something else is done, then to a third place where you are told what to do and what not to do, until gradually you move on. The understanding becomes deeper that 'this cannot be what I am seeking'. Or, it may be your destiny that you go to the final place directly. Some people who have come here have come after twenty years of seeking, while some others have come directly here.

TAAVI The seeking or the opening seems to be very natural in the presence of the guru.

RAMESH That is the traditional Eastern concept. It is still a concept. It is part of the phenomenality. So the guru's grace happening is still a part of phenomenality. It is part of the process. It is part of the Energy functioning. But the traditional Eastern way is to say that for the seeking to progress substantially, the guru and his grace are necessary. Whether it happens or not, again depends on the destiny of each body-mind organism.

SINGH But even coming here, what you get is still not in your control.

RAMESH That is correct, actually, even coming here was not in your control or what you get out of it. Coming here was in your destiny and what you get out of it is also your destiny.

[The guru] does his best to put into words what truly cannot be put into words. He does this for only one reason, and that is he hopes that there will be perhaps a single word or a single sentence that may reveal the Truth and remove the obfuscation that has appeared on the disciple's real nature. He repeatedly avers that all there is is Consciousness and that therefore the disciple, like the guru, cannot possibly be anything but Consciousness; further that all phenomenal objects – including the guru and the disciple – are nothing but the subjective Noumenon in its objective expression as the manifestation. But the realization of this truth at the intellectual level is just not sufficient because at the root of the intellectual comprehension, the culprit is still there as the individual comprehender! The individual outside crust has to be shattered before the intellectual comprehension can be transformed into intuitive apprehension or apperception. And this individual crust can be shattered only by the disidentifying of the pseudo-subjectivity through a subjective experience of the sheer absence of a separate individual entity.

The 'doer' is indeed the obstruction, the bondage which is to be cut asunder by the word of knowledge. It is a deep intuitive understanding in which the comprehender (the split-mind, the ego) is absent. This 'happening' is not in the hands of either the individual guru nor the individual disciple. It can occur only at the appropriate time and place in the totality of functioning when the divine relationship between the guru as Consciousness and the disciple as Consciousness is ripe enough to fructify, when the guru and the disciple meet face to face like two mirror surfaces facing each other.

The step before enlightenment

RAMESH Manfred, what was it that was not clear before, which now has become clear?

MANFRED When I was here last year there was a desire for enlightenment, that if I came to see you, you could give me enlightenment.

RAMESH In other words, you came here expecting me to give Manfred enlightenment.

MANFRED Exactly. And then after ten days of listening I thought, 'What's happening here?'

RAMESH So last year you came here expecting 'me' as an individual to give 'you' as an individual enlightenment?

MANFRED Not 'you' as an individual, but you as a sage and this energy – all this would give me enlightenment.

RAMESH So Manfred as an individual came to see another individual with *powers* to give Manfred enlightenment.

MANFRED This was my idea, yes.

RAMESH And then you found that this ruddy sage was just another individual who could give nobody anything.

MANFRED This was totally clear.

RAMESH Now, did that bring about a sense of freedom?

MANFRED Maybe. Yes. The experience of the sense of freedom was also after Lucknow – *sadhana* was stopped, meditation was stopped, therapy was stopped, group was stopped, Pune was stopped.

RAMESH But as you just said, Manfred was still seeking enlightenment.

MANFRED Yes, of course! That's why existence brought me here, to seek this desire. I did not know that this desire was still there. I thought, 'I'll go to India again for the winter months, and I'll also stop and see Ramesh.' And then after a couple of days here this desire again came up.

RAMESH So you've understood the basic teaching which happens here?

Manfred Yes.

Ramesh What has this understanding done for Manfred? This understanding that Manfred cannot be enlightened.

Manfred Much more freedom. All spiritual clearing has gone. Spiritual seeking has gone. Life is much simpler. Misery is gone.

Ramesh Yes. You know, the others listening here are impressed when you say, 'The misery is gone,' rather than my saying, 'Your misery will go.' So would you say then that the misery was in the seeking *done* by Manfred?

Manfred The seeker was the misery. Manfred as the seeker was the misery. And now the seeking just happens – spontaneously.

Ramesh In other words, what you are saying is now there is no longer any seeker.

Manfred I think so.

Ramesh So there is no longer any Manfred as a seeker. If the seeking continues *let it continue*.

Manfred Yes!

Ramesh Manfred is not concerned.

Manfred Yes.

Ramesh Yes. But you are quite right. Manfred as the seeker does not have to do anything. That happens only when Manfred comes to the undeniable and unconditional acceptance that Manfred is *not the doer*. Isn't it? That has to come first from personal experience.

[*Speaking to another person.*] This is the whole point, Stan. Stan exists because Stan acts. So when Stan comes to the conclusion that Stan does nothing, then Stan doesn't exist.

Stan exists because Stan acts. And when you come to the conclusion *from personal experience* that Stan *does not act*, then how

can Stan exist? You see? Stan doesn't exist, but the body-mind exists. And through the body-mind, actions that were happening before will continue to happen strictly according to the will of God and the destiny of this body-mind organism. This is really simple, isn't it?

That is why Ramana Maharshi said that Self-realization is the simplest thing. And I'm saying, 'All you have to do is to find out from personal experience if Stan is the doer.'

YOGANAND Ramesh, you just said that all you have to do is to find out from personal experience that you are not the doer.

RAMESH Wait a minute, the deepest understanding is that even this is not in your control. That is the whole basis – nothing happens unless it is the will of God.

YOGANAND Nothing I can do. Nothing.

RAMESH The most relevant point is only this: Yoganand does not act, therefore Yoganand does not exist. That is the only relevant point. If Yoganand does not act, 'Who acts?' the intellect asks. Then the answer, 'God acts', is merely a sop, a pacification, something given for the intellect. But it is irrelevant. This conceptual answer is irrelevant.

You see, what is Self-realization? Self-realization is the annihilation of Yoganand as the doer. When that happens the rest of it doesn't matter.

YOGANAND I have an image of a dog chasing its tail. And when I have the realization, I see the dog stop the hunting after its tail. At one point he stops chasing.

RAMESH No, no. The dog doesn't exist. The dog disappears because the dog chasing its tail is merely a creation of the intellect. It's an image created by the mind – so the dog disappears.

[*Speaking to another person.*] Everything just happens. Robert

188

is not the doer, that is the only relevant point. If Robert is not the doer, then Robert doesn't exist. What exists? Only a programmed body-mind organism that exists at the will of the Source. The Source creates body-mind organisms. The Source creates actions. And the totality of actions through the totality of manifestation is *What-is, Now*, this *apparent* creation which is *lila*, the divine play.

The only relevant point is that Robert *does not act*. That is the *only* relevant point. If there is total unconditional acceptance that Robert does not act, then it means at the same time that Robert does not exist – then what exists is *only the Source* doing whatever it wants to do, and there is no Robert concerned with what is happening, except as an instrument.

So if there is someone thinking 'he' has got the understanding, then the understanding is not total. The *total understanding* is that kind of understanding in which there is no *individual understander or comprehender*. The understanding that 'one' may have – that he is not the doer – is the acceptance by the intellect that what Ramesh has said, what has been heard, is logical – no intellectual objection to it. This is where the intellect says, 'I accept.' BUT when it happens from personal experience, then the intellect collapses, the individual is annihilated. The individual is no longer there to observe. Then what happens is the impersonal witnessing of whatever is happening through the body-mind organism. The important thing to realize is that there is no 'one' existing as the witnesser. There is only *impersonal* witnessing. Let there be no confusion.

Is there a step just prior to enlightenment or Self-realization? Yes. That step is the individual not caring whether enlightenment happens or not. That is the penultimate step for the final under-standing to happen. No 'one' to care. Who cares? A thought will arise, 'Will there ever be enlightenment in this body-mind organism?' And promptly, 'Who cares?' You see? So 'who' cares? There is no 'who' to care!

NARAYANI When I realize that enlightenment has nothing to do with me – I was just sitting here and thinking that it has nothing to do with me. But still I am seeking. I'm not seeking enlightenment anymore, yet I don't know what I'm seeking anymore.

RAMESH Confused?

NARAYANI I couldn't say it makes me more free or more happy. Yes, it gets more confused now.

RAMESH You see, the confusion is still the ego, isn't it?

NARAYANI Sure. I never would have thought I would lose this interest in enlightenment and still have the ego.

RAMESH Why? Because it was the ego who wanted enlightenment as an object. So Narayani wanted enlightenment as an object which would give Narayani …

NARAYANI And then I understood that enlightenment is no object.

RAMESH Nothing to get hold of, because 'to get hold of' Narayani has to be there, and enlightenment means the annihilation of Narayani. That is why I keep saying that if you had the choice, and you don't have the choice, choose to seek one million dollars because when you get it there will be a Narayani to enjoy it. But if enlightenment happens there will be no Narayani to enjoy enlightenment.

NARAYANI What happens to me is I realize that enlightenment is no object, and this confusion happens. There is some guilt arising, saying I'm so lucky in a way, but I feel confused. It's getting more dark, it's not getting …

RAMESH The point to understand here is that this reaction which you are having now is the ego getting perturbed. The ego knows that if this process continues it will no longer be there. The ego is resisting. The ego does not give way easily. The ego resists. To what extent the ego resists is the will of God and the destiny of this body-mind organism.

So what does Narayani do when she finds the ego causes confusion? What Narayani is doing now is saying, 'I don't want to be confused. I am getting confused.' The alternative is, 'All right, there is confusion, I can do nothing about it. Let the confusion be there. Who cares?' Then the confusion will become less and less, and the ego will become weaker and weaker.

NARAYANI So in a way it is none of 'my' business whether there is confusion or not.

RAMESH That is the point! So accept the confusion. Don't fight it!

NARAYANI When I used to come to see you I always knew I came because I wanted enlightenment. And now this time I knew that enlightenment was not possible anymore. So there is this feeling, why am I sitting here? It is also none of 'my' business why I'm sitting here. I'm just sitting here.

RAMESH It's just happening. So having understood that Ramesh as an individual can give *nothing* to Narayani as an individual, see what happens next time. You may not come here or you may still come here. You may still come here and wonder, knowing, 'I get nothing here. Why am I here?' Let whatever happens, happen!

NARAYANI Thank you.

RAMESH You're welcome. Yes, Vasant?

VASANT I just have to thank you for the increased acceptance of what you are saying.

RAMESH So be grateful to the Source. And when I say, 'Be grateful to the Source,' what I'm saying is that gratitude to the Source *arises*. Let it arise.

Vasant After this total acceptance there is no doubt.

Ramesh And more important, Vasant, there is nothing to appear and disappear. Something which appears as an experience will disappear.

Vasant And it's such a relief.

Ramesh Nothing appears, nothing disappears. No experience happens, no experience disappears.

Vasant And the war is over.

Ramesh You see, the point is this: an experience happens and the ego says, 'Ah, I am enlightened.' Then the experience disappears after a week. 'I am unenlightened now.' Terrible frustration, confusion.

Vasant Yes. And I think this is the process, this coming and going, until it stays there.

Ramesh So this flip-flop comes and goes which is the confusion about which Narayani was speaking. Let that flip-flop happen. Accept it. The confusion happens. Accept the confusion. Don't fight it.

Vasant There was nobody there anymore who could do anything, and in that relaxation something started happening. I had been doing everything, and then the attitude happened, just forget about it.

Ramesh You know the story of Lao Tzu and his disciple? A disciple, his face shining with the glory of achievement, came to Lao Tzu saying, 'Master, I have *got* it!' Lao Tzu placed his hands on the disciple and said, 'My son, you have *not* got it.' So the disciple went away dejected but completely accepting what the master had told him. Time passed and eventually the disciple returned and fell at the master's feet, 'Master, it has happened.' So Lao Tzu raised him up and asked what had happened. The disciple replied, 'You told me that I had not got it, and I accepted it as the total truth. I had not the slightest doubt in what you said. But I also had no doubt at all that I had done everything that I could possibly do. So I just let life happen without wanting enlightenment and without wanting to do something about enlightenment. Then there was the sudden, spontaneous apperception in the heart that it had happened. There was no "me" left wanting enlightenment, wanting anything.'

Effect of the teaching on daily living

RAMESH How has the understanding been affecting your daily life? Unless a teaching affects your daily life in some beneficial way, that teaching is useless.

Life becomes simpler, not easier

RAMESH Do you think because of this understanding that life will become easier – easier in the sense of fewer difficulties?

MICHAEL It may so happen. I don't really care.

RAMESH Yes. But if it does, it is *not* because of the teaching. That you understand?

MICHAEL Yes.

RAMESH Whether it becomes easier or not, you don't know. But if it does, and you and I both hope it will, it has nothing to do with the teaching.

MICHAEL Right.

RAMESH That would have been so whether you came here or not depending on your destiny. But life does become *simpler*. It may not become easier, life may be as hard as it used to be or as easy as it used to be, but life becomes simpler. Doesn't it? Would you say that?

MICHAEL Absolutely.

RAMESH Why would life become simpler, Michael? In what way will life become simpler? Because there is less involvement.

MICHAEL Exactly.

RAMESH Isn't that right?

MICHAEL There was a point where it was clearly seen that I could not possibly have the overview of all creation. Only the Creator could have that overview.

RAMESH That is correct.

MICHAEL So I better leave the rudder to him.

RAMESH Again quite right. Which means Michael gets less and less involved in what is happening. Isn't that right?

MICHAEL Absolutely.

RAMESH Which means Michael accepts life as it happens. Michael accepts What-is at every moment as it is, without wanting to change it. That's right, isn't it?

MICHAEL That's right.

RAMESH So life becomes simpler because there's less involvement. There is less involvement because there's more acceptance of What-is. Really simple, isn't it? Then why do you think people find it so complicated? If this is so simple, why do you think ...?

MICHAEL As long as there is a belief in having to do things, then it is bound to be like that.

RAMESH Quite right.

MICHAEL And that can be changed – only by grace.

RAMESH Again, yes. So basically the whole problem is the sense of personal doership, which is really what is meant by 'ego', although various definitions are given for the ego. But by 'ego' what is really meant is the sense of personal doership.

Someone rang me from Madras and she said, 'Am I right in saying that you say we are all puppets?' I said, 'Yes, and a very wise man called Rumi agrees with me, that we are all puppets.' So she asks, 'Why is it so difficult for me to accept that we are all puppets?' What do you say, Michael?

MICHAEL Again, it is the sense of personal doership.

RAMESH Yes. It may be possible to think in terms of all the people being puppets, but it is difficult for the 'me' to imagine being one of those. And the doership is with the sense of free will, isn't it? People find it difficult to accept that they are puppets because mainly they are not prepared to accept that there is no free will.

Who cares?

CARMEN Ramesh, I don't understand how you can say, 'Who cares?' It's bothering me. There is so much suffering and people not caring what happens to each other. Sometimes it comes to the point that I can't take it anymore, and then you say, 'Who cares?'

RAMESH Now wait a minute! You don't understand the context in which 'Who cares?' is said. The context is meant for the apparent seeker who thinks 'he' or 'she' is doing the seeking – the seeking of God, or enlightenment, or whatever. 'Who cares?' is *not* about life in phenomenality. 'Who cares?' means: who cares whether God is taking me along the path quickly or slowly – *who cares*? That's his business. This attitude has nothing to do with practical life.

To what extent does the meaning of the words, 'Who cares?' have to life in general? An example is that you have two people: one cares a lot and the other cares very little. The one who cares a lot will not stop caring even if he's told to stop caring for others. And the one who is not able to care for others, even if you tell him to do so, will not be able to. Why? Because each body-mind organism has a certain nature – not a nature which 'he' has acquired, but which comes with the body-mind organism. One body-mind organism has been created with a deep sensitivity where the caring is part of its nature. If another body-mind organism has been created by the same Source, by the same God, with much less sensitivity, then much less caring will be its nature – over which he or she has had no control. The way one is programmed, one's natural characteristics – sensitive or insensitive – is not in the control of anybody. I'm not suggesting that the attitude in living life be, 'Who cares?' Rather, these two words refer to the seeker's attitude towards spiritual progress.

What the understanding brings

RAMESH How will you live? You will live exactly as you have lived so far. Earlier you made decisions. Life means making decisions, so you will continue making decisions. But earlier when you made decisions – and you expected those decisions to be according to your will – you felt frustrated if those decisions turned out to be wrong. With the understanding from the teaching happening here, you will continue to make decisions and put those decisions into practice. But subsequently, the consequences of those decisions will be accepted as something over which you had no choice.

That is the only difference. Life isn't going to change for the better unless it is the destiny of this body-mind organism for it to do so. This teaching is not going to make life easier for you. If I said this, the ego would have expectations – now that I know this intellectually, maybe, and I've got the hang of the matter, my life should be easier. It won't be. If it would be, then there's a reason.

I mention this repeatedly so that people won't have expectations, and when I do I see a few people becoming a bit restless. So I ask what's the matter? One person said, 'Ramesh, you said life may not ... In my case, at least, life has become a whole lot easier. Not only simpler because of the attitude, but a whole lot easier.' So I asked him, 'Just because it is easier, would you guarantee that it will be easier for others who have got the similar understanding, even intellectually?'

What happens really is this: the understanding basically comes to the importance of the working mind – that it is the working mind and not the thinking mind which is being used. The working mind is the mind that works in the present moment. The working mind in the moment is only concerned with doing a job. The working mind is not interested in the consequences. Whether there will be success or not or whether there will be the money that is expected is the thinking mind. The thinking mind is the ego and the expectations. So the thinking mind always lives in the past or in the future but never in the present moment. The working mind dips into the past to take advantage of past experience, but doesn't project into the future. The working mind dips into the past but remains in the present moment. The thinking mind dips into the past and projects 'its' future, and is always worried about whether what is being done now is right or wrong or could be done better.

So what this understanding does produce, even at an intellectual level, is this – the interruptions of the working mind by the thinking mind become less, even while knowing that consequences are beyond your control. And if the interruptions of the working mind by the thinking mind become less, then the working mind obviously becomes more efficient. And if the working mind becomes more efficient, your work will be more efficient. And if your work is more efficient, your rewards are also likely to be more.

A man comes here usually on Sundays. He told me, 'Look Ramesh, as far as I am concerned, I'm convinced the teaching does make life easier.' He's in marketing. He said that in his case what had been happening earlier was when he went and saw a prospect he would talk about whatever he was supposed to, but at the back of his mind the thinking mind was always active. Now, he says, he knows that what will happen with a prospective customer is not in his hands. What no expectations produces is a more sincere, open dialogue with the customer. He made it perfectly clear that what is happening now is that he is speaking more freely, and he said he is speaking more honestly. The point is that his openness, knowing that the future is not in his control, has somehow impressed his customers so much that they are recommending him to others. And he is doing very, very well. So he says that he cannot accept that the teaching does not make life easier.

The basic point that I'm making is: (1) the understanding almost always has to be intellectual in the beginning and (2) the understanding goes deeper from personal experience. This means investigating and analysing your actions and trying to find out whether they are truly your actions as you have been thinking, or whether they have been *happenings* over which you have had really no control. And as the experience becomes clearer and clearer that no action was really 'your' action, that it was absolutely and essentially a *happening* over which you had no control, then the ego gets weaker and weaker. And as the ego gets weaker and weaker the Understanding-in-action makes life simpler. Why simpler? Because there is less pride, less guilt, less hate, less envy. Not that these won't happen, but when the involvement happens it will get cut off. Until the understanding is truly there, the involvement and its getting cut off may eventually happen almost simultaneously until even the arising of involvement stops.

RAMESH As Ramana Maharshi says, 'All thinking begins with the "I" thought' which is the ego, which is the sense of personal doership. You see? But the sense of personal doership will lead to involvement. That is natural. But the important thing to understand is that if something leads to involvement all is not lost.

The involvement continues horizontally in time – there is a sudden realization that you have been involved, and then the involvement gets cut off. Does it not? In the beginning involvement may not get cut off at all, but when there is some understanding, that understanding produces the sudden realization that there has been involvement. So in a conceptual scale of zero to ten, involvement may begin and get cut off at nine. As the understanding goes deeper, the sudden realization of involvement happens quicker and quicker. Thus it gets cut off at nine, eight, seven, six until finally when the involvement happens there is a sudden realization and the involvement gets cut off immediately. But this sudden realization is not produced by 'you', it is produced by the *understanding*. That is what is to be understood. The sudden realization of involvement is not something which 'you' can produce out of 'your' control. It is the understanding that produces the realization. Let us be clear.

So the understanding does have an effect, a very good effect, not only on your own physical and mental health, but on those with whom you come in contact. But there is a danger! If the understanding is not deep enough, this being considered as the wise man in the group can be very heady stuff. If the 'wise man' wants to continue being the wise man, the spontaneity will be lost and it will not be long before he is found out.

Expectation – importance of doing something

RAMESH The trouble is expectation. That is the whole problem in life. You expect something, you don't get it, you feel frustrated. Money is really the main problem for most people. I personally think one should not lessen the importance of money. If money is no problem, eighty per cent of the problems are not there. Then what remains as problems are what the mind creates out of expectation. If the expectation doesn't materialize there is frustration. So if it is possible to live without expectation, then there is no frustration.

If you meditate without expectation, then there is no problem. I'm not asking you not to meditate, but try to meditate without any expectation. Now what happens is you sit in meditation and all the time you expect something to happen – call it silence, call it being in oneness, or whatever. What you call it doesn't matter. But the problem arises if you meditate with an expectation.

So if there is no expectation, you live your life. Whatever happens. *Why not let life happen?* I can't say this to someone who needs money, who needs money to live, for the family. Talking about spirituality to a hungry man is like adding insult to injury. I can't tell him or her to do something and not expect money. That's why I never underestimate the importance of money. If money is not a problem, then why have any expectations? *Let life happen.* What I say does not apply to those unfortunate people below the poverty line.

LEGAN I feel I have to grow. I have to change. I have to become …

RAMESH That's the whole point! Why?

LEGAN I have to become more spiritual …

RAMESH Why?

LEGAN … or more open, more centred or …

RAMESH That's what I'm saying. So try to live your life or let life happen without expecting anything. The expectation happens because you're bored. The mind is empty, and the thinking mind never allows itself to be empty. The thinking mind always wants something. That's why the thinking occurs and the expectations happen. If you don't have to earn money, then do something to give the working mind a chance – do something to help people. There must be something you can do to help people around you who need help. So if boredom is your problem ...

LEGAN There is always this talking in this fellowship that I'm going to. There's always this talking about transformation and change, and I feel nothing is happening with me. Sometimes it's okay. Sometimes I feel I have to do something.

RAMESH So do it. That is exactly what I'm telling you. And do it without expecting anything. And having done something, if satisfaction arises – fine. If it doesn't arise – that is also fine.

LEGAN Is meditating everyday helpful?

RAMESH Helpful for what? That's the whole problem. Meditation is helpful for what?

LEGAN For peace of mind.

RAMESH Ah! So it is peace of mind that you are looking for, isn't it? And that is the expectation.

LEGAN I think I'm always looking for something.

RAMESH Yes. That is the whole problem. So keep yourself busy doing something, and if you don't need to do anything for money, so much the better. But do something. I'm sure you can't say that there are no people who need some kind of help. There are people around you needing some kind of help. Do they not?

If you are able to help people, they are bound to say, 'Thank you, I am very grateful.' And that expression of gratitude from someone else does bring about a certain satisfaction. What happens when people praise you or express their gratitude? If there is expectation, then pride is the result. But if there is no expectation, then only a sense of satisfaction *arises* that someone has been helped. And if you keep on doing this for a certain length of time, then the continual sense of satisfaction is itself the peace of mind you are seeking. But if there is expectation there is no peace of mind – there is pride.

LEGAN I always want to change. This whole idea about enlightenment and transformation and that I have to change and that I have to feel …

RAMESH You have to improve, and change, and transform yourself – that is the whole problem, isn't it? Why should you transform yourself? Why should you not accept yourself as you are? The peace of mind you are looking for will happen *only* when you *stop looking for it* and *let things happen*. Understand this! This is the very basis of the understanding – that no 'one' is a Self-realized man or woman. It is most important to understand this, according to my concept. No human being can be Self-realized. In fact, so long as there is a belief that 'I' have achieved Self-realization, Self-realization has *not* happened. You see?

Destiny – funny how it manifests

RAMESH You know, the matter of destiny – it's funny how it happens. I have known two people, both extremely nice people, generous people – but both did nothing. One was a man I'd known since Maharaj's time. He had had a successful business selling furs, and when public attitude began to change against such things he decided it was best to sell his shop. As a result he suddenly had a great deal of money, but he also had the wrong impression that he was a very good investor. He began speculating and eventually lost it all. Then he lived on the charity of his parents. He also came here. Everyday I kept impressing on him the necessity to *do* something and not give such a free scope to the thinking mind – to put his working mind in such a position as to be engaged for at least a minimum of time. Since he was such a good salesman I finally said to him, 'Take a job as a salesman.' 'Oh no,' he replied, 'I have owned a shop, how could I work for someone?' So that thinking was the destiny. Regardless of what I said, he continued to do nothing. Also, he had had an unhappy childhood, and as he saw it, an unhappy life. Two or three weeks ago I learnt that he had committed suicide.

There was also a young lady who was very similar. In spite of having a talent for computers, she too used to do nothing, the thinking mind churning away, and as a result she was very often disappointed, frustrated and seriously distressed, living on dole from her country as well as the generosity of a friend and relative. She also used to come here, and I would tell her, '*Do* something. Engage in something with a view to earning your living. Don't just depend on charity. *Do* something! *Do* something and provide opportunity for the working mind rather than the thinking mind.' But the question of destiny is there. Her destiny was unlike the other fellow's. She did manage to get a job, and she is working hard now. She sometimes telephones, and not long ago I asked, 'How are you doing?' 'Oh I'm doing so well now. I work most of the time and perhaps a little harder than I should, but I'm happy.' So she's doing all right. The other committed suicide.

These are two cases where I felt maximum compassion. Each one went his or her own way depending on the destiny. All you can do is show the way, whether he or she is able to go that way depends on the destiny.

There is the story of a Zen master. He grew up living with and listening to his venerable grandfather who was also a Zen master. When he was very young he heard his grandfather often say, 'Whatever is to happen will happen. Everything has a destined life.' One day this boy, hurrying from here to there, knocked over a valuable and favourite vase belonging to his grandfather. The vase broke. So he went to his grandfather and said, 'You know that vase you like very much?' 'Yes.' 'Well, it's life ended three minutes ago.'

Life does become simpler

FEROZE You are taught that you are responsible for everything, but this teaching is exactly the opposite – 'you' are responsible for nothing. It has happened already. I think the advantage is as you've said – it may or may not make your life easier, but at least you'll stop thinking about it.

RAMESH That's well put – 'you stop thinking about it'.

FEROZE You become very relaxed, I think.

RAMESH Has that been your experience, Feroze?

FEROZE Yes, in the last few weeks I would say it certainly has been more relaxed. Let it happen rather than do.

RAMESH You have to come to the conclusion that you really have nothing to do with it. Ramana Maharshi made this clear when he was asked, 'I can accept that the most important things may have been predetermined. But is a small thing predetermined? If I take this fan which I'm using and put it on the ground, do you mean even that action is predetermined?' And Ramana Maharshi said, 'Certainly.' You see? Every single action is predetermined – every split second.

FEROZE From what you have said, it has to be because if this is all like a movie, you can't have a movie in parts. The whole thing has to be there. It's all over and done with.

RAMESH That is exactly it. The movie is there in the can.

FEROZE So it does make things much simpler.

Responsibility

RAMESH What does one really mean by responsibility? Usually responsibility for most people depends on the consequences. When people say, 'I am responsible for my actions,' what is presumed is that the actions will have certain consequences for which 'I' shall be held responsible.

PETER I was not thinking so much of society punishing or rewarding but one's own …

RAMESH So it's really both. Responsibility is based both on what 'I' think 'I' should do and on the consequences 'my' actions are liable to have on others. So responsibility, as far as my own convictions are concerned, will depend on my conditioning at that moment about what is right and wrong – by and large what one calls moral standards. And how do moral standards happen? They happen over a period of time through conditioning.

PETER But there are different standards for people in different societies, different groups …

RAMESH So the basic point I would make is that there is no universal standard of morality and discipline. There may be a standard within a society if it imposes one. But the one I am *truly* concerned with is my sense of fairness and right and wrong. And if what I consider right or wrong differs from that of society, then all I can do is be true to myself. All I can do is what I think is right in the circumstances. That is the only option left to me.

PETER Then again this could be induced by conditioning.

RAMESH Certainly! It *is* conditioned. One's own standards of right and wrong are part of the conditioning, which is part of the programming. Programming is DNA plus conditioning. There is a sense of right and wrong. In fact, what I say is, if there is a question, 'Do I do this or do I do that?' then my answer has always been to do whatever you think is right or wrong at that moment. Why? Because 'you' are not doing it anyway. There is *no individual doer*, neither you nor anyone else.

If at that moment you think that you should do one thing as against the other, it will be based on the conditioning. And who has produced that conditioning? Have you produced it? No! That conditioning is part of God's will and the destiny of that body-mind organism. This is precisely what the Buddha is reported to have said: 'Deeds are done, there is no individual doer thereof.' But there is an individual doer in society. Without individual doers society will not function. So as far as society is concerned there are doers. You can't say no.

PETER What about punishment?

RAMESH Actions and the consequences. It's a peculiar thing. You know that no individual exists either in this body or any other body, but you also know that society doesn't know this.

PETER I thought I heard you say the other day, 'Do what you want.' There seems to be quite a difference between doing what you want and doing what you think is right.

RAMESH What you like to do at any particular moment according to your sense of right or wrong is exactly what the Source wants you to think at that moment. Otherwise 'you' have initiative, and my point is that there is no individual at all.

In life you cannot live without making decisions, and my answer is to make decisions *as if* you have free will. Consider all the consequences and alternatives – then come to a decision. But deep down you know that that decision could not have been different from God's will; otherwise, that decision wouldn't have happened. A decision will not happen if it is not God's will; a decision will not turn into an action unless it is God's will; and a decision will have consequences strictly accordingly to God's will. Where do 'you' come in apart from the fact you make a decision *as if* you have free will? The difficulty happens with – what will happen to 'me'? There is no 'me'! Therefore make decisions knowing deep down it is not 'my' decision, it is God's will.

The responsibility is taken by the fact you act *as if* you have free will. By acting *as if* you have free will you have assumed responsibility for the consequences, but deep down you know that whatever the consequences are, they are the destiny of that body-mind organism.

According to my concept the question of responsibility is not there – BUT, all in capitals, living one's life in society you cannot ignore the sense of responsibility. Therefore, what do you do? Act as responsibly as you are programmed to do.

Cannot avoid pain in the manifestation

PRATIMA Actually nothing ever really happens. Everything is just a manifestation of Consciousness and appears to happen.

RAMESH So if somebody hits you it's only an appearance?

PRATIMA Yes.

RAMESH You don't feel it? Nobody feels it? If somebody hits somebody else, doesn't the one feel the hit being made by the other?

PRATIMA On the relative level, yes, there is the appearance of pain, but really there is no separate individual to actually feel ...

RAMESH So you say there is really no separate individual, yet the individual says, 'Dammit, if somebody hits me on the face, I feel it.'

PRATIMA So somebody hits me. That is one thing, hitting occurs. The point is to what extent do I identify that as a problem.

RAMESH No. To what extent is the being hit and being hurt real or illusory?

PRATIMA There is no problem with being hit as such. The problem only arises when the mind interprets that.

RAMESH No. The problem arises when somebody hits me and I feel the pain.

PRATIMA But it's only the mind's interpretation of the pain as negative that creates the problem.

RAMESH The problem is that I feel the pain, and you are telling me it's illusory! And what is more, if I hit you, you will feel the pain. Will you not? Will you stand there and take more illusory blows?! Let us be clear. Let us not be confused.

PRATIMA So hitting occurs. There is no problem in that ...

RAMESH Oh, there is a problem for the person who is being hit ...

PRATIMA Only when the mind comes in and interprets it as a problem.

RAMESH 'Oh no! I don't care about the mind!' the person will tell you, 'I feel the hurt! I feel it and you are telling me that this hurt is illusory?!'

PRATIMA Well maybe I should rephrase it and say that everything which occurs is apparently real. Many things happen in life and they're all part of Consciousness. Maybe being hit is a wake-up call that is required to kick you out of the thinking of the mind.

RAMESH Are you telling me, Pratima, that this would be accepted?

PRATIMA I don't know what might be accepted or not, but the fact remains that without identification with this, knowing that the body-mind organism is not one's own ...

RAMESH Pratima, the answer will be, 'All right, I do identify, and I cannot *not* identify. I have to identify with this body, and therefore *the pain I feel is real.*' You say that all this is illusory. My answer to all of this is that the manifestation and all of its functioning are both real and unreal just as the shadow is real in the sun and doesn't exist when you come into the house. The totality of manifestation is real in the waking state. When the sun shines in the waking state the manifestation is real. But when you are home, in deep sleep, the manifestation does not exist.

The valid question I put to you, Pratima, is this: how can you *avoid* the waking state? And the answer is you *cannot* avoid the waking state. Therefore you cannot avoid the manifestation and the *pain* in the manifestation. The pain will be felt in the body-mind organism.

Can only surrender to the mystery

RAMESH Meister Eckhart put it beautifully: 'All that the human being can do is wonder and marvel at the magnificence of God's creation.' Thousands and thousands of varieties of objects, each with a different programming. In other words what he says is, the Lord's creation is a mystery and all that the human object can do is surrender to the mystery and not try to solve it.

No purpose in listening – just enjoyment

RAMESH Listening again and again is not necessary with a view to trying to understand. You see? You enjoy it. It may be that what has been said is enjoyed without any purpose. Where's the purpose in listening to Beethoven's music or Mozart? Some people don't like Beethoven because he is too violent. Many prefer Mozart. Or quite a few prefer Leonard Cohen. Why do people listen again and again to Leonard Cohen's music? They like it. There's *no purpose* in listening to it.

Who cares?

About the two questions that you ask: (1) sexual distractions –
'who' is distracted?! Remember Yang Zhu: 'Let the ear hear what
it longs to hear, the eye see what it longs to see, the nose smell
what it longs to smell, the mouth speak what it wants to speak, let
the body have every comfort it craves, let the mind do as it will.'
Why associate yourself, why identify with the body at all? Sometimes it may be that you are less hungry than at other times. Why
think in terms of 'you' being less hungry or more hungry – why
not there is less hunger or more hunger? Then, when there is
disassociation or disidentification with whatever happens to the
body-mind mechanism – including a greater or lesser tendency
towards sex – the prevailing tendencies of the body-mind are
merely witnessed *without any comparing or judging*. In such witnessing, the fact that certain changes are taking place is witnessed,
without even relating such changes to 'my' body. This is the point:
to whichever body such changes may relate, the basic point is that
it is the body to which the changes relate.

This same perspective may be carried over to your other point:
(2) 'In times of ill health, I occasionally wonder if what was
started when the head went into the tiger's mouth will be allo-
cated sufficient time to arrive at its ultimate conclusion in this
particular body-mind apparatus.' My very dear friend, DOES IT
MATTER? It can only matter to an entity who is desirous of such
a consummation, and the entity is itself the ultimate barrier to the
happening of the event called enlightenment or awakening. The
entity is inherent in any desire or expectation, whether the desire
is for a lowly object or for a 'holy' event like liberation. Consciousness is all there is, and whatever appears or happens is
merely a movement in Consciousness. So how can there ever be
any 'one' to want even enlightenment? Both the tiger and the head
in its mouth are concepts which disappear, merge and melt in the
very understanding. It is in this sense that Nisargadatta Maharaj

used to repeat all the time, 'UNDERSTANDING IS ALL.' In such understanding the entity itself gets dissolved, leaving no 'one' to want or expect anything.

It is difficult for an ordinary person to understand and appreciate the subtle but nonetheless significant differences between enjoyment of sensual pleasures and the attachment to sensual pleasures. It is not that, after enlightenment, the body-mind organism ceases to enjoy sensual pleasures. The difference between the sage and the ordinary person, in regard to the enjoyment of sensual pleasures, is that while the ordinary person is continually in search of such pleasures, the sage does not hanker after such pleasures but enjoys them with zest when they happen in the ordinary course of life. The sage does not seek pleasure, nor does he reject it when it happens. In other words, he does not deliberately discriminate between the acceptable and the unacceptable: he is open to both in the ordinary course of daily life. When there is choice, the body-mind organism continues to choose according to the circumstances, according to its natural characteristics and tendencies, without thinking in terms of good and bad ...

Thus the sage, Ashtavakra, says: 'Absence of attachment (not enjoyment to be eschewed) to sense objects is liberation; passion for sense objects is bondage. Understand this fact, and then do as you please.'

RAMESH Your real question is, 'How will I ever know if I have the final understanding or not?' It bothers you, doesn't it? It does bother most people. Would you like an answer? The answer, again, is very simple. When that final understanding is about to happen, the one who is so anxious to know whether the final understanding has happened or not will finally say, 'Who cares?' Has the understanding happened or not? Who cares?

When that stage is reached it is almost synonymous with the understanding having happened because there is no 'one' to care anymore.

CLAIRE I think what bothers me is that sometimes the understanding exists and then it is not there anymore and then it happens again and then it's not there anymore.

RAMESH The answer is let it happen. There's a flip-flop – 'Sometimes I think I've got it. Sometimes I think I haven't got it.' So let it happen. The involvement happens only if you say, 'I don't want this flip-flop to happen.' Then there is involvement. If the flip-flop happens, let it happen. How long will it happen? Who cares?

Talking about the teaching

BRUCE Ramesh, when we go away from here, there may be people I would like to tell about these kind of experiences who will have difficulties with certain aspects of it. I wonder if you've found a gentle way to share this knowledge with people. How can we tell people without scaring them? I cannot just walk up to somebody and say, 'You're a fiction, buddy!'

RAMESH The whole point is that if the talking happens, let it happen, and the effect of that talking will depend on the destiny of the hearer! People sometimes ask me, 'Should I talk to them?' and my answer is, 'Don't talk to them, but if talking happens, let it happen.' If you want to talk to them, there is a 'me' wanting to talk. But whether the talking happens or not is again not in your hands.

Enjoy life

Once it is realized that the Self, the I AM, Consciousness – which is What-we-really-are – is the doer and the witness, it will be seen that it is not only unnecessary to renounce our daily activities but that it is desirable to continue our normal life. We continue with the deep understanding that we (as phenomenal objects) are 'being lived' in the totality of the functioning of the manifestation. The supposed doership of the 'me' is nothing but an illusion. *Normal daily activities, continued without a sense of doership, are the best possible preparation for sudden enlightenment to happen.*

CHAPTER FIVE

CONFUSION NO MORE

One morning I had a visitor, one wearing ochre-coloured robes, a swami. He had written a few books, the blurb on one of which said: 'After graduation with honours from the university, he spent several years in monasteries and caves practising raja yoga and meditation. Ultimately, he realized the core of his being, which is beyond the boundaries of individual self.'

He started by saying that he had read several of my books and that he was a 'fan' of mine! One of the first things he said was that he was appalled by the number of fake gurus he had come across who did not have even the rudiments of true understanding. Then he went on to say that he was astonished to read that Nisargadatta Maharaj not only used to get angry very quickly, very often, but that he was a smoker, smoking locally produced cigarettes called bidis; and to add to that, he said, he made and sold these bidis in his shops!

I told him that, according to my concept, no 'one' gets angry but that anger arises, varying in intensity and frequency, according to the 'programming' in the body-mind organism, which is a psychosomatic apparatus (genes plus conditioning, over neither of which anyone has had any control). Oh, he said, that is only a play on words which a fake guru hides behind, in order to hide his lack of control over his own physical and mental weaknesses. Surely, he said, a sage must have total control over all his desires and all his actions. Then, he said, he would like to present me with a copy of his book. I asked him what the book was about. He said, it was about the mystical wisdom of non-doing, which means, he said, that everything happens and therefore the principle of non-doing means that no one has the power of control over the body and mind! I could not believe my ears. This is what this man tells me about what his book was all about, and yet, only a few minutes ago, he had condemned Nisargadatta Maharaj for his anger and his habit of smoking. He suddenly came to his senses when the other visitors could not help laughing.

He quickly got up, said his goodbyes and left, saying he had another appointment.

This is an area of enormous confusion: what does Self-realization mean and how does a Self-realized human being live his daily life? Conditioned as they are by hundreds of years of confusion, the spiritual seekers have come to have the idea that the Self-realized sage is a kind of superman, a 'perfect' human being, totally in control of his mind and body, totally disciplined, whom everybody looks up to for advice and guidance in all situations in life, and who will protect his disciples from all difficulties in life. And, of course, there are plenty of people in this world who do not fail to take full advantage of this fact. Hence so many prosperous ashrams and millionaire gurus.

The area of confusion for most spiritual seekers is thus around two questions: (1) What exactly is Self-realization? What does it precisely mean? And (2) How does a Self-realized being live his daily life? Does he have a daily life like any ordinary human being? Curiously enough, though, it is not very often that the spiritual seeker asks himself: what do I expect Self-realization to do for me for the rest of my life that I did not have before? And, truly, this is the vital question. What is more, from what I have read about the talks between a guru and his disciples, I have never come across this specific question being asked by a disciple to his guru: after Self-realization, Sir, what did you get for the rest of your life that you did not have before?

It is, actually, the great Buddha who gave specific answers to these two questions:

1 Enlightenment means the total acceptance of the fact: events happen, deeds are done, but there is no individual doer of any deed.

2 Enlightenment means the end of suffering. 'Suffering', obviously, cannot include the pain that everyone – including the sage – has to suffer from moment to moment, depending upon his destiny, or God's will, according to the Cosmic Law. What the Buddha meant by 'suffering' was, again obviously, the suffering that the human being has created for himself because of his mistaken belief in his sense of volition, free will, his responsibility for his own actions: the load of guilt and shame for his own actions and the load of hatred and malice towards the 'other' for his actions. The disappearance of this load is what the Buddha means by 'end of suffering'.

There is another area of confusion which is felt not by all spiritual seekers but by those who have had the dubious privilege of having had an 'experience of ecstasy'. What these people forget is that that experience was in the moment, which merely proved to that person that the separate entity was an illusion and that Reality is oneness. But what that experiencer forgets is that it is the illusory separate entity which must live the rest of his life in the illusory phenomenal manifestation, and it is this forgetfulness which leads the spiritual seeker to seek, not the Ultimate Understanding, but a repetition of that experience. And in this seeking – which can prove to be unbearably frustrating – the seeker forgets that the experience itself was a 'happening' over which he had never had any control. And, therefore, he tries all kinds of methods and disciplines in order to 'achieve' that experience of oneness which had actually 'happened', perhaps because of the very fact that when it happened there was no seeker trying to achieve it.

It is an undeniable fact that enlightenment, Self-realization, the Ultimate Understanding or whatever can only *happen*, that it is not something which one can achieve through self-effort. As the Buddha has stated, there is no individual doer. No one does anything, no one achieves anything, everything happens according to the Cosmic Law.

The area in which the spiritual seeker should turn his attention to, therefore, is how to be in that mental state of total relaxation, in which the vacant mind would be able to receive the happening called 'enlightenment'.

The traditional approach is from the periphery inwards, and through time, practice, discipline and renunciation, gradually to come upon that inner beauty and 'love' – in fact to do everything not to make oneself narrow, petty and shoddy; peal off little by little, no hurry, take time; tomorrow will do, next life will do – and at last when one does come to the centre, what does one find there, at the end of twenty, thirty years? Nothing but frustration. Why? For the simple reason that the mind has been made incapable, dull and insensitive. What is really necessary is a total revolution, a complete mutation in our minds, in our way of living, in the activities of our daily living.

What is our daily way of living? Is there any time or inclination to understand oneself – self-knowledge – and observe one's behaviour in our relationship with the 'other'? What actually happens is that in daily living you are pursuing a self-projection. You are *this*, which is not acceptable, so you want *that*. It is only because you do not have a clear understanding of *this* that you create *that* to understand, or to escape from *this*. So your action is strictly within the limits of your own projection, whether it is the 'other', or God, or the state. Such activity is the activity of a dog chasing its tail.

The *this* includes what we take ourselves to be in the spiritual field. For example, I am ignorant, I am a sinner. How can I improve myself? I must find myself a guru, and so on. The *that* includes my projected ideal of God-realization, attainment of a permanent state of 'bliss' (how can we live our daily life in a state of bliss?!), absolute Truth, knowing Ultimate Reality, liberation from the cycle of rebirths, and so on. Just as a treasure lost in a dream cannot be found by the most efficient authority for the simple reason that the treasure has no existence at all apart from my mind, exactly so, ideals like moksha, mukti, *kaivalya*, God-realization etc. cannot be reached or acquired with or without the aid of a guru, for the simple reason that they are only products of one's own mind. There can only be an Ultimate Understanding within oneself – one can only be a beacon within oneself.

I am this and I want to become that. In trying to become that, there is conflict, struggle. In this struggle we are inevitably concerned with fulfilment by gaining an end. Fulfilment is the goal, the drive behind it is the effort put in by the 'me', the seeker – whatever the goal. Desire creates its own opposite, and transformation is not a matter of being centred in one desire, but of being free from the conflict which craving and pursuing brings. Only with the dissolution of conflict can there be tranquillity, and only then can Reality come into being.

Thus we find that man is always seeking: seeking a purpose, seeking a goal, seeking satisfaction, and the highest satisfaction he calls God. We always feel that something is missing, and so we try to fill that void in ourselves, that loneliness, that emptiness with lots of ideas, purposes, with significance, culminating in a permanency that we call God, samadhi – one keeps on inventing names. We need something to cling to, and we keep seeking – and we are in conflict.

Conflict cannot arise unless there is the consciousness of the 'me'. There is awareness of the conflict only when the 'me' suddenly becomes conscious of itself. So long as everything is moving smoothly without any contradictions, there is no consciousness of a 'me' in action and effort. The moment I am blocked in any way, I am aware of myself and become miserable. The fact of the matter is that we want to live without being blocked, and conflict, *suffering will exist so long as I do not understand myself.* Therefore, to understand oneself is surely more important than overcoming sorrow and conflict.

How does the 'me' arise? A. Gesele, the psychologist, has observed the development of the self in children at various stages in the early years of life. He says:

> *Up to eighteen months of age, the child is self-engrossed but not self-aware, since he does not very clearly recognize the 'not-self'. At two years, he begins to use self-reference words, 'mine', 'me', 'you', 'I', in that order. At three years of age, the idea of 'persons' becomes clear. At five and six the child begins to see even in terms of individual qualities.*

It is necessary to see the whole movement of the 'me', the 'self', the 'what I am' non-analytically so that in the very observation itself there can be instant understanding. If you see the action of the 'me' which is in relationship, the seeing itself is the ending of the 'me'. This seeing frees one from the conditioning of the 'me'. It is an interesting fact that the brain is the result of time: it is conditioned to protect itself physically; but when it tries to protect itself psychologically, then the 'me' begins, and our misery starts. It is this effort to protect itself psychologically that is the affirmation of the 'me'. Knowledge acquired psychologically by the brain, it asserts itself in relationship as the 'me' with its experiences, its will, its violence. And then comes division, conflict and sorrow in relationships.

There are various concepts about how the psyche, the ego, the self, the 'me'-person has come into being; and all perhaps have in them certain facts, which together constitute the self. Where there is any kind of possession there must be the beginning of the self. And, from this reaction, this instinct, the self gradually increases in strength and vitality and soon becomes well established. The gradual increase in possessions gives the feeling of separations as an individual.

It is a basic fact that the self is put together by thought (intellect), which is not an individual possession. Thought is the content of the impersonal Consciousness. It is the Consciousness which has identified itself through intellect as the individual 'me'-self. For this reason, too, the 'me' can never become a better 'me'. It is this self, this separative self-centred activity which imagines that one day it will make itself something that it is not. What is to be understood is that there is no 'becoming' of the self; there can only happen the ending of selfishness, of anxiety, of pain and sorrow, which are the context of the psyche, the 'me'. There is only the ending of all that, and most importantly, *such ending is not a matter of duration*. It is actually a matter of apperceiving that there never was a 'me' as the doer of any deed, and such apperception is of the moment, never any duration.

The cause of all conflict, anxiety is the belief – a wrong one – that an action happens as a result of someone doing something. Actually, as the Buddha has put it so succinctly: 'Events happen, deeds are done, but there is no individual doer of any deed.'

Relationships between human beings are based on the image forming and a defensive mechanism to protect oneself from the action of the 'other'. In all our relationships each one of us builds an image about the other and these two images have relationship, not the human beings themselves. The images are fictitious and one cannot live in an abstraction. All our relationships – whether they be with property, ideas or people, are based *essentially* on this image-forming, and hence there is always conflict, at all levels of being.

To observe ourselves without the image of personal doership

– which is the past, our accumulated experience and knowledge – happens very rarely, but when this does happen, there is a state of mind that is wholly alone and pure – not in isolation – in stillness. And such stillness is purity, beauty without the corruption of any image-forming.

It is only when we see anything or anyone without any pre-conception, without any previous image, that we can be in direct contact with anything in life. All our relationships are actually imaginary, based on images formed by thought. It is only when we understand the true relationship between each other, *based on non-doership*, that there is absence of any guilt and shame for one's own supposed action, and absence of hatred and malice, jealously and envy towards the 'other'. Such a clean, innocent relationship – possible only on the basis of non-doership – may be termed peace, tranquillity, love.

The accumulations, the stored up memories – all based on personal doership – are indeed the 'me' and the 'other'. It is this sense of personal doership that makes the 'me', the ego, the self build a wall around itself. It is the sense of personal activity of the 'me' that leads to isolation. Becoming aware of its isolation, it begins to identify itself with anything other than the 'other' doer: with virtue, with good deeds, with an ideology. And such identification, with anything other than the 'other' causes further isolation, which means escape from the present moment. If one wishes to be free from sorrow, one must stop running away from the What-is, and this can happen only with the *total* acceptance that no one does any deed, that everything is a happening, depending on the Cosmic Law.

It is an interesting fact that sorrow, memory, the thought of 'me', everyone of them, all belong to time, and when we happen to stay in the present moment – when one is attending to some-thing with the working mind totally engrossed in what is being done, something extraordinarily pure and beautiful happens: the 'me' is absent. In fact, the 'me' – even as *mere* identification with a name and form – exists only in relationship with the 'other'. Therefore, when time is absent, and the 'other' is absent, the 'me' cannot exist either. There is only the present moment and the 'Presence'. It is only the arising of thought – and the arising of the 'me' together with the thought – that destroys the present moment and the 'Presence'. In other words, when the 'me', the spiritual seeker is absent, there can never be any question of any confusion: the 'me' as the seeker-doer IS the confusion. The only way to avoid confusion is to avoid thinking – horizontal thinking by the 'me'. Simply being aware of the arising of the horizontal thinking – the confusion – removes the confusion.

Unnecessary confusion

Most masters have clearly stated that it is necessary for the spiritual seeker to keep the body *reasonably* fit and healthy for the spiritual effort to have the maximum effect. They have also warned that it is as much necessary not to pamper the body, but to try to control it as much as necessary.

And then you come across, in the daily newspaper, the pronouncements of a half-baked guru, and you are amused. They are:

1 'The human body is the temple of God. You have to take great care of your body.'

2 'There is no point in subjecting your body to torture (through various disciplines) – *since God dwells within*, you must take good care of it and protect it.'

3 'When your body is *well cared for*, you experience great and divine love in it … great divinity dwells in this very structure, in this very system.'

4 'This body is a gift – so you have to understand that it is not

really yours. Once you understand that it is a gift of love from God, your attitude towards it will change for the better.'

5 'Instead of putting your body down, through meditation you elevate yourself and develop healthy feelings *towards yourself*.'

6 'The body has to be strong for you to experience joy and self-esteem.'

7 'If you care for the body with great love, with great joy, as the gift you have received from God, *it will reveal the Truth to you*.'

8 'When you see the light in this body, that very light will provide you with shelter and security.'

9 'When you respect the body ... it becomes one with the universe; there is no wall when you see another person, only love throbs between you.'

And then, my amusement turned to amazement when I gathered that the writer was the head of a prosperous, million-dollar ashram!

Satchitananda

The Hindu concept of *satchitananda* can create considerable confusion unless it is clearly understood. Unfortunately, it is usually explained in a way that cannot avoid confusion.

As the 'swami' has tried to explain it, 'Hey, I'm in Nirvana!' We talk like this when we feel good. But what is it like to actually attain Nirvana, otherwise known as moksha or Self-realization?' This very question raises the hopes of the seeker that the supreme state of Self-realization means 'happiness' of the kind and of the intensity that one has never experienced in life. Surely, thinks the spiritual seeker, such happiness compared with which, sexual orgasm must be nothing!

There is a joke about this misconception. Every Sunday afternoon, four philosophers used to meet for lunch. One Sunday, one of the philosophers announced: 'Last night God appeared to me in my dream and offered me total happiness or total knowledge. I, of course, chose total knowledge.' Promptly, the other three, with great expectation, said: 'Come on, come on, tell us all about it.' Came the answer: 'I'm afraid, it was the wrong choice.'

'*Satchitananda*' is supposed to be the ultimate state of Self-realization. *Sat* is existence; *chit* is Consciousness. In this state of *satchit*, what is supposed to happen is the condition of *ananda*: supreme bliss, *pure and permanent bliss and joy*. This is what causes the confusion. The confusion arises because the very basis of life and living in phenomenality is not clearly understood. Life can never be anything other than a mix of both pleasure and pain – one thing one moment and the other the next moment. Pleasure and pain go together not because, as the 'swami' explains, 'The world is imperfect and man also is imperfect'! Pain and pleasure go together because the basis of manifestation, and its functioning that we call 'life' and 'living', is the existence at any moment of both the polaric counterparts – interdependent opposites – of every conceivable kind, beginning with male and female. The 'swami' suggests: 'For real and permanent happiness one needs to rise above petty desires and seek Ultimate Reality. There is supreme bliss and satisfaction there – an indescribable joy and peace.'

The poor misguided 'swami' does not realize that 'bliss', (or 'joy') and 'peace' cannot go together: 'bliss' or 'joy' is in the moment and cannot be but momentary, whereas peace is the anchor which the Self-realized being has, while facing life from moment to moment. This is the unfortunate confusion. As Ramana Maharshi has declared: 'Peace is much higher than joy.' A sage cannot live his life in phenomenality – no one can – if he is in 'permanent bliss'. But a sage can and does live his life, anchored in peace and harmony, while facing life, like everyone else, from moment to moment.

To crown his total misconception of the whole matter of Self-realization, the 'swami' declares:

Whichever the figure (of Self-realized people), I have little doubt that most of them are from India.

As my young, modern grandson studying in the USA said, 'Holy shit.'

Confusion for the spiritual seeker cannot arise if the conceptual basic principles in the happening of the manifestation – and the functioning of that manifestation that we call 'life' and living – are deeply engraved on his psyche. They are:

1 Phenomenal manifestation is the activization of the Noumenal Potential Primal Energy-Source-Consciousness – or by whatever name known; when the energy generated by the 'Big Bang' exhausts itself, sometime or the other, the activized manifestation will go back into the potential, until a similar happening happens in due course.

2 The totality of the phenomenal manifestation is the total of all the three-dimensional objects of every conceivable type or species, for example, a stone, a growing plant, an animal, a human being. All are part of the totality of manifestation, all basically three-dimensional objects.

3 Whatever happens at any moment to any manifested object can happen – in fact, according to the principle of pre-determination, whatever has happened in the eternal picture – can only be according to a conceptual Cosmic Law which has been in operation from day one till eternity. No one can ever possibly know the basics of this impersonal Cosmic Law.

4 The Creator – Energy or Consciousness or God or Whatever – has infused in the three-dimensional object called the human being: (a) life-animus as an animal, with senses, with sentience or active consciousness which is the functional element functioning through the senses of the animal; (b) mind-intellect which creates the ego-identification with a particular body and name as a separate entity with the sense of volition or personal doership.

5 The basis of the functioning of manifestation is duality: the existence at any moment of both the polaric counterparts of every conceivable kind, beginning with male and female and going on to the dualities like beauty and ugliness, good and evil, health and illness, ignorance and knowledge, light and darkness, etc. The sage is a sage because he has accepted this fact; he has realized that his own programming is a combination of several positive and negative elements, that he himself cannot be a perfect human being, nor can anyone else, and therefore is able to accept whatever happens without too much of a critical eye and without too much judgement. In other words, he is able to accept the What-is in the moment without any difficulty.

   The ordinary person, on the other hand, is not generally able to accept this duality as the basis of life and living, views everything with a very critical eye and prefers one against the other among the many dualities in life. And is, therefore, usually dissatisfied and frustrated and generally unhappy.

   In other words, the sage lives his life having accepted the duality as the basis of life, with a very tolerant attitude and is, therefore, generally at peace, contented and tranquil. The ordinary person on the other hand lives in *dualism*, continuously comparing and judging, wanting one thing in preference to the other. And is, therefore, discontented, disgruntled, unhappy, confused.

6 An aspect of the basis of life that is not clearly understood is the uncertainty in life. No one can know what the next moment will bring – pain or pleasure – and no one can avoid it either. Spiritual seeking has nothing to do with this. Not realizing this, many a seeker has wasted considerable time and effort in going to some godman or other hoping to lessen such pain – physical or psychological or financial. Actually this really cannot be called 'spiritual' seeking at all but considerable confusion is caused by not understanding this aspect of life. The best of sages have had to bear the suffering of such pain themselves. If this is understood, considerable confusion and frustration could be avoided.

If one does any kind of spiritual effort with the object of lessening one's suffering of this kind, it is bound to end in frustration, and confusion too. There is the case of a prominent politician who regally announced that he had 'lost his faith in God' because, before leaving on a journey, his wife had visited a particular, famed temple, and yet during that journey, she had died in an accident. There was another spiritual seeker who was proud of the fact that he had never missed even a single day's pooja of just about an hour every day. Then one day, his only son died. He bravely accepted this fact, and adopted a relative as a son. This adopted son, too, met with an accidental death. This fact so confused and frustrated him, that he went to the pooja room, collected all the god figures in a piece of cloth and threw them in the well (this was sometime ago, in a village), and thereafter never did any pooja himself, nor did he attend any pooja, ever.

This is one aspect of life, a spiritual seeker would ignore at his own peril: everything is predetermined, and no one can reduce the pain, or increase the pleasure, that has been assigned to him by the Creator, according to a Cosmic Law.

7   The Buddha had announced: 'Enlightenment means the end of suffering.' This could cause a certain amount of confusion if it is not clearly understood that the 'suffering' referred to by the Buddha was not the day-to-day pain and grief, but the suffering caused to an individual by his belief in volition and free will, by his belief that all action happening through his body is his action, for the consequences of which he himself was responsible. This suffering is the load of guilt and shame for one's own actions, and the load of hatred and malice, jealousy and envy one feels towards the 'other' for his actions. Only the full and total acceptance of non-doership – there is no individual doer of any action – would remove this kind of suffering.

Finally, there is the ultimate question: what precisely does a spiritual seeker want? The answer is clear: what he wants is to be anchored in peace and harmony while facing life from moment to moment. This is where the spiritual seeker's seeking ends. But ultimately, the question could remain: with the mind settled, most of the time, in peace and tranquillity, is that the end of the seeking? The answer, again, is: yes. Yet again the enquiry continues: the seeker's seeking has ended. But is there something beyond the seeker's seeking that could happen in that state of contentment, peace and tranquillity, that is unknown to the seeker? This really is a most absorbing question: the state of the mind.

   The human mind is perhaps the most mysterious and interesting thing in the universe with which the human being is primarily concerned. Perhaps the most outstanding characteristic of the human mind is its lack of stillness and silence. This is because the mind is like a machine which is constantly 'on', everlastingly busy whether awake or asleep. Even when we are alone by ourselves, not engaged in anything specific, what happens? There is hardly ever any stillness, silence. We talk to ourselves, actually uttering words without any audible sounds, silently vocal. We also see images, even with closed eyes, entertaining things, events, persons in the mind, and this is how the perennial conflict begins between opposing desires and urges.

The restless mind is ready to be influenced by anything that attracts its nature, the programming in the organism. There is actually no basic difference between the so-called religious person whose mind is occupied with the 'higher values' like virtue or God, and the ordinary man whose mind is occupied with money, fame, wine or women. The one will be generally regarded as a holy man, an extraordinary being, whereas the man who is concerned with material, worldly matters will be regarded as just an ordinary man like the rest of us. But the pertinent point is that in both cases the mind is occupied: what the mind is occupied with is not relevant. Can the occupied mind ever be able to receive something 'new'? It is absolutely essential for the mind to be vacant, to be empty, and to be unoccupied to be able to move into unknown depths, into untrodden spaces. Only out of this emptiness of the mind can anything fresh, creative arise.

There is no space in the structure of the mind, as it normally is, for the simple reason that it is too crowded with fears, hopes based on the future. Only when there is silence, stillness can there be immense, timeless space. Only then can there be a possibility of coming upon that which can be considered as the sacred, the eternal, the real. This can happen only when there is total freedom from the perpetual dualism between 'What-is' and 'What-should-be'. This can happen only when one is completely alone – not isolated – when 'one' is all there is, representing all humanity. This can happen only when there is an awakening of intelligence that events happen, deeds are done, but that there never has been an individual doer of any deed.

Throughout the world, human beings are constantly seeking security and the very basis of phenomenal living is insecurity. In this seeking after security, an illusion, one is caught in certain patterns of belief, dogma, ideology, the same belief from childhood, the same traditional rituals. We get attached to people, to ideas, to symbols or concepts because in them we seem to find some sort of security.

Once one is able to accept that there is really no such thing as security in life – to realize that psychologically there can be nothing permanent – gives one a totally different approach to life. No one can deny that it is essential to try to have outward security – food, clothing and shelter – but it is absolutely necessary to see very clearly that the outward security has nothing to do with psychological security. One can try to discipline the mind, control it, shape it but such torture does not make the mind quiet. As it clearly mentioned by Lord Krishna, in the *Bhagavad Gita*:

> *Even for a wise man, the energy within the body-mind organism produces actions according to his own natural characteristics. All living creatures follow their natural tendencies. What is the use of any external control or restraint?*

(III. 33)

It is only when you really observe and listen, out of silence, that the mind can be quiet. It is not something you can cultivate, because it is not the product of time or of effort or of comparison. It is clearly the product of observation in daily living, the observation of your thoughts and the understanding of thought. It is only when the mind is totally aware, passively aware, that it can be extraordinarily silent, quiet – not stagnant but highly awake in that silence. Such a mind is, of course capable of using the experience of the past, but it has actually left the past – and the future – completely.

If you really want to understand something, there suddenly arises a quietness in the mind; when you wanted to listen to music or look again at a painting you have loved, you will have noticed that there has arrived suddenly a deep quietness of mind. In that alert yet passive state of mind, there is receptivity, understanding.

So long as the mind is in conflict, condemning, blaming someone – oneself or the 'other' – for some happening or other there can be no understanding, no transformation. It is only in the passive awareness of the mind that regeneration can happen – transformation, revolution, total apperception.

Here again, there is a specific area for confusion: a still mind does not mean concentration of mind, but rather freedom, self-knowledge and deep silence. A mind that is sought to be made still through meditation, through compulsion, through conformity, through ritualistic discipline, is not a still mind but a dull mind. The mind that can be open to fresh creation has to be, on the other hand, not a dull, stagnant mind but a mind that is very very attentive, very much aware of every thought, word and feeling which reveals our innermost natural state. This is the real confusion.

Concentration means exclusion, and therefore, distraction: there is a constant conflict going on when you are trying to concentrate on something while you mind flies off in various directions. Meditation truly does not mean a seeking, a probing, an exploration. It does not mean taming of the brain to conform to a discipline, nor is it a self-analytical introspection. On the contrary, meditation must happen naturally; thought happens naturally, and all that needs is a very keen awareness of the thought as it appears and disappears. Out of such awareness of thought, arises keen all-inclusive attention, not concentration and exclusion. It is attention that is open to stillness and silence, leading to something creative, something sacred, something infinitely holy, whereas concentration is a process that causes the mind to build a wall to stop other thoughts arising.

It is so very necessary to see the clear distinction between true meditation which brings about the natural state of mind, the *Sahajavastha* of Patanjali. It comes into being when there is a clear understanding, an apperception that naturally overcomes all wanting and desire, including the desire for personal emancipation.

True meditation brings about at times the most refreshing feeling of lightness, and sometimes, its depth is beyond measure. Its very essence is extraordinary freedom, without the slightest desire to possess any recollection or experience. Meditation simply cannot be any private personal pleasure or experience. It is freedom itself in its essence.

The total acceptance of non-doership leads to the acceptance of What-is, leads to a state of mind in which there is no dualism of any kind; on the other hand, there is a total negation of the past, of the tradition, so that the mind becomes very keenly aware of the present moment, without any choice, without any distortion, without any resentment, bitterness. The mind is totally free to *receive* the Truth, the sacred, the unknown.

It is important to realize that an experience is not Reality. Considerable confusion has been caused by the concept that experience is the final authority for the acceptance of a concept, but the fact of the matter is that Reality and Truth cannot be experienced. It is What-is. All knowledge or experience is only an illusion. As has been said, 'Knowledge bends experience and experience shapes knowledge.' Also, there is the fact of what is known as 'virtual reality' which again confirms the fact that what seems like Reality, what is apparently experienced as Reality could well be an illusion. Many people have been led astray by chasing an experience and have ended in awful frustration. The only Reality is the What-is, in which there is no preference; it includes both the polaric counterparts of every conceivable kind.

In our educational system we are hardly ever taught to look at life impartially – just looking impartially at the various happenings in our daily living, just observing them without a critical, judgemental attitude – witnessing – can be an astonishingly beautiful and fruitful happening. This is what can lead to what may be called 'fulfilment' – transcending the background of tradition, habit and prejudice, which is actually what constitutes confusion and suffering for the spiritual seeker. A mind filled with beliefs, conclusions, previous experience cannot be receptive to the truth of any matter.

The fact of the matter is that the mind that would have genuine insight, penetration, discernment, must necessarily be very clear, without any distortions or prejudices or ready-made conclusions. A mind capable of insight must necessarily be free from escapes, free from suppression. Freedom implies an emptiness to observe. It is only this emptiness, this vacancy that can bring about insight. The mind has become conditioned to be aware of only those things, events or facts that stand out distinctly from their background. If there is no discrepancy or anything special or different, then the mind is conditioned to ignore it. It is this very conditioning that one needs to be fully aware of, for the insight to happen.

For the mind to be free of all its burden of distinctions and prejudices, it is absolutely essential for the mind to accept *totally* – not just intellectually – that events happen, deeds are done but that there is no individual doer of any deed. This view has received unqualified support not only from mystics for hundreds of years but, for some time now, even from the most honoured physicists, including the famous mathematician, Stephen Hawking, that everything is 'predetermined'. If everything is predetermined, everything has already happened (as Lord Krishna says in the *Bhagavad Gita*), then no one does anything. But each one has to test the concept of non-doership in the fire of his own experience for the concept to turn into Truth for him.

If the concept of non-doership is accepted totally, then the mind becomes totally free of any guilt or shame for one's own apparent actions, and also totally free from any sense of hatred and malice, jealously and envy for the 'other'. In other words, the mind becomes totally free and vacant, so that whatever happens is merely witnessed, without blaming anyone for anything. When something is happening, it is merely witnessed – the mind is in a witnessing state. If at any moment, there is nothing to be witnessed, the state of mind would be what may be called the non-witnessing state. And if, for any reason, the non-witnessing state is not disturbed, it would go into a deeper state that could be called an impersonal Awareness, in which the separate entity all but disappears. And that must be the deepest kind of Awareness in which there is no vestige of the ego, which has already lost its sense of personal doership, and has thus become what Ramana Maharshi called 'the remnants of a burnt rope', totally harmless and ineffective.

It is interesting – and instructive – to observe clearly the actuality of our living. What the actuality of our living amounts to is trying to escape from What-is, and it is this that causes pain and sorrow in life, and turns life into a constant struggle and conflict: the ambition, the search for fulfilment, gaining and losing an argument, and, of course, the endless pursuit of pleasure. What many of us do is to try to escape from this What-is into its opposite, which is sometimes called religion or spirituality.

It is strange that we do not realize that escaping from the What-is can never be successful. However hard we may try to escape from ourselves, the conflict, the pain and the pleasure, the basic fear and so on never leave us; they surface again and again. The fact of the matter is that the problem cannot have a solution: the solution itself has an opposite! The only answer is to face the problem itself, to analyse it truly objectively, without any personal conditioning: one simply cannot escape from life. The very basics of the phenomenal manifestation – and its functioning that is 'life' as we know it – is the existence of polaric counterparts, or interconnected opposites all the time. If we keep on choosing one against the other all the time, we are bound to be frustrated. 'What-should-be' simply does not exist. All there is, is 'What-is'. It is this 'What-is' that we must comprehend in its totality, not creating the opposite, or escaping from it. It is this effort to escape from the reality of What-is that causes enormous confusion.

Another cause of confusion in the spiritual seeking – as in all seeking – is the fact that most of us, most of the time, do not listen totally; nor do we see, observe something with totality. If we are listening to a concept being detailed by a speaker, how often do we listen totally? What actually happens is that while we think we are listening – or observing – our mind is so busy, *at the same time*, refuting it or collecting arguments against it. Total listening can happen only when the mind is quiet; only when there is no intervening screen of our own previous convictions and prejudices, only when the mind is in a state of 'alert passivity', in a state of sensitivity. This does not mean allowing ourselves to be brainwashed. In fact the concept we are listening to needs to be tested thoroughly in the fire of our own experience, but not while we are listening to it. This is really important, in order to avoid confusion.

A serious cause of confusion is the fact that we take 'fragmentation' as the basic fact of life. It is not. We may have to divide the whole into parts in order to study each part separately, but it is a total mistake to take separation as the basis of life. The moment one says one is a Hindu or a Muslim and keeps thinking in that perspective, one forgets that one is being constantly conditioned wrongly. Similarly, fragmentation happens when there is a *continuous* comparison with the 'the other'. Unfortunately, measuring ourselves against something or someone has been the basis of most systems of education. To avoid confusion, it is absolutely essential to understand – and keep in mind – that fragmentation is not the essence of 'What-is' or Reality.

It must be clearly understood, therefore, that the problem is not how to get rid of classes or sects, but to understand that it is the mind or thinking or conceptualizing which brings about fragmentation. It is this passive awareness of things as they are – the highest form of true intelligence, true wisdom – without the fragmentation, that brings about peace and harmony in our daily living. Such peace, the absence of fragmentation, is the source of spontaneous action, the most effective action.

It is generally accepted that the real creator of the problems is the 'me' in relation to the 'other', but it is not realized that it is the process of thinking, of conceptualizing that creates the 'me'. When there is no conceptualizing, no distinguishing, no fragmentation, there is no 'me'. The stillness of the mind, the source of spontaneous action, has its own creative understanding of 'What-is', for the very reason that in the still, quiet mind, where there is no movement of thought, there is no observer, no experiencer, no 'me'. The 'me' is the accumulation of past experiences, memories of the past, a totally worthless collection of mental garbage.

What causes the mind to stray from its stillness, its silence? Not 'desires' as you may be inclined to think. A little investigation will reveal that the 'desire' itself – the arising of a thought, a desire – is not in anyone's control, not the ordinary person, nor the sage. *It is the pursuit of the desire that brings out the 'me' into action,* in the case of the ordinary person. The sage witnesses the desire arising in his body-mind organism. If the desire is satisfied, as part of What-is, the sage has no hesitation in enjoying the pleasure *to the full* (and hence is known as *Mahabhogi*, super enjoyer) but if the desire is not fulfilled, he does not pursue it. He accepts that the satisfaction of that particular desire is not part of 'What-is' in the moment, and does not pursue it – as the ordinary person does.

It is only the negation of the past conditioning, with its tradition and its discipline and its authority that means freedom – freedom to die to the moment, freedom from the doership of the 'me'.

Finally, the area of the deepest confusion is perhaps the notion or concept of 'time'. This is because it is not clearly recognized that there are, basically, two distinct kinds of time: (1) time by the clock: this 'time' is obviously a necessary part of the mechanism of living; (2) psychological 'time', created by thought or conceptualizing: I must do this; I must achieve that. There is only chronological 'time', all else is deception created by the thinking mind.

The 'me', the thinking mind, the experiencer, coming in after the experience of the present moment, creates 'time' wanting to continue the experience if it is pleasant, or hoping that the night-marish experience will not happen in the future. So 'time' is considered as a means of evolving into something better. It is absolutely necessary to realize that 'time' cannot bring about trans-formation, and in so thinking, we are only avoiding the 'What-is', the only Reality, in the present moment. There is psychological 'time' only when one moves away from the 'What-is'.

In order to avoid confusion and frustration, it is absolutely necessary to understand that there is really no psychological 'time' at all. The religious, the evolutionary books have told us that we need time to improve, to change from What-is to What-should-be. The distance is time, and we have unfortunately been following this pattern blindly, without questioning. Hence the confusion, the frustration, the pain in life.

The understanding, the Self-realization, can never come tomorrow. It can only be now or never. In fact, there is no 'never', only 'now'.

It is only when the mind-heart is free from the burden of pride and arrogance, and guilt and shame on account of one's own deeds, and also free from the burden of hatred and malice towards the 'other' for his deeds, that the mind-heart can be open and receptive to that experience in which you are steadily anchored. In fact that experience then turns out not to be an experience but in fact our true nature. This real experience is indeed a harmonious blending of the head and the heart, when the mind-heart becomes pure, with the removal of the dirt of personal doership.

The different fields in which the human being has his experiences are: (1) thinking, (2) doing, (3) perceiving, (4) feeling. These experiences keep changing from moment to moment, but the one experience, constant without any change, is the changeless experience of the 'I AM principle', the screen on which the other experiences appear and disappear. With this deep understanding the sage ignores the fleeting experiences and stays anchored at the central I AM experience, in peace, harmony and contentment, in beauty and love.

When the thinking-doing-perceiving feeling disappears, the apparent thinker-doer-perceiver-feeler also disappears, and I remain as pure Consciousness. The ignorant person, in his confusion, believes that the body-mind lives, while in fact it dies at the end of every perception, thought, feeling or action. It is the I AM principle that continues unchanged throughout this process.

The fact of the matter is that that I AM principle and the manifest phenomenal 'reality' can only be the One and not two. The actual 'Reality' is neither the known nor the unknown, but the basis of both. In other words, the subjective I AM and the objective manifestation are one and the same.

THE SAGE ALSO HAS AN EGO

RAMESH Yes, Ronald. What's on your mind? Something we talked about yesterday?

RONALD Not something we talked about yesterday. Actually it's more about the past twelve years. It seems that the search started with the search for quietus, no movement. That's what I was aiming for, that was what was attracting me …

RAMESH What you were aiming for was quietness of mind? Peace? Harmony?

RONALD Yes, eventually it definitely was peace of mind. That's the word for it. And I joined this philosophical school in Holland which, after some time, appeared to be a sort of Advaita school. I didn't know that in the beginning.

RAMESH Do you remember the name of the school?

RONALD It is the School of Economic Science in English. And in Holland it is called the School of Philosophy. It has a direct link with the Shankaracharya.

RAMESH I see. And this was how long ago?

RONALD It started tewlve years ago. And it was very hard work. Lot of practising, exercises, meditation … lot of volition, I think you would call it. But there were some very clear experiences of peace of mind.

RAMESH Can you give me an example please, Ronald?

RONALD These experiences occurred while working in the gardens, during those exercises … but they were always temporary. So on the one hand, it was very inviting, very stimulating for me. On the other hand, looking at the people, looking at myself, I realized, 'You have nothing to tell!' That was very clear. That was one thing that meditation told me … it told me that I have nothing to say. There can be very nice experiences of peace of mind but you never know when they come or how they come …

RAMESH One moment. 'Experiences' and 'peace of mind', according to my concept, are totally different. Experiencing is in the moment. Peace of mind is not in the moment. Peace of mind, according to my concept, is a sort of anchor. You are anchored in peace while facing life from moment to moment. You are anchored in peace and harmony while having experiences from moment to moment. And, the experience can be good or not good, pleasant or not pleasant. So while you are experiencing whatever the moment brings there is still a feeling of being anchored in peace.

RONALD Well, definitely it was not an anchor. I would perhaps call it an experience of peace. So that's one thing meditation taught me … that it's not providing you that anchor.

RAMESH In other words, what meditation gave you was a sample of what could be had.

RONALD Exactly. That was the motivating part of it, very invigorating. But at some moment it became clear that, exactly like you say, it was not an anchor. And this organisation, the School of Philosophy, was very volitional and there was a lot of hierarchy in organizing things and there were spiritual-level hierarchies right up to the Shankaracharya. But then something else happened. About four years ago, there was an experience which came as a result of an exercise. It was very brief yet it brought about a complete change in the way I looked at things. It happened suddenly while I was driving my car. I felt as if I was driving through myself. The whole world was you, me. And it was not conceptual; it was not thought about or created.

RAMESH What you are saying is, it was an experience, not something imagined. I accept it. So it was an experience.

RONALD And it disappeared.

RAMESH How long would you say it lasted?

RONALD It lasted at least ten minutes and gradually disappeared. And it was so completely different from anything I had known before, it was a total change of perception. And ever since it gave me the idea – as you have said somewhere in your books – 'I exist as phenomenal absence but the phenomenal experience is myself.' And I have the idea that the latter part of that sentence is what I experienced. But the first part was not there. Because I was still there. I was having the experience.

RAMESH The absolutely basic point, Ronald, is that at any moment one or the other can be present. If the 'me' is present, 'I' as the impersonal Awareness cannot be present.

RONALD One or the other ...

RAMESH Yes, one or the other. In deep sleep Ronald is never there. And yet when Ronald wakes up he is able to say, 'I slept well,' or 'I did not sleep well.' Therefore when Ronald was not there in deep sleep there was something present and that was the impersonal Awareness. It was still that same impersonal Awareness which became the personal Awareness in the waking state.

RONALD Becoming personally aware or being personally aware I can still experience the world as myself.

RAMESH Yes! But the point is, one or the other. Ronald as identified Awareness can never be aware of the impersonal Awareness. In other words, Ronald sitting down cannot at the same time be Ronald standing up. Same Ronald, same Consciousness – but either impersonal or personal.

RONALD I understand you when you have this line in your book. 'I exist as phenomenal absence …' It's either that part or …

RAMESH The understanding is, what exists in my absence is the absence of 'me' as an independent individual entity. So What-is is my absence, absence of the 'me'. One or the other. Either 'I' or 'me'. And having understood, having truly accepted that, the 'me' stops chasing the 'I'. Which, in your case, is what had not happened. That's where the frustration comes from. Ronald the 'me' wants to be or experience 'I' as the Source. Can't be done. Ronald sitting down cannot be Ronald standing up. One or the other. But the understanding is, Ronald, whether sitting or standing, is the same Ronald. And what is important is the understanding. Sitting, standing, running, lying down – it is still the same Ronald. Once that understanding is there, that is all you need to have. Once the understanding is there, for practical purposes I suggest that Ronald forget it.

RONALD Sorry?

RAMESH Having understood that, I suggest that Ronald, while he is functioning in daily living as Ronald, I suggest that Ronald forget what is his real nature. Forget his real nature. Otherwise, if Ronald keeps reminding himself that he is not Ronald, he is impersonal, then Ronald will never be able to concentrate on what he is doing in the present moment. Let me give you a simple example. Ronald has a home, he has his possessions, he has someone living with him. All that is there; you will *know* that. So when you leave your home and go to your office you don't have to keep reminding yourself – that is where my home is, that is my address, that is my telephone number. You don't have to remind yourself; you know it. Similarly, when you are living your life as Ronald during the daytime I suggest that you forget your real nature. You *know* it. Where can it go, where can your home go? You know where your home is. Therefore, I suggest that you stop thinking about your real nature. Stop *thinking* about your real nature when you know that there are millions and millions of Ronalds but there is only one Source. Everybody's home is where it is. Having understood that, while I am living my life as Ramesh I don't have to remind myself. That is the real point. And the shadow chasing the substance is the whole problem. Therefore, I have never been able to accept the concept of the master telling the disciples 'never forget your real nature'. I say, forget it. But, in order to forget, you have to know it!

RONALD 'I' has to forget it.

RAMESH The 'me' has to forget the 'I'. Having understood that the 'me' functioning in this life is not truly an independent, separate entity with a sense of doership, but this 'me' functioning in life is merely a separate entity and every separate entity is a separate instrument, through which the same Source or God or Consciousness functions and brings about whatever is supposed to happen, according to the Cosmic Law. Having understood that, you let the Source function through this body-mind organism as an instrument. Consciousness functions through all the human instruments precisely as electricity functions through all the various electrical gadgets and produces what each gadget is designed to produce. So all that you have to know is that you are not doing anything. Whatever is happening through anybody is a happening that is brought about by the Source or Consciousness or God strictly the way it is supposed to happen according to the

Cosmic Law. Nobody does anything. Life is like a movie scripted by Consciousness, produced and directed by Consciousness. Every character is played by Consciousness and is being witnessed by Consciousness. The movie is already 'in the can'.

RONALD Can I go back to my experience because I think that the understanding of what you are saying, the true realization of that, should bring back that experience …

RAMESH It may, it may not. Personally I would rather not have the experience.

RONALD Rather not have the experience? You mean, you would rather not have phenomenal experiences yourself … ?

RAMESH No. The experience that 'I am not what I am, I am the Source'. Why? Because Ronald has an experience or two and since then all that Ronald has been doing is to chase that experience.

RONALD That was my fear. That and the spiritual materialism. But it was such a complete shift in perception …

RAMESH Indeed!

RONALD … that I thought I must do something. Especially because, as I realized later, this single, personal experience showed me that everything in the scriptures is true. I remember there was a sign indicating 'Amsterdam'. I was struck by it really; that you can drive within yourself and there could be a signpost pointing to something within something which is One.

RAMESH You live in Amsterdam?

RONALD Yeah.

RAMESH Amsterdam and arrow mean nothing. You don't need to have an arrow pointing to Amsterdam all day, do you? You know where Amsterdam is.

RONALD What I meant was, it was so different from usual, I thought there must be something there ... but it's not! [*Laughs.*]

RAMESH I think the experience, unless you have the right perspective, can be like a drug. You have an experience – 'I know I am not Ronald' – so Ronald keeps chasing that experience. But what I'm suggesting to Ronald is: you cannot live your life as Ronald if you have that experience all day.

RONALD Ummm ...

RAMESH So, if you have that experience, my point is, what you have is the total acceptance which does not need a perennial experience. The total acceptance that you are not the doer, everything happens through every body-mind organism, every separate entity is a separate instrument through which the same Source functions. That is the total acceptance. Once that total acceptance has happened – I am Ronald, I live in a particular place, I have this address, I have so many people living with me – then you don't have to keep it in mind. Similarly, the deep acceptance that Ronald is a separate entity, separate from billions of others but the separation refers only to the separation of the separate entity as a separate instrument. So the true understanding is: I am a separate entity and for a separate car to run the separate car has to be filled with petrol. Therefore, the separate instrument has to be fed. But it is still an instrument. So I live as a separate entity, see whatever goes on as a separate entity but with the total acceptance that the separate entity is truly only a separate instrument through which the same Source is functioning. So with that understanding, Ronald is a separate instrument, Ramesh is a separate instrument. Once that is understood there can be no question of Ramesh blaming either himself or Ronald or any of the millions of other Ronalds for something that is happening.

RONALD That's why your concept appears for the spiritual seeker in the indirect way ... appears to be. You start looking for peace, so you really work on it and you try to experience it. That seems direct whereas you are, of course, taking the direct way by cutting out the ego …

RAMESH [*Laughs.*] Now, tell me, Ronald which is the more direct method? Telling you who you are …

RONALD For the seeker, at first it appears to be indirect …

RAMESH But what I am telling you – Ronald, the spiritual seeker – is: let us go to the most direct point. What does the spiritual seeker want? Can anything be more direct? You learn that Ronald is a spiritual seeker seeking something and Ronald is told, 'Oh, you are not an individual, you are an illusion, as a part of the illusion. Understand that and keep remembering that.' So I say, '*Who* is the spiritual seeker?' Ronald! 'And who is the seeker?' *The ego!* Make no mistake!

Therefore the most direct approach I have is, who is seeking what? And you cannot get away from the direct answer that 'I', the ego identified with this body-mind organism as a separate entity, is seeking. What am I seeking? I have enough money, I have good health to enjoy everything life can give me and yet, why do I have a sense of emptiness; why do I have a sense of a lack of fulfilment; what is it I don't have in spite of having good health and all the money I need?

RONALD Yeah, that was what took me to this philosophical school …

RAMESH That is how you started but the school made you forget it.

RONALD Yeah, first it gave me motivation but then …

RAMESH How did you start, Ronald? You wanted something. So what I am saying is, let us start with that. Ronald, try to understand what it is that you want. This is as direct a method …

RONALD Is it right to say, try to understand what is required to get what I want?

RAMESH Indeed. First, go back even before that, Ronald. You want peace of mind. Now what I am saying is you have decided what you want. Second thing is, how do you know that what you want is not an illusion? That is as direct as you can get. Let me give you an instance. What do I want? I want something. Second, is it an illusion I am seeking? For example, if I decide I don't want any more pain in my life – physical, psychological or financial pain – you can't get it. So if you keep chasing someone or something to remove pain from your life altogether you are chasing an illusion. Never in a million years can Ronald expect to get it. Similarly, this peace of mind, being anchored in peace of mind, is it or is it not an illusion? And then we come to the conclusion that it is *not* an illusion. For two reasons.

One, you say to yourself, I have myself experienced that peace of mind, not as an experience of the moment but as an experience. I agree the experience didn't last, but there were certain moments of being anchored in peace. And when I had that experience of being anchored in peace, it was not that I was in the best of health. When I experienced those moments of being anchored in peace, I had a slight backache. And yet I had that feeling of being anchored in peace, which is I wanted for the whole of my life.

Two, everybody knows one or two people who have and live that peace of mind. I have it temporarily, but knowing at least one or two people who are able to live their life seemingly anchored in peace, I know it can be done or, more appropriately, it can happen. So what you are seeking is not an illusion.

Step by step. What do I want? I want this anchoring in peace. Is it an illusion? No. Then we proceed further. You say you had the experience of being anchored in peace. Why did you lose it? You had it, you say so yourself. Why did you lose it? You couldn't help it. Why couldn't you help it? What happened that made you lose that experience? Do all the investigation you want and you will come to the conclusion that a thought happened and smashed the peace. What kind of thought? Any investigation will reveal to you that the thought which smashed the peace had nothing to do with what the moment brings; it had nothing to do with the pleasure and pain of the moment. It was something much deeper. So you investigate and come to the conclusion that the thought which smashed my peace was ...

RONALD 'I have the experience, I have the peace ...'

RAMESH No, no. You have the peace, it's there. What smashed that experience is a thought of something you did to someone and hurt him or something you could have helped someone with and didn't help him ... he committed suicide, take an extreme case. In other words, what I am saying is, every single time, whenever that experience happened, that experience was smashed by a thought, a memory of something you did to hurt someone or something you did not do to help someone. Or the other way around.

RONALD Can this experience not be smashed by the thought 'I am having this experience'?

RAMESH No, because at that time you do have the feeling ... who is experiencing? It is Ronald, make no mistake. But what I am telling you is, instead of Ronald making the investigation – 'Why did I lose that?' or 'I had that experience and then I lost that. Therefore I must find it again' – instead of that, Ronald must investigate ...

RONALD I had one question. You say here and I didn't under- stand [reads from a book by Ramesh] there is no difference between What-is and What-appears.

RAMESH What I'm saying is, What-is and What-you-are-look- ing-for is peace. What appears in the moment disappears in the

248

moment. Pain and pleasure in the moment appear and disappear. Therefore, you are not really concerned with what happens in the moment. You know it comes and goes. Therefore, what you are really concerned with is to be anchored in peace when you are facing life from moment to moment. And that peace you had experienced and what shattered the peace. That is what we are investigating. That is a separate matter: Ronald having an experience, and not forgetting it and chasing something. So Ronald chasing that experience is chasing an illusion. Why? Because you didn't create that experience, that experience happened, over which Ronald had no control. Therefore chasing something over which Ronald had no control, that's what's been happening to Ronald so far. So what I'm telling Ronald is, forget the experience! Go to the root of the problem. And what is the root of the problem? It is Ronald considering himself the doer of his action and the other, the doer of *his* action, with the result that the sense of personal doership, I do what I do and you do what you do, that relationship between me and the other based on doership ...

RONALD Can I go one step back? When I said that the thought that smashed the experience was that it was me that was having the experience, you said, 'It is you who had that experience ...'

RAMESH You can't get away from it. It is Ronald who had the experience, therefore, Ronald knows that an experience has happened, therefore, it's not an illusion. I am not saying that ...

RONALD Is that what you mean by there's no difference between What-is and What-happens ...

RAMESH Yes. What-happens, as separate from, What-you-are-doing. The whole point is, everything happens. It's not anybody doing anything. And that is the core of the Buddha's teaching. I am not talking about Buddhism. The core of the Buddha's teaching is, events happen, deeds are done, and there is no individual doer of any deed. And my point is, the basis of life is the relationship between 'me' and the 'other'. Therefore, the peace of mind which I am seeking cannot happen unless the relationship between 'me' and the 'other' is smooth as marble. The relationship between 'me' and the 'other' must be smooth. Only then can the peace happen …

RONALD So you say there is a 'me' and the 'other' …

RAMESH Indeed, Ronald! Despite whatever the masters might have said! 'You don't exist!' So who the bloody hell is suffering? Me, Ronald, Ramesh is suffering. Who is the seeker? The ego is the seeker. Make no mistake. 'Begin killing the ego.' 'You don't exist.' I don't see the point in it. And millions of seekers in awful confusion, suffering because of this. The ego being told, you don't exist!

RONALD So you want to say the ego is an illusion?

RAMESH No, what I am saying is, the ego is an illusion if the entire manifestation is an illusion. So if the entire manifestation is an illusion, then I am an illusion, you are an illusion. And if we accept that, we stop. No more words, no more sops. But that can't happen. Therefore, so long as there is an ego functioning in life, let us assume that everything we are talking about is an illusion but which is actually real. So if the total acceptance is that there is no creation, all this is an illusion … if I accept everything is an illusion and we are all part of the illusion – then, no more talk! Stop talking!

RONALD Go home!

RAMESH Indeed, go home! But that is not happening. Therefore, *who* is talking to me? Who is seeking whatever he is seeking? The ego. The moment we are talking, the moment we are conceptualizing, we cannot get away from the ego. Therefore, the ego has to be accepted. But let us examine, what is the ego?

RONALD You said that the ego has to be accepted?

RAMESH Yes! The ego has to be accepted. That's what I am telling you. Now again basically what is happening here at this moment? Two egos are talking.

RONALD Two?

RAMESH Two egos … You see the amount of confusion that is happening in Ronald's case. And the confusion was such … Ronald, believe me, I could see it in your face.

RONALD Absolutely. I mean, I wouldn't dare to think you have an ego!

RAMESH You see, that's what the masters have been saying. I cannot presume that the masters didn't know what they were saying. All I can say is the masters did not make as clear, as I am trying to, what they knew.

RONALD Could you repeat that, please?

RAMESH I am not saying that the masters who said that the ego is the problem did not understand it. Maybe many of them didn't, but at least some of them must have understood exactly what they were saying but the limitations of speech made them say something without clarifying it to the extent that I am doing.

The question before Ronald is this: all the masters have said that the ego is a problem. The ego has to be destroyed. And here you are telling me, 'Accept the ego. Don't try to kill it.' And Ronald is wondering, 'Don't tell me all the masters were wrong?!' That's why I am saying that the masters were not wrong but there was a confusion between the egos of the masters and egos of the listeners. There was confusion. What is the confusion? The confusion is about the ego. What is the ego? 'Destroy the ego, kill the ego.' The master who said that didn't bother to talk about the ego itself, did he? They assumed something and … 'Kill the ego'!

In order to get rid of this confusion let us first talk about the problem. The problem is the ego. So who's talking to whom? The ego of the teacher, the ego of the student. So you say, 'Do you have an ego?' Yes, I confess I do have an ego. Then Ronald's next question would be, 'If I have an ego and you have an ego and you are supposed to be enlightened, where's the difference?' This is precisely the question the seekers have not asked their gurus. Therefore this horrible confusion.

See the point? Ronald asks me, 'I am an ego and you say you are an ego and we are talking and yet you are supposed to be enlightened and I am supposed not to be enlightened. What is the difference?' This is precisely the point, Ronald, which has never been discussed. My point is, I have an ego as much as you. So what is the common element in the two egos and what is the element which is not there? Valid question. 'I have an ego, you have an ego. You are enlightened, I am not. How come?'

RONALD It's the other way around! [*Laughter.*]

RAMESH I am talking for Ronald! [*More laughter.*]

RONALD This is absolutely my question. Yeah, you are right.

RAMESH That has been the cause of confusion. We are playing a game of cricket. I know the rules, you don't. How can we play a game of cricket? So, let's first clear the ground. Let's talk about what we are talking about. You see the question, 'Where is the difference between the seeker and the master if both have egos?' Very, very valid and most pertinent question. And the answer is, I consider myself a separate entity, I have my separate family, I have my separate possessions, I have my separate destiny exactly as you do. But the only difference is that Ronald considers that he is the doer of his actions and I don't. So what do I believe? I believe that each of us is a separate entity but none of us has the real power to do anything. I am an ego, you are an ego but the difference is, Ronald's ego thinks he is the doer of his actions, but my ego is totally convinced that no one is the doer, neither me nor you …

RONALD Neither me nor you. So, 'me' and 'you' …

RAMESH … Neither me nor you. Nor anyone else. So on what basis will the relationship between me and the other continue? On this basis: I do nothing, everything happens through me. You do nothing, everything happens through you. How can there be any problem between 'me' and the 'other'? And the whole problem in life, including the spiritual problem, is the relationship between 'me' and the 'other'. Why? Because it is the relationship between 'me' and the 'other' which is the cause of enormous hatred. I do something, I remember doing something which I should not have done and since that moment I hate myself. You did something you shouldn't have done and you hurt me, therefore, I hate you. So, in most cases, in almost all cases, Ronald, the relationship between 'me' and the 'other' is based on hatred – hatred of oneself, hatred of the other – most of the time. With this total understanding, that no one does anything, in order to live my life in society, I have to accept responsibility for my actions as far as the society is concerned …

RONALD What I seem to be doing is forgetting this point of not being the doer …

RAMESH Therefore, the entire problem is the problem of doership. The problem is not that we are all an illusion. The real is real. How does it help the ego of the seeker to be told, 'You don't exist. Nothing exists.' So what I am saying is, 'Yes, we do exist, as independent entities. But we are independent entities as independent instruments through which life is happening.'

RONALD Does that mean that you experience the group here as about twenty individual, separate egos?

RAMESH Yes, indeed. Have no confusion. I do indeed consider each of us a separate entity. I do not pretend to say, 'Oh, we are all One.' I don't. We are all separate entities through which the

One functions. We are all separate entities, separate instruments through which the One operates.

RONALD And if I go back to this last part of this sentence, I exist, the phenomenal appearance is myself …

RAMESH Myself, as the ego. Therefore, let me go back. Ronald has an ego, Ramesh has an ego. Where's the difference? Ramesh's ego has been able to accept totally that he is not capable of doing the simplest thing. Whereas Ronald says, how can I live if I am not responsible for my actions? That to me, Ronald, is the only difference. This ego has been able to accept totally that no one does anything. Whereas Ronald has firmly accepted that each one is a doer and responsible for his or her action. So the result of Ronald's thinking that everybody is a separate doer is that all the time, every moment he is judging someone or the other. Every moment something happens, he is judging himself and hates himself, he judges the other and hates him too. Whereas, having accepted that 'I don't do anything neither does Ronald', therefore immediately with this understanding I stop blaming either you or me.

RONALD That point seems very clear. But, still, what do you mean when you say that the phenomenal appearance is myself …

RAMESH I am Ramesh, I have my own home, I have my own property, I have my own family, I am interested in my son succeeding. I would also like your son to succeed but if they are in competition, I would like my son to succeed. [*Laughter.*] Make no mistake. That is as separate as I can be, isn't it Ronald?

What I am saying is, who is talking to me? One ego is talking to me. Ego is identification with a particular body-mind organism as a separate entity. Therefore 'me' is talking to the 'other'. Two egos talking to each other. And ego is merely the sense of identification with a particular body-mind organism and a particular name as a separate entity …

SWAMIJI When this system dies … ?

RAMESH Then when this body-mind organism dies, the ego dies with it.

SWAMIJI So there is no reincarnation?

RAMESH You tell me who is to be reincarnated?

SWAMIJI I am asking you, Sir …

RAMESH I am saying, this body dies and the ego dies, nothing remains. So if you want to tell me, some soul goes … okay, then, *you* know about the soul, I don't.

SWAMIJI Suppose I murder someone and I am not caught in this lifetime and I die without being punished. Nothing is going to happen? The whole system collapses there and everything stops because the ego has died with the body?

RAMESH The body dies, the ego dies. That is my simple concept.

SWAMIJI There is no karma?

RAMESH As far as I am concerned, there is no beyond for the ego. Because the ego is no longer there.

SWAMIJI But you quote Buddha and Krishna. If I am not wrong, they did believe in this philosophy of karma and reincarnation. Could you elaborate on what they meant … ?

RAMESH I cannot know what somebody meant. I cannot explain what somebody said. I can only tell you what I am saying.

SWAMIJI Right, right. But sometimes you do quote Buddha, like 'Deeds happen, and there is no individual …'

RAMESH The Buddha said something, I quote it to you. But I cannot know what Buddha thought!

Swamiji So you do not know about this philosophy of karma? What Krishna and Buddha meant?

Ramesh First of all, you used the word karma. What do you understand by the word karma, Swamiji?

Swamiji Karma means ...

Ramesh Karma means action.

Swamiji Right.

Ramesh Karma simply means action. And what I am saying is, an action happens. Action happens because the Source creates that action through a particular body-mind organism according to His will or Cosmic Law and the body-mind organism through which that action happens has nothing to do with the action. It is the Source that creates the action. *Twameva karta, Twameva harta, Twameva bhogta* ... You are the doer, You are the saviour, You are the experiencer.

Swamiji In my understanding, karma is not simply the action. Karma also implies the effect of these actions and if the body-mind organism is wiped out for some reason ...

Ramesh And that implication I don't have.

Swamiji Okay, sure, sure ...

Ramesh The implication that 'I am doing', that is exactly the thing I have totally got rid of.

Swamiji Okay. And do you have any thoughts about '*Brahma satyam, jagan mithya, jeevo brahmeya naparaha* ...'? If you could comment on this ...

Ramesh All I know is, that at the basis of it there is no creation, therefore no dissolution ...

SWAMIJI But in the moment, you are an ego, I am an ego – so there is creation, right?

RAMESH Therefore, there is a creation, we *know* the creation. I am talking about this illusory creation in which these illusory egos are suffering. I am talking about this illusory world in which the illusory egos are suffering and the illusory egos are asking how their illusory suffering can be removed …

SWAMIJI Does the illusory ego that is called Ramesh have any awareness of this Brahman?

RAMESH No!

SWAMIJI No?!

RAMESH Why? Because the individual cannot have an experience of the Brahman …

SWAMIJI Right. So those who talked about these were either deluded or they meant something that you don't understand … ?

RAMESH I don't know. What the others said I don't know. But I can quite easily understand that in my dream there is a world which is illusory. When I wake up, the world that I wake up to itself can be an illusion. That I accept. But, my point is that I am concerned with this illusory world and the illusory egos which are suffering and, therefore, I as an illusory ego am talking to another ego who is suffering and I am telling that illusory ego that his suffering is entirely based on his thinking that he is the doer. And I am telling that illusory ego that if he is able to accept that no one is the doer, no more illusory suffering.

EUGENE If all is Consciousness, where does the thought 'I am the doer' come from?

RAMESH If all is Consciousness, Eugene, where could anything have come from?

Eugene Consciousness.

Ramesh Simple.

Eugene Therefore, Consciousness can lead us to the understanding that we are not the doers. At the time our mind still says we can get certain things done ...

Ramesh Consciousness is functioning through every body-mind organism and at any moment is producing such action as is supposed to happen according to a Cosmic Law. A Cosmic Law which none of us could possibly ever understand.

Eugene But it's the same Cosmic Law that gives us the discomfort or anger at certain things that happen in this so-called illusory world?

Ramesh Yes. That goes with the ego, Eugene.

Eugene But then how can you have the peace? I am talking of looking at seven thousand people a day dying of AIDS in Africa. I am uncomfortable ...

Ramesh Where does the discomfort arise?

Eugene From observance ...

Ramesh No. Where does the discomfort arise? The discomfort arises in a psychosomatic apparatus which is the body-mind organism called Eugene. The amount of discomfort that happens in Eugene may not happen in somebody else. Two people seeing the same thing. Much discomfort arises in one; in the other case ... he says, well, that's how life goes on. Discomfort arises in one; discomfort does not arise in another. Why, Eugene? That's what we have to find out, isn't it? Discomfort arises in the case of the body-mind organism called Eugene. This body-mind organism has been designed with sensitivity far more than the others. Where did he get this sensitivity that makes him uncomfortable? It came with the body-mind organism. Eugene is the name given to a particular body-mind organism and that body-mind organism consists of genes plus conditioning. Eugene had no control over being born to particular parents. Therefore, Eugene has no control over the genes in this human object. And as you know, research says, more and more, that whatever you think you were doing, the research says, no, you weren't doing it … it was your genes. You are a homosexual, not your fault. Genes. So, my point is, you had no control over being born to particular parents; therefore, you had no control over the genes in this human object. Similarly, you have no control over being born to particular parents, in a particular geographical environment, and a particular social environment – in which environment this body-mind organism has been receiving its conditioning from day one. Conditioning at home, conditioning in school, conditioning in society … that relevant society … conditioning in church or temple. Continuous bombardment of conditioning. At home, in school, society, and church or temple. This is good, that is bad. You must do this, you must not do that.

EUGENE All from the Source …

RAMESH So, I make bold to tell Eugene, at any moment, whatever Eugene thinks, let alone does, is precisely what God wants him to think. I repeat, I make bold to tell Eugene whatever Eugene thinks at any moment is precisely what God wants him to think and, therefore, God created Eugene, a body-mind organism, with those genes and that conditioning which makes him think the way he does. In other words, whatever Eugene thinks at any moment depends, according to my concept, entirely on his genes and up-to-date conditioning which God made. Think, Eugene, think. I make bold to tell you this: even what Eugene *thinks* at any moment, and every Eugene in the world, is precisely what God wants him or her to think. Because what you think depends on programming. Genes plus conditioning over which you have no control. God made the conditioning. That is my basic concept. And I repeat it is a concept, it is my concept. [*Laughs.*] I agree, it is a revolutionary concept for you. With the result, I say, that even what I think, God wants me to think.

EUGENE I accept and believe that. But I'm still concerned that once you accept the idea of Source and Source being sovereign and even that my own thoughts came from the Source, I wonder why the Source ... that He is making this! [*Laughter.*]

RAMESH That is why you want to know why the Source creates handicapped children, why the Source creates war, why the Source creates so many problems for Eugene?! [*Laughter.*]

And I'll tell you why the Source creates. Eugene, you and I and everybody, we can only think with an extremely short perspective. Our view or perspective is so short, so limited. Whereas whatever is happening has been happening according to a Cosmic Law which deals not with Eugene and me but has been dealing with the entire universe for eternity. So how can we ever know the basis on which the Cosmic Law functions? We can never know. We can only accept. That is why I remember the beautiful words of Meister Eckhart: 'The human being, being the human being, can only wonder and marvel at the magnificence and the diversity of the creation but cannot possibly know why.' Because the 'why' is based on the Cosmic Law which has been applying, has applied for eternity. Therefore the smallest thing – a leaf falling from a tree, or an entire planet being demolished – is strictly according to the Cosmic Law. Not a leaf will fall unless it is supposed to fall according to the Cosmic Law.

EUGENE That's a big swallow ...

RAMESH Indeed. That's why there are very few people who have been able to accept what I'm saying. Most people will say, if no one is a doer, how can the world function? The world functions only because everybody thinks he is a doer and liable to the society for his actions. So your question can be put in a specific way, Eugene. What Eugene really wants to know is, if I am totally able to accept, totally accept, that no one does anything, how do I live my life in the society?

And I am saying, I live my life in society having totally accepted that the society does not share my concept of non-doership. The society holds me responsible for my actions and I have to accept it. Therefore, I live my life in society doing at any moment whatever I think I should do in that moment. I repeat, I do at any moment whatever I think I should do in that moment. Thereafter, whatever happens has never been in my control and whatever happens on that as my action, the society will judge my action. Therefore, I do at any moment whatever I think I should do and thereafter, I accept the society's verdict.

Say, if an action happens through this body-mind organism and the society says it is a very good action, Ramesh should be honoured. Then what happens? When I come to know of the society's decision, a sense of pleasure arises in this body-mind organism. I read about it or I hear about it and the brain reacts to that reading or hearing, and a sense of pleasure arises in the body-mind organism. And what arises in the body-mind organism, no one has control over it because that depends on the programming – genes plus conditioning. So an action happens and the society accepts. Sense of pleasure arises in this body-mind organism. But the ego, knowing that it is not his action, while the pleasure arises in this body-mind organism, a sense of pride never arises in the ego. I repeat that a sense of pleasure arises as a natural biological reaction in the body-mind organism but knowing that it is not his action, pride cannot arise in the ego.

Similarly, take another action. The society decides it is a bad action, Ramesh should be punished. Knowing the society's decision, a sense of regret or pain will arise in the body-mind organism as something in the moment. Good action, pleasure in the moment. Society says bad action, pain or regret in the moment. But the ego, knowing that it is not his action, while the pain will arise in the body-mind organism, the ego will never share any sense of guilt or shame: not my action! Pleasure in the body-mind organism in the moment, no reaction in the ego about pride. Pain or regret in the moment in the body-mind organism but no guilt or shame in the ego.

If I am hurt, earlier I used to think: so-and-so hurt me, I hate him. Now with the total acceptance that no one is a doer, I accept that hurt as my having to suffer according to the Cosmic Law, which no one could have averted. And if I am hurt because I am supposed to be hurt, through which body-mind organism an action has happened which has hurt me is irrelevant. The relevant point is, I was supposed to be hurt and I am hurt. Through which body-mind organism an action has happened which hurt me depends on the Cosmic Law. I have nothing to do with it. Therefore, I accept the hurt as my destiny, Cosmic Law, and do not blame anyone.

So the result is, as far as my actions are concerned, the ego is not bothered with the weight of pride or guilt or shame. And as far as the other is concerned, the ego does not have to carry the weight of hatred towards anybody. So I live my life doing exactly what I think I should do at any moment, accepting the pain and pleasure in the moment but without the load of pride and arrogance, guilt or shame, hatred or malice, jealousy or envy towards anybody. And that is precisely the peace which is usually associated with the sage. And my idea of the sage is one who has been able to accept totally that no one is a doer. As simple as that, Eugene. Whether you are able to accept it or not, it is your destiny, Cosmic Law. You are able to accept your destiny – Cosmic Law. You are not able to accept it, and you have to carry the load of pride and arrogance, guilt and shame, hatred and malice – you'll do so.

Swamiji What is the cause of differences in our genes if there is only one Source and one Consciousness as you are saying?

RAMESH The cause is God's will or Cosmic Law.

SWAMIJI What is this God? You say it is pure Consciousness, one Consciousness. And you are so different with your characteristics and I am so different from others ... What is the cause of this differentiation in our tendencies and destinies ...

RAMESH The cause of this, Swamiji, is only one: God's will and Cosmic Law. Neither of which any human being can understand at all.

SWAMIJI Could you elaborate how did you come to this idea or concept that it is God's will and not our individual actions that we are carrying as a consequence ... ?

RAMESH Yes, I came to this conclusion because of God's will, my destiny, Cosmic Law. If you are not able to come to that conclusion it is your destiny, God's will, Cosmic Law.

SWAMIJI So there are differences in our genes for no reason other than it is God's will ... ?!

RAMESH For the reason that, that was exactly what is supposed to be according to the Cosmic Law which no one can understand.

RONALD Perhaps one minute to understand this final sentence. Perhaps, it's just the English ... I hope so ... where it says, 'Phenomenal appearance is myself ...' Does it mean the appearance of phenomena is myself? I mean, Consciousness ...

RAMESH 'Myself' as Consciousness. Therefore, the very first thing: when you talk, what are you talking as? Almost every single time you will be talking as the ego. And whom will you be talking to? Another ego!

RONALD I heard you say it is the ego that arises ...

RAMESH What I said was that the reaction in the body-mind organism is biological, mechanical, natural. The eyes see something good, the ears hear something good, pleasure arises in the body-mind organism but knowing that what has happened is not my action, the pleasure in the body-mind organism will not be accompanied by a sense of pride in the ego.

RONALD And in my ego pride arises, in your ego it ...

RAMESH ... doesn't! Exactly! But the pleasure arising is the same in both the body-mind organisms. But the reaction in the ego is different.

RONALD And in my old perspective, paradigm, I interpreted this line of the 'phenomenal appearance' as the whole world and everything which is myself. And you say it is ...

RAMESH Myself as Ronald. But then whoever has written or said that means the Source ... confusion. When you read Nisargadatta Maharaj, most of his stuff, you will never really know whether he is speaking as 'I' or 'me'. So *I Am That* can cause considerable confusion.

RONALD Sorry, I didn't get that.

RAMESH Nisargadatta Maharaj used to talk spontaneously but you never knew when he used the word 'I' as the Source or 'I' as the individual entity. That, you had to read between the lines.

EUGENE How do you get from 'me' to the Source?

RAMESH How does 'me', this ego, get to the Source? Has there been in my power to do *anything*, Eugene? What you are asking is ... You go out there in the sun, there is a shadow. How can the shadow go to the substance? Therefore the shadow can disappear only if Eugene goes indoors. So this ego with the sense of doership can disappear only if I am able to accept totally no one is a doer. Which is going home. Away from the sun.

Therefore, as I said earlier, there is either the 'me' as the ego or 'I' as the Source. Both can't be together. Therefore the 'me' can never be the 'I'. You can only understand that truly the 'me' is not there; all there is, is the 'I'. No 'me' can ever be there, all there is, is the 'I'. But the problem is the enormous frustration and unhappiness because the 'me' wants to know the 'I'. And 'me' wants to become the 'I'. There is a whole lot of confusion there. So, it is the 'I' that has become the 'me'. How can the 'me' become the 'I'? Six billion 'me's … how can they, everybody, become the 'I'? [*Laughter.*] That is the whole problem, Eugene.

Therefore, what can the 'me' do? Very simple. I accept that basically all there is, is the 'I' and so long as the 'me' is there I live my life thinking and doing whatever I think I should be doing at any moment and leave the 'I' to itself. Forget the 'I'. Live my life with the one understanding that whatever happens is what the Source does. I am not the doer. With that understanding I live my life thinking and doing whatever I should be doing at that moment, with the total understanding that whatever I think of doing at any moment is precisely what God wants me to think. Therefore, there is no question of my committing any sin. No question of anyone committing any sin.

EUGENE Where did the concept of sin come from except that it came from the Source?

RAMESH Yes, indeed! Quite right. So the Source created the concept of sin so that most of the people should worry about how not to commit a sin. And one of them suddenly realized, 'Hey, I am not doing anything. How can I commit a sin?' Then this one who understands this, he and God have a big laugh. [*Laughter.*] And the Lord said, 'At last you have understood what the whole game is about!' [*Laughter.*] I am glad to see a smile on your face, Ronald.

RONALD I am serious, huh?

RAMESH How could you not be? How could you not be? With that problem and that confusion, how could you not be? Yes, Ronald, grim – grim as death! [*Laughter.*]

MANOHARLAL Is there any difference between full acceptance and complete understanding?

RAMESH Full acceptance and total understanding are the same thing. But the question is, what do I mean by total acceptance? That is the important question. Now tell me ...

MANOHARLAL First the acceptance will come and then it will lead to understanding ...

RAMESH That depends on each case. In one case, it can go direct to the heart ... rare case. But in most cases, the understanding will first have to be at the intellectual level. And what is the intellectual concept? Nobody does anything and I truly accept that no one does anything. Therefore, at any moment I do not hold myself responsible for anything and I do not hold anybody responsible. Therefore, any moment I do not carry a load of hatred either for myself or anybody else. Total absence of hatred. Life goes on. I live my life without any load of hatred for me or the other. How can anyone not accept this lovely concept? If I can live my life without the load of sin, without hatred for anybody, how can anybody not intellectually accept the concept? So intellectual acceptance is not difficult. It's easy. The real problem is, how can that intellectual acceptance be total acceptance? How can this intellectual understanding be total understanding? How can this intellectual acceptance be total acceptance? Only if this intellectual understanding, a concept, is tested by the ego from its own experience.

MANOHARLAL By analysis? By investigation?

RAMESH Yes, by investigation. What I suggest is, at the end of the day, assuming you are busy throughout the day, take twenty to thirty minutes off to sit quietly. But be comfortable. Really comfortable, physically and mentally relaxed. And if for that you would like a glass of beer, have it. Then when you are comfortable, investigate.

You are not sure about most of the actions during the entire day, but select one action which you are absolutely convinced is your action. And take that one action, investigate that one action. If it is my action as I think, did I decide to do that at any particular moment? If it is my action I must have decided to do that, from out of the blue, at a particular moment. Then you will feel: no, I didn't. How did that action happen? I happened to have a thought. And I have no control over what thought arises next. Therefore, my investigation leads me to accept if the happening of that thought had not happened, my action would not have happened. So what I call my action depends on something over which I have no control. How can I call it my action? Then you take another action, and another and another. And what I am telling you with confidence is, every single time, without exception, you will come to the conclusion that if something had not earlier happened my action would not have happened. For instance, if at that particular moment I had not happened to be at some place and seen something, what I call my action now would not have happened. Or if I had not happened to be at a particular place and heard something – two people talking, I overheard them – and that led to my action. So what I am saying is, the process happening continuously, coming to the inevitable conclusion, what I thought was my action turns out to be not my action. Five actions, fifty actions, one hundred actions, any number of actions. You come to the inevitable conclusion: it could not have been my action. Then, at some point of time it is likely that a flash of acceptance happens: I cannot be the doer. How can I be the doer? I have investigated fifty actions. In not a single case could I accept that I was the doer. The flash of acceptance can only happen. When it will happen? Your destiny, God's will, Cosmic Law. But when that flash of total acceptance happens, you know: 'I simply can't be the doer.' And if I cannot be the doer, no one can be the doer either, whatever he may think. You say, I have come to the conclusion, by investigating my own experience, I cannot be the doer. Then what was the intellectual acceptance has become total acceptance. And if at that moment, a flash of acceptance has happened, do I rely on that flash of acceptance?

MANOHARLAL The flip-flop is there ...

RAMESH So if flip-flop is there I suggest Manoharlalji goes to a doctor and undertakes a lie detector test. Then he will know. [*Laughs.*] Then there will be no flip-flop. The doctor, after the injection has taken its effect, asks Manoharlalji, 'Do you really believe nobody is a doer?' and the answer will be, 'Of course I do and you should too!'

EUGENE Accepting the happening does not necessarily lead to an action, to try to alter the happening, does it?

RAMESH The final total acceptance that you are not the doer simply means that after that, Eugene merely watches any action happening to anybody not as the individual's action. He witnesses any action happening through anybody without blaming any-body – either himself or anybody else. So he witnesses all actions as happenings or events over which he has no control.

EUGENE That's not what the newspaper says!

RAMESH Newspapers? You believe newspapers, Eugene?! [*Laughter.*]

ERNEST You say you have an ego and at the same time everything is God's will. So there is no individual doer ...

RAMESH This ego believes nothing can happen unless it is God's will, Cosmic Law. Another ego will say, that's bullshit ...

EUGENE But when you use the word ego ...

RAMESH I mean identification with a particular body-mind organism and a name as a separate entity. But for me that separate entity has no volition. The separate entity is a helpless separate instrument through which the Source, Self or Consciousness functions. Whereas your ego believes that you are the doer, everybody is a doer. That is the only difference according to me. My ego has been able to accept totally no one is a doer, whereas Ernest's ego still believes everybody is a doer, is responsible for his action. That is the only difference. We both have egos, but what the ego has been able to accept differs fundamentally between yours and mine.

EUGENE Could you repeat that last bit please?

RAMESH My ego believes no one is a doer. Your ego believes everyone is a doer. That is the only difference. But both have egos.

EUGENE But my point is more than the ego, an identification with a certain body-mind organism ...

RAMESH ... as a separate entity.

EUGENE As a separate entity?

RAMESH Yes.

EUGENE That experience might also disappear. That might be there or might not be there ...

RAMESH No, it *cannot* be there. You see, if I function in life, someone calls me Ramesh. I respond, don't I? The fact that I respond to my name being called means there is identification with this body-mind and this name as a separate entity. Jesus Christ, if you had called him by his name, he would respond, would he not? Ranjit Maharaj, if you called him by name, would he not respond? So he would respond as what? As God? Ranjit Maharaj if called by name, would respond as the Source or Ranjit Maharaj as a separate entity?

EUGENE It depends, no?

RAMESH It depends on nothing.

EUGENE Or it's always Ranjit Maharaj or Ramesh?

RAMESH Any sage in order to live the rest of his life as an individual entity has to have ego but that ego of the sage has been able to reject totally the idea of doership. That is why I started with it – Ronald saying: he has an ego, I have an ego; he thinks he is a separate entity, I think I am a separate entity. Where is the difference? And that's how we started. The difference is, this ego has been able to accept totally, no one is a doer. Whereas that ego still believes that everyone is a doer.

EUGENE But those separate entities might have …

RAMESH Separate entities may have different experiences. So what? Who has different experiences? Separate egos!

EUGENE Yeah, that has no meaning further …

RAMESH Therefore, it is very simple. If the sage lives his life as a separate entity, doing whatever his normal doing is – he may be a cobbler, barber, doctor, solicitor, lawyer, engineer, tennis player – the sage continues to live his life in the same occupation as a separate entity. Therefore the ego as identification with a separate name and form must continue. And if a sage says, I don't have an ego, then he has not understood the meaning of the ego. So you have to explain to the sage that what I mean by ego is a separate entity with doership. Then he will say, 'I am not.' But then you tell him that the ego means merely identification as a separate entity, then he will say, 'Of course, I am there. If you will call me, I will respond.' This is the basic cause of considerable confusion. The sage must have an ego but the sage's ego does not anymore have the sense of volitional personal doership. Therefore the sage's ego is harmless …

EUGENE … and has barely any meaning also. I mean, it is just the way of talking, in fact.

RAMESH No, it has deep meaning. The deep meaning being, the sage knows totally that no one does anything. With this understanding the sage does not hate anybody. The sage does not fear anybody as an enemy. But the sage has to live his life as a separate entity. So if you have been hearing that the sage has no ego … big, big mistake. Cause of considerable confusion and frustration. The sage also has an ego. The ego means basically identification with body-mind and the name as a separate identity. The difference lies entirely in doership. Aside from doership, both are identification with a separate body-mind, as a separate entity. And this is so very important, Eugene, and unfortunately, as you say, this was not clear to Eugene and it is not clear to thousands of people. Therefore so much confusion.

EUGENE I related also to different kind of experiences. If you see different kinds of masters, they act in different ways, they experience different things …

RAMESH And yet they are all sages.

EUGENE And yet they are all egos …

RAMESH They are all egos. Absolutely! [*Laughter.*]

EUGENE They are separate egos …

RAMESH But you were under the impression that Ranjit Maharaj had no ego. Isn't that right? If Ranjit Maharaj told you that he had no ego, I would say he didn't know what he was talking about. How can he say he has no ego? When he responds to his name being called, he lives as Ranjit Maharaj.

EUGENE Well, I think I understand what he means when he says he has no ego. It's just that ego becomes part of Consciousness so in reality the ego does not exist.

RAMESH Ego cannot live without existing.

EUGENE No, I understand that, but from the point of view of the ...

RAMESH You are trying to tell me what Ranjit Maharaj was thinking?

EUGENE Yes. [*Laughter.*] Now it is more my understanding than ...

RAMESH So if your understanding was that the sage has no ego, your understanding was wrong. Now your understanding will be, if you accept my concept, that the sage also has an ego. He lives as a separate entity, responds to his name being called, but he knows that as a separate entity he is helpless as far as any doing is concerned.

EUGENE Yeah, that's what makes the difference.

RAMESH That is the difference.

EUGENE Because that ego is as it is nothing, as if it has no ...

RAMESH I will tell you exactly what I feel. My wife, she said I shouldn't say it. You know what I say? The ego of the sage is like the male penis after the sexual act. Helpless. The roaring bull has become a little mouse. That's as clear an example as I can give you. Ramana Maharshi is more decent. He says the ego of the sage is like the remnants of a burnt rope. So you take it as a burnt rope or a penis after sexual intercourse, whichever has a clearer idea.

EUGENE Well, mine is still standing! [*Laughter.*]

RAMESH Therefore, your sense of doership is very much there! [*Laughter.*]

Let there be no confusion:

You cannot commit a sin;
You cannot commit a mistake.

Whatever has happened, whatever is happening, whatever will be happening is precisely what is supposed to happen, in every respect, according to God's will: Cosmic Law.

Any event – and its consequences – affect whoever is concerned, strictly, according to the respective destiny: God's will: Cosmic Law.

When the ordinary person uses the personal pronoun 'I', he means 'me' both to himself and to the 'other'. When the sage uses the word 'I', he means 'me' in regard to the 'other' as far as the society is concerned, but he 'knows' that there is really no 'me', nor the 'other', but only the 'I' forever.